Eric Hobsbawm was a Fellow of the British Academy and the American Academy of Arts and Sciences. Before retirement he taught at Birkbeck College, University of London, and after retirement at the New School for Social Research in New York. Previous books include *Age of Extremes*, *The Age of Revolution* and *The Age of Empire*. He died 1 October 2012, aged 95.

T0299678

# On Nationalism

## ERIC HOBSBAWM

Edited by Donald Sassoon
with an introduction

abacus
books

ABACUS

First published in Great Britain in 2021 by Little, Brown
This paperback edition published in 2022 by Abacus

7 9 10 8 6

A CIP catalogue record for this book
is available from the British Library.

ISBN 978-0-349-14350-7

Typeset in Baskerville by M Rules

Printed in Italy by Elcograf S.p.A.

Papers used by Abacus are from well-managed forests
and other responsible sources.

MIX
Paper | Supporting
responsible forestry
FSC® C104740

Abacus
An imprint of
Little, Brown Book Group
Carmelite House
50 Victoria Embankment
London EC4Y 0DZ

The authorised representative
in the EEA is
Hachette Ireland
8 Castlecourt Centre
Dublin 15, D15 XTP3, Ireland
(email: info@hbgi.ie)

An Hachette UK Company
www.hachette.co.uk

www.littlebrown.co.uk

# Contents

## II: THE PERILS OF NATIONALISM

# Introduction

*Donald Sassoon*

Eric Hobsbawm did not like nationalism. As he wrote in 1988 in a letter to a left-wing nationalist historian, 'I remain in the curious position of disliking, distrusting, disapproving and fearing nationalism wherever it exists, perhaps even more than in the 1970s, but recognising its enormous force, which must be harnessed for progress if possible. And sometimes it is possible. We cannot let the right have the monopoly of the flag. Some things can be achieved by mobilising nationalist feelings . . . However, I cannot be a nationalist and neither, in theory, can any Marxist.'[1]

His anti-nationalism is not surprising. He was a Jew opposed to Zionism. He was British but born in Egypt in the year of the Russian Revolution. His grandfather was Polish. His mother was Viennese. His father was born in England. His parents married in Switzerland. His wife, Marlene, was born in Vienna and brought up in Manchester. He grew up in Vienna and Berlin, and was a boy in Germany when the Nazis took over – an experience that left an enduring impression. He wrote in his autobiography that Berlin made him a lifelong Marxist and communist, a political project which, he acknowledged, had utterly failed. 'The dream of the October Revolution,' he wrote, 'is still there somewhere inside me . . . I have abandoned, nay rejected it, but it has not been obliterated.'[2] It was not a happy childhood: his father died when he was twelve and his mother when he was fourteen.

It is almost as if the term 'rootless cosmopolitan' had been coined for him were it not for the fact that he was so very English in his mannerisms, albeit an Englishman with a command of five languages. With this kind of background it is not entirely unexpected that he should have looked at conventional wisdom (including conventional historiography) with a good deal of scepticism.

In this collection of Hobsbawm's writing on nationalism, we see some of the critical historical insights he brings to bear on this contentious subject, which is more than ever relevant as we stand on the doorstep of an age when the internet and the globalization of capital threaten to blow away many national boundaries while, partly as a reaction, nationalism seems to re-emerge with renewed strength.

Historians, he explained, 'have a responsibility to historical facts in general, and for criticizing the politico-ideological abuse of history in particular'.[3] He possessed, if I may use the expression, a powerful 'bullshit' detector – an essential tool in a profession where a critical mind is as important as wisdom and a wide knowledge. Hobsbawm had all of these.

There is little doubt that he took some pleasure (I can still see his mischievous smile) in pointing out that stuff peddled as ancient is actually quite recent: whether it is the festival of the Jocs Floral (Floral Games) re-established in Catalonia in 1859, with the theme of *Patria, Fides, Amor* (Country, Faith, Love), at a time when Catalan nationalism was not concerned with the linguistic question, or its Welsh equivalent, the eisteddfodau, revived in the same year while Welsh was not standardized until the twentieth century ('Are All Tongues Equal?' in this collection).

History challenges beliefs to an extent unequalled in other disciplines. To argue that the earth is not in the middle of the universe and that the sun does not go round it, or that our ancestors were apes, may be destabilizing for Abrahamic religions since the science appears to invalidate the accepted stories concerning the Creation, but, in our times, most religions have learned to put up with the science. In any case, for most (not all) people, whether the sun goes round the earth or the other way round is of no great importance. Life goes on. One's identity is not threatened. But to be told, in the modern age, that is to say since the nineteenth century, that Italy or Germany are recently 'invented' nations; that Clovis, 'the first Christian King of France', was born in Belgium (which did not exist then) and did not speak French, and nor did Charlemagne; that Pakistan was 'invented' in the 1930s (Hobsbawm mentions with irony, and more than once, a popular book called *Five Thousand Years of Pakistan* written by the British archaeologist Mortimer Wheeler) may well be upsetting for those who have been taught such things at school and for whom a national identity is important, and, nowadays, identities, and not only national identities, are more important than ever.

He is equally scathing about Zionists who 'skate lightly over the last 1800 years to get back to the last fighting inhabitants of Palestine'. People can identify as Jews even though they do not live in the territory, do not speak the same language, do not follow the same religious rituals (or any), do not have the same historical background or the same culture, etc. For him, 'no serious historian of nations and nationalism can be a committed political nationalist'. And he doubted, for instance, that a Zionist could write 'a genuinely serious history of the Jews'.[4] Nationalists believe nations have been around since time immemorial. The business of historians is to refute such assertions.

The best historians have always been aware of the dangers of myth-making. Thucydides, in the first chapter of his *History of the Peloponnesian War*, wrote that, at a time of turmoil, 'Old stories of occurrences handed down by tradition, but scantily confirmed by experience, suddenly ceased to be incredible.'

Hobsbawm too was perfectly aware of the power of history. He was fond of saying that there was a time when he thought, consolingly, that historians, unlike architects and civil engineers, could not cause disasters. He eventually recognized, as he admitted, that history, in the hands of nationalists, can kill more people than incompetent builders. Hence the responsibility which befalls the historian for, as he often wrote: 'Historians are to nationalism what poppy-growers are to heroin addicts: we supply the essential raw material for the market.' Or variants of this: 'History is the raw material for nationalist or ethnic or fundamentalist ideologies, as poppies are the raw material for heroin addiction.'[5]

He would then add: 'Nations without a past are contradictions in terms, for the past legitimizes. What makes a nation is the past, what justifies one nation against others is the past, and historians are the people who produce it. So my profession, which has always been mixed up in politics, becomes an essential component of nationalism. More so even than the ethnographers, philologists and other suppliers of ethnic and national services who have usually also been mobilized.'

This never led him to decry nationalism and patriotism as simply absurd. One can see the effort he made to understand the phenomenon (unlike so many on the left) reading a text he produced during the Falklands War. In an article published in the Communist Party journal *Marxism Today* (in this collection), he accepted that the Argentine claim on the islands, which led to their invasion in 1982, *was* absurd, since no Argentine ever lived there. Equally he noted that the British government cared very little for these islands and that, indeed, most British people had never heard of the Falklands until the Argentine invasion. But when it happened, many in the UK were genuinely outraged, displayed their patriotism, and sang 'Rule, Britannia!' rather than the official anthem, the non-nationalist but also non-democratic 'God Save the Queen' which implores God to 'scatter her enemies' and not *our* enemies, hoping that 'long . . . may she defend our laws' instead of hoping that we did the defending ourselves.

At the time, many on the left were appalled and even surprised by this outburst of British nationalism. Not Hobsbawm: 'anyone on the left who was not aware of this grass-roots feeling, and that it was not a creation of the media ... ought seriously to reconsider their capacity to assess politics'. And, as a historian, he reminded his readers that patriotism cannot be neglected, and that it should not be left to the right. Not approving of something does not entitle one not to try to understand it.

Hobsbawm's starting point was the relatively recent construction of nationalism and of the idea of a nation. He regarded it (see *The Age of Revolution*) as mainly a European phenomenon. There was, in the nineteenth century, little nationalism in Latin America, and what existed was the work of patrician elites, while the Catholic masses remained passive, almost as much as the indigenous population. One could not to speak of a Colombian or Venezuelan consciousness, not in the first half of the nineteenth century and probably not until the twentieth century. Japan, however, was an exception: the Meiji Restoration of 1868, aimed at resisting European colonialism and building up Japan's power, was the sign that the national problem had reached the Far East (*The Age of Capital*), though even there it was the work of the elites. To a large extent, nationalism outside Europe was a consequence of European imperial power.

There was, in the late eighteenth century, an American nationalism of a sort, but it had to do with freedom from England and has little in common with its current version. The Civil War was fought to preserve the unity of the nation. If the Southern secession had succeeded, muses Hobsbawm, it would have probably given rise 'to a proud Southern Nation'.[6]

In Europe, nationalism was the product of the 'dual revolutions', the French Revolution and the British Industrial Revolution. Some, such as the historian Elie Kedourie (who defined nationalism as a political religion), suggested that the invention of nationalism could be traced back to German Enlightenment thinkers such as Immanuel Kant and Johann Gottlieb Fichte in response to Napoleon's occupation of German territory. One's identity as a 'German' before the unification of Germany, was, at best, cultural and linguistic (though most spoke a variety of German dialects). Thus German-speaking inhabitants of the Austro-Hungarian Empire may have thought of themselves as 'German' as well as Austrian and Catholic. Modern German identity was developed under Bismarck as a consequence of the wars against the Danes (1864), the Austrians (1866) and the French (1870), and the establishment of the German Reich. 'True' nationalists were dismayed since they regarded this as the *Kleindeutschland* (Lesser Germany) solution, much preferring *Grossdeutschland* (Greater Germany), which would have included all German speakers, including the Austrians. To demonstrate how recent is the birth of German nationalism, Hobsbawm chronicled the ceremonies held in German schools in 1895–6 for the twenty-fifth anniversary of German unification.[7] Not so differently, American citizens, many of whom, by the end of the nineteenth century, had no common national identity, were 'Americanized' by a similar process of drumming into them rituals commemorating an America which had preceded them such as the 4th of July and Thanksgiving.

Nationalist ideas, however, grew more powerfully in the decades after the French Revolution. It was not necessarily a revolutionary movement: though, at the time, most nationalists tended to be members of the liberal elites. In fact, the continuing appeal of nationalism has been its adaptability. One could be, in Tsarist Russia, a reactionary, anti-modernizing Slavophile and, on that basis, a fervent supporter of a Holy Russia trying to keep the detested west at bay. Or one could be a revolutionary patriot whose goal was to relieve the suffering of 'the people' from reactionary and clerical rule, or liberate one's motherland from foreign rule. In much of the nineteenth century, though, nationalism tended to be identified with liberalism. Then it became mainly associated with the patriotic right,[8] and later in the twentieth century nationalism was far more a banner of

Introduction

the extreme right (fascism and Nazism being the most obvious examples), though communists in Spain and France in the 1930s also waved the national flag. During the Second World War left-wing resistance fighters fought the foreign occupiers in the name of the nation and treated those who collaborated with the Nazis as traitors. The absence of stable nationalist ideology continued after 1945: decolonization movements could be patriotic as well as socialist; Fidel Castro and Che Guevara fought the Cuban revolution under slogans such as *patria o muerte* as did, decades later, Hugo Chávez in Venezuela, who added the word *socialismo*.

In nineteenth-century century Europe, the 'real' people, i.e. prevalently those working on the land, were barely aware that they were Poles or Italians (or Irish, or Hungarian). The most traditional, backward or poorer sections of the population were the last to be captured by nationalism, though eventually they were be awakened by its growing cohorts, usually intellectuals, burghers and the lower gentry – in other words, the educated classes. These were the ones who, at least initially, constructed nationalism. Nationalism usually preceded the nation, a real or potential state, but there needed to be an ideological criterion for nationalism and, in mid-nineteenth-century Europe, this tended to be radical, liberal, democratic, even revolutionary.[9] The Czech or Polish or Finnish or Irish nationalists did not want to return to some ancient monarchy or primitive state of affairs. Each felt themselves to be victims, be it of the English, or the Russians, or the Austrians. They felt themselves to be distinctive. Language mattered, but most Irish spoke English, many Finns spoke Swedish, few Italians spoke Italian. The main issue was that they felt they were victims, victims who blamed 'the other' for whatever predicament they were in. The hope that united them was the belief that matters would improve if only they were separate, autonomous, more independent (one can see how modern such feelings are, since they resurfaced during the 2016 Brexit referendum in the UK).

Nationalists in mid-nineteenth-century Europe wanted to be

progressive and modern, however often they collected ancient myths and folk songs – 'Myths and invention are essential to the politics of identity . . .'[10] Italy and Germany had never existed as states, but German and Italian nationalists felt that to be modern, to be like the nations they envied (usually Great Britain and France), they needed to have their own country. Thus Hobsbawm distinguished between the ideology of nationalism and the ways this ideology was conscripted to serve a political purpose, namely the construction of a state that would be a 'nation-state'. Such constructions required, eventually, the instruments of state institutions which could impose national uniformity: public employment, state schools teaching the 'national' language, a 'national' history and, often, national conscription.[11] One can easily imagine a Sicilian peasant conscripted into the Italian army in 1915, barely aware of being Italian, speaking only a dialect, being given a uniform, ordered about in Italian (itself a Tuscan 'dialect') by a Piedmontese officer, and told to shoot, under the 'national' banner, at Austrian soldiers on an Alpine border he barely knew existed.

The dominant role in the construction of nationalism, however, was held by primary education. Between 1870 and 1914, Hobsbawm explained, the number of primary school teachers trebled in Sweden and increased by almost as many in Norway. The number of children in primary schools in the Netherlands doubled; in the UK it trebled. In France, primary education was made compulsory in 1882. Its function was not just to teach literacy and numeracy, but also national values: 'be proud of your country' was the educational basis of primary schools. It is still the desired aim of some: in Britain, Michael Gove, when Secretary of State for Education, bemoaned the lack of emphasis on Churchill, eminent Victorians and 'Britain and her empire' in the history curriculum. 'This trashing of our past has to stop,' he said, complaining that 'the current approach we have to history denies children the opportunity to hear our island story'.[12]

The nation, however, is not purely constructed from above. It develops unevenly among social classes and regions. It must resonate with people who have something in common. Hobsbawm is reluctant to map out a rigid path, though he suggests that there often is an initial 'cultural-literary-folkloric' phase, one in which romantic intellectuals such as Johann Gottfried Herder are prominent. They are followed by a small band of enthusiastic nationalists with a distinct political programme of nation-building, people such as Adam Mickiewicz in Poland, Giuseppe Mazzini in Italy, Daniel O'Connell in Ireland and Lajos Kossuth in Hungary. By the 1890s, even within well-established nation-states we witness the growth of separatist national movements such as the Young Wales movement organized by David Lloyd George, the future Liberal Prime Minister, or the Basque National Party.

Paradoxically, at the time of its construction, that is to say in the nineteenth century, there is very little theoretical work on nationalism. A possible exception is John Stuart Mill, who in his *Considerations on Representative Government* offered a somewhat tautological but not inaccurate definition of nationalism: 'A portion of mankind may be said to constitute a Nationality if they are united among themselves by common sympathies which do not exist between them and any others – which make them co-operate with each other more willingly than with other people, desire to be under the same government, and desire that it should be government by themselves or a portion of themselves exclusively.' Of course, explains Mill, this works only for 'civilized' nations, and, it must be recognized, at the time he was writing, national identity existed mainly (though not exclusively) in Europe and North America.

Mill then added that the feeling of nationality may have various causes, such as 'race and descent', language, religion, a territory or a common foe. He added that 'it is ... a necessary condition of free institutions, that the boundaries of governments should coincide in the main with those of nationalities'. In other words: one nation, one state. That a nationalist is someone who thinks he or she is part of a nation was axiomatic for Mill, and though it is, as Hobsbawm writes, a 'fuzzy concept' and Mill's is a somewhat circular argument, it provides only an *a posteriori* guide to what a nation is. It is a perfectly reasonable initial working assumption that all that is required for nationalism is that a 'sufficiently large body of people ... regard themselves as members of a nation'. If that happens, we have a nation. Something might unite them: living in the same region, speaking the same language, belonging to an equally indefinable 'ethnic' group, being persecuted by others. So far there is little that divides the Marxist Hobsbawm from the liberal Mill. But Mill added that 'the strongest of all is identity of political antecedents; the possession of a national history'. For Hobsbawm (and for many historians) a national history is not a given: people can identify as members of a nation even though they do not live in the territory, do not speak the same language, or share the same culture.

The other major nineteenth-century British thinker who dealt with the question of nationalism ('theorize' would be too strong a word) was Lord Acton. Acton, a liberal Catholic, took issue with nationalists who sought to make the principle of nationalism the foundation of the construction of states. In the past, he explained, social unrest was aimed at returning to a previous state of affairs. Since the French Revolution, the masses wanted something new – a new world – and that was dangerous. The principle of nationality had 'converted a dormant right into an aspiration and a sentiment into a political claim' and had become 'the most powerful auxiliary of revolution'.[13]

The one nineteenth-century theorist Hobsbawm identifies with, in a quote he repeats throughout his work on nationalism, is Ernest Renan, who in his famous 1882 lecture at the Sorbonne, *Qu'est-ce qu'une nation?* ('What is a Nation?') defined it as a 'great solidarity constituted by the common understanding of the sacrifices made in the past and those to make in the future'. But this past, he added ominously, was often a constructed past for it assumed 'oblivion' (*l'oubli*), adding that '*historical error* is a crucial factor in the creation of a nation, which is why progress in historical studies often constitutes a threat to the nation'.[14] Hobsbawm interpreted this to mean 'getting history wrong is an essential part of being a nation', adding that it was 'the professional business of historians to dismantle such mythologies, unless they are content – and I am afraid national historians have often been – to be the servants of ideologists'.[15]

Renan had added that 'the existence of a nation is like a daily plebiscite', meaning that national unity must be constantly constructed and reconstructed. So though the nation is the work of an elite, without popular support it would be virtually impossible ever to develop a nation and a broad national consciousness. Of course, nationalists did not just want to celebrate a nation, a community which holds itself to be a nation, but they wanted the transmutation of a nation into a sovereign state, the idea being that the state embodied the people, something quite different from the states of old, embodied in a sovereign. The new sovereigns of the nineteenth century adorned themselves with the patina of popular legitimacy, thus while Queen Victoria was Queen of the United Kingdom and the Tsar was the Tsar of All Russias, Napoleon was the Empereur des Français, Leopold I was the first Roi des Belges, and George I of Greece (son of a German prince and born in Copenhagen) was styled King of the Hellenes. Nietzsche saw this quite clearly in 1881 when, alarmed at the conflation of state and people, he exclaimed in his *Thus Spoke Zarathustra*:

> The state? What is that? Well then! Now open your ears, for now I shall speak to you of the death of peoples. The state is the coldest of all cold monsters. Coldly it lies, too; and this lie creeps from its mouth: 'I, the state, am the people.'[16]

Others in the nineteenth century, such as Arthur Schopenhauer, decried nationalism without explaining it: 'The cheapest sort of pride is national pride ... every miserable fool who has nothing at all of which he can be proud adopts, as a last resource, pride in the nation to which he belongs.'[17]

The fact that nationalism, in the nineteenth century, was the prerogative of the educated classes does not to entail, explained Hobsbawm, that, in some cases, there existed feelings of belonging to something one might call a nation also among the popular classes. Russians, in the nineteenth century, regarded themselves as Russians, and this included many Ukrainians and Belorussians, today zealous defenders of their national identity. Many French 'felt' French, as did some of the English, but not yet the Italians. Such identities, however, owed much to territory or religion or language. One could think of oneself as German without aiming for a united Germany, just as one could think oneself a Yorkshireman without aiming for an independent Yorkshire, or regarding Yorkshire as a nation.

Apart from religion, the main identity, in pre-industrial societies, was largely confined to the village and the region (where people spoke a similar dialect). Migration, which increased dramatically in the course of the nineteenth century, still meant uprooting from one's village or town, not from one's country. Venetians who immigrated to the Americas in, say, 1880, might long to return to Venetia, but not to 'Italy' (a state established only in 1861). Italy would have been for them a relatively meaningless term, but, paradoxically, they would be regarded as 'Italians' by the locals because the distinction between Venetia and Italy would not be made in such distant lands.[18] So our Venetians would become more 'Italian' overseas than if they had remained at home, though in this case their newly acquired 'national' consciousness would not be inspired or constructed by nationalists, but by 'the others', just as anti-Semitism might transform secular and non-observant Jews into 'real' Jews and perhaps even Zionists. A common enemy helps nationalists, but those in the Balkans who fought against the Ottoman Empire before the First World War were not fighting for a Yugoslav nation (which did not exist then) but against what they regarded as an oppressor. The same could be said about the Sikhs against the British of the East India Company in 1845 and 1846.

Rebellions by peasants against foreign rule could not be called nationalist, when those who fought were united only by the consciousness of oppression, by xenophobia (theirs or of others) and by attachment to ancient tradition, to their 'true faith' and a vague sense of ethnic identity.

The Greeks, perhaps, Hobsbawm concedes, were the exception to the rule in their struggle for independence in the 1820s. And because of this exception, a 'brave' (Christian) people fighting against the Muslims (Ottoman Turks) could also obtain the sympathies of philhellenes throughout Europe, including Shelley, Byron (who died in Greece), Leigh Hunt, Thomas Moore and Jeremy Bentham – even though the struggle of Greeks against Turks had as much a religious dimension as a national one.

Elsewhere, nationalism had little mass basis. The idea that there was strong 'national' feeling among, say, the Germans during the Napoleonic Wars was, in Hobsbawm's view, 'patriotic mythology'. The failure to realize that the people lacked the proper patriotic spirit is what caused the near-impossibility of mobilizing the peasantry around the idea of the nation throughout Europe. Take the case of Carlo Pisacane, an Italian patriot follower of Mazzini who, in 1857, sailed with twenty-four volunteers to Sapri in southern Italy, hoping to lead the locals against the authorities in what was then the Kingdom of Naples. Not only did Pisacane fail miserably but the local inhabitants, believing them to be bandits, overpowered the 'invaders' and killed Pisacane and most of his comrades.

Peasants could be mobilized against taxes, against landlords, against Jews, but not for the 'fatherland'. Basque-speaking peasants remained unenthusiastic about Basque nationalism (the Basque National Party was founded only in 1894), which was largely an urban-based, middle-class movement.[19] Romania came into being in stages largely because of the Congress of Berlin of 1878, but official history attributes a much greater role to Romanians themselves, though the Romanian peasantry was never propelled by nationalist spirit. When Romanian peasants revolted, as they did in 1907, it was because of their deteriorating economic conditions due, in part to the collapse of the international price for wheat at the end of the nineteenth century (in turn due to the far greater productivity of American wheat farmers). This peasant tax revolt, brutally repressed, took at first a specifically anti-Semitic form since a large proportion of estate farmers or *arendaşi* (originally moneylenders who acquired land) were Jewish.[20] Patriotism had very little to do with the revolt.

In what was regarded as the era of nationalism (which Hobsbawm sets at 1870–1914), relatively few new states emerged: Germany in 1870; Italy in 1861 (though further unification with Rome as capital took place in 1870, and the absorption of the South Tyrol and Trieste only after the First World War); then Montenegro, Bulgaria and Serbia, which became recognized as states in 1878; Romania, which became a fully fledged independent kingdom in 1881; and Norway, which separated from Sweden in 1905. None came into being because of a popular uprising or even a mass nationalist movement.

Nationalism may not have been much debated by liberal scholars in the nineteenth century, allegedly the century of nationalism, but it was not much debated by socialists either. Hobsbawm mentions some of the exceptions: Karl Kautsky, Rosa Luxemburg and, later, Otto Bauer. It was almost ignored by Marx and Engels (who, famously, had urged workers of all countries to unite), by Plekhanov and by Lenin. Stalin, it is true, wrote his unremarkable *Marxism and the National Question* (1913), in which he listed the characteristic features of a nation: a common language, a common territory, a common economic life and a common psychological make-up. Many pre-1913 'nations' would have failed at least one of the tests, including Spain, Italy and Switzerland. On the whole, however, the left was 'internationalist' only in the sense of supporting those who fought for a cause it approved. Otherwise organizations such as the Second International and, later, the Communist International were based on states. Even revolutionary Russia recognized 'nations', and with the November 1917 Declaration of the Rights of the Peoples of Russia established, at least formally, the rights of the peoples of what was the Tsarist Empire to secede and form separate states – hence the constitution of Soviet republics in 1922 (they became fifteen in 1940 with the absorption of the three Baltic Republics and Moldavia).

The use of the term 'nationalism' increased throughout the twentieth century, reaching a temporary plateau during the Second World War – what Hobsbawm calls 'the apogee of nationalism'. Writing in 1990, and hence before the current explosion of the term, he believed that nationalism had become less important, that it was no longer a global political programme as it had been in the nineteenth century. He believed, perhaps wrongly, that nation-states were on the retreat, and that they would be absorbed by the new supranational restructuring of the globe. He was perhaps over-optimistic when he concluded his *Nations and Nationalism* by assuming that the phenomenon of nationalism had passed its peak: 'The owl of Minerva which brings wisdom, said Hegel, flies out at dusk. It is a good sign that it is now circling rounds nations and nationalism.'[21] And he certainly did not and perhaps could not have envisaged in 1970 that the Welsh and Scottish nationalism he discussed somewhat dismissively would become so significant a few decades later (see the essay on the Celtic Fringe in this collection).

In the last two decades the uses of the term 'nationalism' has increased steeply with the rising tide of nationalist parties – almost in parallel with the growing use of the term 'globalization'. As Hobsbawm wrote rather presciently, 'The paradox of nationalism was that in forming its own nation it automatically created the counter-nationalism of those whom it now forced into the choice between assimilation and inferiority.'[22] In the nineteenth century nationalism was mainly about uniting regions into larger states which were called nations. In the twentieth century, especially after 1945, the characteristic nationalist movements were no longer in favour of unification (as in Germany and Italy in the nineteenth century) but turned increasingly towards separation. The secessionist movement began with the break-up of nineteenth-century empires. The end of the Tsarist Empire gave birth to Poland, Finland and the three Baltic Republics; that of the Austro-Hungarian Empire to Austria, Hungary, Czechoslovakia and the Kingdom of the South Slavs (Yugoslavia after 1945); the Ottoman Empire was reduced to Turkey. The trend towards national secession continues to the present. Some have been successful: for instance Bangladesh from Pakistan, Kosovo from Serbia and South Sudan from Sudan; others (so far) failed – for instance Biafra, Katanga and Kurdistan. Following the break-up of the Soviet Union and of Yugoslavia more states were created, all assuming to be coterminous with nations, though the UK, Belgium and Spain, among others, have recognized 'nations' inside their borders (Scotland, Wales, Flanders, Wallonia, Catalonia, etc.) – nations which might secede, creating more states. Today the main international organization of states is called, misleadingly, the United *Nations*, but it is an organization of states (as Hobsbawm once said, one could not very well call it the United States . . .).

In the nineteenth century, Hobsbawm noted, there was a prejudice, even among nationalists, against the pulverization of states into mini-nations. Petty German principalities or Central American republics were jokes; 'Balkanization' was a term of abuse. Today states, however small, are regarded as quite viable.[23] Many Austrians after 1918 did not think their small Alpine republic could be viable once it was separated from the Austro-Hungarian Empire, and were in favour of joining Germany. Few Austrians today would hold such views. And no one regards Singapore, with half the population of Moscow, as not viable. On the contrary, it is one of the richest states in the world.

Hobsbawm took on board Benedict Anderson's remarkable *Imagined Communities*, where a nation is defined as:

> ... an imagined political community – and imagined as both inherently limited and sovereign. It is imagined because the members of even the smallest nation will never know most of their fellow-members, meet them, or even hear of them, yet in the minds of each lives the image of their communion ... [the nation] is imagined as a community, because, regardless of the actual inequality and exploitation that may prevail in each, the nation is conceived as a deep, horizontal comrade-ship. Ultimately, it is this fraternity that makes it possible, over the past two centuries for so many millions of people, not so much to kill, as willing to die for such limited imaginings.[24]

Hobsbawm uses this to define modern states where, at least since the end of the nineteenth century, the inhabitants have imagined themselves (with considerable help from state insti-tutions and political organizations) as being bonded together, by language, culture and ethnicity, as a homogeneous commu-nity – a standing invitation to get rid of 'the others' by 'ethnic cleansing'. This is what makes the 'concept of a single, exclusive, and unchanging ethnic or cultural or other identity a dangerous piece of brainwashing'.[25] A single national language, he added, becomes significant only when ordinary citizens become of some importance. In pre-industrial societies, it did not matter which dialect a peasant spoke. A single language becomes important when there is a strong state, a bureaucracy, and a written language is established. This is why Turkey under the nationalist leader Kemal Atatürk adopted Roman script in 1929, even though Turkish had been written using Arabic script for centuries, and Romania changed its own script from Cyrillic

to Roman only when it became a sovereign state in 1863.[26]
Vietnamese was once written in a variant of Chinese characters.
The present Roman script was devised in the sixteenth century
by missionaries hoping it would help them learn the language.

None of this mattered when the vast majority of the population was illiterate. National linguistic homogeneity in
multi-ethnic and multi-lingual areas does not simply evolve,
but is achieved by mass compulsion, expulsion, or genocide.
As Hobsbawm explained, Poland, which in 1939 had a third
of its population classified as non-Polish, became overwhelmingly Polish-speaking only because its German population was
expelled to the west, its Lithuanian, Byelorussian and Ukrainian
inhabitants were detached to form part of the USSR in the East,
and its Yiddish-speaking Jewish population had been murdered
by the Nazis. This is what made Poland into a relatively homogeneous nation speaking a single language.

The idea that there should be one language per nation is an
'explosive' factor, since it ignores the fact that it is historically
quite normal for there to be different languages within the
boundaries of a single state, as is the case today in many countries such as Belgium, Spain, Switzerland, Canada and India.
Even Irish nationalists were not able to get the vast majority
of Irish to speak Gaelic (the Gaelic League was founded only
in 1893) and Zionist Jews started to use a language, Hebrew,
that Jews had not used except for religious purposes, and even
then the Hebrew word for 'nationalism' had to be invented.[27]
'Once again,' Hobsbawm wrote, 'Zionism provides the extreme
example' of a borrowed nationalist programme which had no
precedent in, or organic connection with, the actual tradition
that had given the Jewish people permanence, cohesion and an
indestructible identity for some millennia.[28] The key factor in
establishing a national language was political power.

Even nineteenth-century European monarchs had to accept
the principle of nationalism, although many of them did not
entirely 'belong' to the nation they ruled. Queen Victoria's

children had a German father; Tsar Nicholas's mother was
Danish, his wife German; the first king of Greece came from
Bavaria; Kaiser Wilhelm II's mother was Queen Victoria's
daughter; Victor Emmanuel II, first king of Italy, had an Austrian
mother, his son, Amedeo, became king of Spain, his daughter
queen of Portugal and his grandson, King Victor Emmanuel
III, married Elena of Montenegro. The European royal families
were true cosmopolitans, 'citizens of nowhere'. This continued
until recently: Queen Elizabeth II's husband, Prince Philip,
was born in Corfu, his mother was a German princess (Alice of
Battenberg) and his father, a member of the House of Schleswig-
Holstein, was the son of King George I of Greece and Olga
Constantinovna of the Russian Romanov family. This came to
an end with the present British royal family: the four children
of Queen Elizabeth II all married British people, though two
of her grandchildren married foreigners (a Canadian and an
American). Hobsbawm would probably find it even more ironic
that, apart from what is left over from nineteenth-century aristocratic families, the one unmistakably cosmopolitan element in
today's world is not the internationalist left he had embraced in
the 1930s, but international capitalism, free to roam the world
at will, with Facebook having more 'members' than Islam or
Catholicism and the internet uniting what, in the words of the
*Internationale*, is the human race.

## Notes

1 Cited in Richard Evans, *Eric Hobsbawm: A Life in History* (London, 2019), p. 551.
2 Eric Hobsbawm, *Interesting Times* (London, 2002), pp. 55–6.
3 Eric Hobsbawm, *On History* (London, 1998), p. 7.
4 Eric Hobsbawm, *Nations and Nationalism since 1780. Programme, Myth, Reality* (2nd edition; Cambridge, 1990), pp. 12–13.
5 *On History*, p. 6.
6 Eric Hobsbawm, *The Age of Capital* (London, 1975).
7 'Mass-producing traditions: Europe, 1870–1914', in *The Invention of Tradition* (Cambridge, 1983).

8   Eric Hobsbawm, *The Age of Empire 1875–1914* (London, 1987), p. 159.

9   *The Age of Capital*, p. 106.

10  *On History*, p. 9.

11  *The Age of Capital*, p. 117.

12  Michael Gove: 'All pupils will learn our island story', 5 October 2010, http://conservative-speeches.sayit.mysociety.org/speech/601441.

13  J. E. E. D. Acton, 'Nationality', in J. N. Figgis and R. V. Laurence (eds), *The History of Freedom and Other Essays* (London, 1907), pp. 270–5.

14  Ernest Renan, *Qu'est-ce qu'une nation?*, available online in French at http://www.rutebeuf.com/textes/renan01.html and in English at http://ig.cs.tu-berlin.de/oldstatic/w2001/eu1/dokumente/Basistexte/Renan1882EN-Nation.pdf (my emphasis).

15  *On History*, p. 35.

16  Friedrich Nietzsche, *Thus Spoke Zarathustra*, trans. J. R. Hollingdale (London, 2003), p. 75.

17  'The Wisdom of Life', *The Essays of Arthur Schopenhauer* (1890), ch. 4.

18  *The Age of Empire*, pp. 153–4.

19  Ibid., p. 155.

20  Philip Gabriel Eidelberg, *The Great Rumanian Peasant Revolt of 1907. Origins of a Modern Jacquerie* (Leiden, 1974), p. 204; Daniel Chirot, *Social Change in a Peripheral Society. The Creation of a Balkan Colony* (New York, 1976), p. 150; Keith Hitchins, *Rumania. 1866–1947* (Oxford, 1994), p. 178; Catherine Durandin, *Histoire des Roumains* (Paris, 1995), p. 192.

21  *Nations and Nationalism since 1780*, p. 192.

22  *The Age of Capital*, p. 120.

23  Eric Hobsbawm, 'Socialism and Nationalism: Some Reflections on "The Break-up of Britain"', *New Left Review*, 105 (1977), pp. 3–23.

24  Benedict Anderson, *Imagined Communities: Reflections on the Origin and Spread of Nationalism* (London, 1991), p. 7.

25  'Are All Tongues Equal?' in this collection, pp. 261–75.

26  *Nations and Nationalism since 1780*, p. 112.

27  See Yakov M. Rabkin, 'Language in Nationalism: Modern Hebrew in the Zionist Project', *Holy Land Studies*, 9:2 (2010), pp. 129–45.

28  *The Age of Empire*, p. 147..

# I

# NATIONALISM IN HISTORY

# 1

## *Outside and Inside History*

> This was given as a lecture opening the academic
> year 1993–4 at the Central European University in
> Budapest.

It is an honour to be asked to open this academic year of the
Central European University. It is also a curious sensation to do
so, since, though I am a second-generation English-born British
citizen, I am also a central European. Indeed, as a Jew I am one
of the characteristic members of the central European diaspora
of peoples. My grandfather came to London from Warsaw.
My mother was Viennese, and so is my wife, though she now
speaks better Italian than German. My wife's mother still spoke
Hungarian as a little girl and her parents, at one stage of their
lives in the old monarchy, had a store in Herzegovina. My wife
and I once went to Mostar to trace it, in the days when there
was still peace in that unhappy part of the Balkans. I have had
some connections with Hungarian historians myself in the old
days. So I come to you as an outsider who is also, in an oblique
way, an insider. What can I say to you?

I want to say three things to you.

The first concerns central and eastern Europe. If you come from there, and I assume that almost all of you do, you are citizens of countries whose status is doubly uncertain. I am not claiming that uncertainty is a monopoly of central and east Europeans. It is probably more universal today than ever. Nevertheless, your horizon is particularly cloudy. In my own lifetime every country in your part of Europe has been overrun by war, conquered, occupied, liberated and reoccupied. Every state in it has a different shape from the one it had when I was born. Only six of the twenty-three states which now fill the map between Trieste and the Urals were in existence at the time of my birth, or would have been if they had not been occupied by some army: Russia, Romania, Bulgaria, Albania, Greece and Turkey, for neither post-1918 Austria nor post-1918 Hungary is really comparable to Habsburg Hungary and Cisleithania. Several came into existence after the First World War, even more since 1989. They include several countries which had never in history had the status of independent statehood in the modern sense, or which had it briefly – for a year or two, for a decade or two – and then lost it, though some have since regained it: the three little Baltic states, Belarus, Ukraine, Slovakia, Moldova, Slovenia, Croatia, Macedonia, not to go further eastwards. Some were born and died in my lifetime, like Yugoslavia and Czechoslovakia. It is perfectly common for the elderly inhabitant of some central European city to have had, successively, the identity documents of three states. A person of my age from Lemberg or Czernowitz has lived under four states, not counting wartime occupations; a man from Munkacs may well have lived under five, if we count the momentary autonomy of Podkarpatská Rus in 1938. In more civilized times, as in 1919, he or she might have been given the option which new citizenship to choose, but since the Second World War he or she has been more likely to be either forcibly expelled or forcibly integrated into the new state. Where does a central and eastern

European belong? Who is he or she? The question has been a real one for great numbers of them, and it still is. In some countries it is a question of life and death, in almost all it affects and sometimes determines their legal status and life chances.

However, there is another and more collective uncertainty. The bulk of central and eastern Europe belongs to that part of the world for which diplomats and United Nations experts since 1945 have tried to devise polite euphemisms: 'under-developed' or 'developing', that is to say, relatively or absolutely poor and backward. In some respects there is no sharp line between the two Europes, but rather a slope to the east and to the west of what we might call the main mountain range or crest of European economic and cultural dynamism, which ran from north Italy across the Alps to northern France and the Low Countries, and was prolonged across the Channel into England. It can be traced in the medieval trade routes and the distribution map of Gothic architecture, as well as in the figures for regional GDP within the European Community. In fact, today this region is still the backbone of the European Community. However, insofar as there is a historical line separating 'advanced' from 'backward' Europe it ran, roughly, through the middle of the Habsburg Empire. I know that people are sensitive in these matters. Ljubljana thinks of itself as a great deal nearer the centre of civilization than, say, Skopje, and Budapest than Belgrade, and the present government in Prague does not even wish to be called 'central European' for fear of being contaminated by contact with the east. It insists that it belongs exclusively to the west. However, my point is that no country or region in central and eastern Europe thought of itself as being at that centre. All looked somewhere else for a model of how really to be advanced and modern, even, I suspect, the educated middle class of Vienna, Budapest and Prague. They looked to Paris and London, just as the intellectuals of Belgrade and Ruse looked to Vienna – even though by most accepted standards the present Czech Republic and parts of the present Austria formed part of the advanced industrial part of Europe, and culturally Vienna, Budapest and Prague had no reason at all to feel inferior to anyone else.

The history of backward countries in the nineteenth and twentieth centuries is the history of trying to catch up with the more advanced world by imitating it. The nineteenth-century Japanese took Europe as their model, the west Europeans after the Second World War imitated the American economy. The story of central and eastern Europe in the twentieth century is, broadly, that of trying to catch up by following several models one after the other and failing. After 1918, when most of the successor countries were new, the model was western democracy and economic liberalism. President Wilson – is the main station in Prague named after him again? – was the region's patron saint, except for the Bolsheviks who went their own way. (Actually, they too had foreign models: Rathenau and Henry Ford.) This did not work. The model broke down politically and economically in the 1920s and 1930s. The Great Depression eventually broke multinational democracy even in Czechoslovakia. A number of these countries then briefly tried or flirted with the fascist model, which looked like the economic and political success story of the 1930s. (We are inclined to forget that Nazi Germany was remarkably successful in overcoming the Great Depression.) Integration in a Great German economic system did not work either. Germany was defeated.

After 1945 most of these countries chose, or found themselves being made to choose, the Bolshevik model, which was essentially a model for modernizing backward agrarian economies by planned industrial revolution. It was therefore never relevant to what is now the Czech Republic and to what was until 1989 the German Democratic Republic, but it was relevant to most of the region, including the USSR. I do not have to tell you about the economic deficiencies and flaws of the system, which eventually led to its breakdown, and still less about the intolerable, the increasingly intolerable political systems it imposed on central and eastern Europe. Still less do I have to remind you of the incredible sufferings it imposed on the peoples of the former USSR, particularly in the iron age of Joseph Stalin. And yet I must say, although many of you will not welcome my saying so, that up to a point it worked better than anything since the break-up of the monarchies in 1918. For the common citizens of the more backward countries in the region – say Slovakia and much of the Balkan peninsula – it was probably the best period in their history. It broke down because economically the system became increasingly rigid and unworkable, and especially because it proved virtually incapable of generating or making economic use of innovation, quite apart from stifling intellectual originality. Moreover, it became impossible to hide the fact from the local populations that other countries had made far more material progress than the socialist ones. If you prefer putting it another way, it broke down because ordinary citizens were indifferent or hostile, and because the regimes themselves had lost faith in what they were pretending to do. Still, however you look at it, it failed in the most spectacular manner in 1989–91.

And now? There is another model which everyone rushes to follow, parliamentary democracy in politics and the extremes of free-market capitalism in economics. In the present form it is not really a model, but chiefly a reaction against what has gone before. It may settle down to become something more workable – if it is allowed to settle down. However, even if it were to do so, in the light of history since 1918 there is not much likelihood that this region, possibly with marginal exceptions, will succeed in joining the club of the 'really' advanced and up-to-date countries. The results of imitating President Reagan and Mrs Thatcher have proved disappointing even in countries which have not been laid waste in civil war, chaos and anarchy. I should add that the results of following the Reagan–Thatcher model in the countries of its origin have not been brilliantly successful either, if you will permit a British understatement.

So, on the whole, the people of central and eastern Europe

will go on living in countries disappointed in their past, probably largely disappointed with their present, and uncertain about their future. This is a very dangerous situation. People will look for someone to blame for their failures and insecurities. The movements and ideologies most likely to benefit from this mood are not, at least in this generation, those which want a return to some version of the days before 1989. They are more likely to be movements inspired by xenophobic nationalism and intolerance. The easiest thing is always to blame the strangers.

This brings me to my second and main point, which is much more directly relevant to the work of a university, or at least to that part of the work which concerns me as a historian and university teacher. For history is the raw material for nationalist or ethnic or fundamentalist ideologies, as poppies are the raw material for heroin addiction. The past is an essential element, perhaps *the* essential element, in these ideologies. If there is no suitable past, it can always be invented. Indeed, in the nature of things there is usually no entirely suitable past, because the phenomenon these ideologies claim to justify is not ancient or eternal but historically novel. This applies both to religious fundamentalism in its current versions – the Ayatollah Khomeini's version of an Islamic state is no older than the early 1970s – and to contemporary nationalism. The past legitimizes. The past gives a more glorious background to a present that doesn't have much to celebrate. I recall seeing somewhere a study of the ancient civilization of the cities of the Indus valley with the title *Five Thousand Years of Pakistan*. Pakistan was not even thought of before 1932–3, when the name was invented by some student militants. It did not become a serious political demand until 1940. As a state it has existed only since 1947. There is no evidence of any more connection between the civilization of Mohenjo Daro and the current rulers of Islamabad than there is of a connection between the Trojan War and the government in Ankara, which is at present claiming the return, if only for the first public exhibition, of Schliemann's treasure of King Priam of Troy. But five thousand years of Pakistan somehow sounds better than forty-six years of Pakistan.

In this situation historians find themselves in the unexpected role of political actors. I used to think that the profession of history, unlike that of, say, nuclear physics, could at least do no harm. Now I know it can. Our studies can turn into bomb factories like the workshops in which the IRA has learned to transform chemical fertilizer into an explosive. This state of affairs affects us in two ways. We have a responsibility to historical facts in general, and for criticizing the politico-ideological abuse of history in particular.

I need say little about the first of these responsibilities. I would not have to say anything, but for two developments. One is the current fashion for novelists to base their plots on recorded reality rather than inventing them, thus fudging the border between historical fact and fiction. The other is the rise of 'postmodernist' intellectual fashions in western universities, particularly in departments of literature and anthropology, which imply that all 'facts' claiming objective existence are simply intellectual constructions – in short, that there is no clear difference between fact and fiction. But there is, and for historians, even for the most militantly anti-positivist ones among us, the ability to distinguish between the two is absolutely fundamental. We cannot invent our facts. Either Elvis Presley is dead or he isn't. The question can be answered unambiguously on the basis of evidence, insofar as reliable evidence is available, which is sometimes the case. Either the present Turkish government, which denies the attempted genocide of the Armenians in 1915, is right or it is not. Most of us would dismiss any denial of this massacre from serious historical discourse, although there is no equally unambiguous way to choose between different ways of interpreting the phenomenon or fitting it into the wider context of history. Recently Hindu zealots destroyed a mosque in Aodhya, ostensibly on the grounds that the mosque had been imposed by the Muslim Moghul conqueror Babur on the Hindus in a particularly sacred location which marked the birthplace of the god Rama. My colleagues and friends in the Indian universities published a study showing (a) that nobody until the nineteenth century had suggested that Aodhya was the birthplace of Rama and (b) that the mosque was almost certainly not built in the time of Babur. I wish I could say that this has had much effect on the rise of the Hindu party which provoked the incident, but at least they did their duty as historians, for the benefit of those who can read and are exposed to the propaganda of intolerance now and in the future. Let us do ours.

Few of the ideologies of intolerance are based on simple lies or fictions for which no evidence exists. After all, there was a battle of Kosovo in 1389, the Serb warriors and their allies were defeated by the Turks, and this did leave deep scars on the popular memory of the Serbs, although it does not follow that this justifies the oppression of the Albanians, who now form 90 per cent of the region's population, or the Serb claim that the land is essentially theirs. Denmark does not claim the large part of eastern England which was settled and ruled by Danes before the eleventh century, which continued to be known as the Danelaw and whose village names are still philologically Danish.

The most usual ideological abuse of history is based on anachronism rather than lies. Greek nationalism refuses Macedonia even the right to its name on the grounds that all Macedonia is essentially Greek and part of a Greek nation-state, presumably ever since the father of Alexander the Great, King of Macedonia, become the ruler of the Greek lands on the Balkan peninsula. Like everything about Macedonia, this is a far from purely academic matter, but it takes a lot of courage for a Greek intellectual to say that, historically speaking, it is nonsense. There was no Greek nation-state or any other single political entity for the Greeks in the fourth century BC, the Macedonian Empire was nothing like a Greek or any other modern nation-state, and in any case it is highly probable that the ancient Greeks regarded the Macedonian rulers, as they did their later Roman rulers, as barbarians and not as Greeks, though they were doubtless too polite or cautious to say so. Moreover, Macedonia is historically such an inextricable mixture of ethnicities – not for nothing has it given its name to French mixed-fruit salads (*macédoine*) – that any attempt to identify it with a single nationality cannot be correct. In fairness, the extremes of emigrant Macedonian nationalism should also be dismissed for the same reason, as should all the publications in Croatia which somehow try to turn Zvonimir the Great into the ancestor of President Tudman. But it is difficult to stand up against the inventors of a national schoolbook history, although there are historians in Zagreb University, whom I am proud to count as friends, who have the courage to do so.

These and many other attempts to replace history by myth and invention are not merely bad intellectual jokes. After all, they can determine what goes into schoolbooks, as the Japanese authorities knew, when they insisted on a sanitized version of the Japanese war in China for use in Japanese classrooms. Myth and invention are essential to the politics of identity by which groups of people today, defining themselves by ethnicity, religion or the past or present borders of states, try to find some certainty in an uncertain and shaking world by saying, 'We are different from and better than the Others.' They are our concern in the universities because the people who formulate those myths and inventions are educated people: schoolteachers lay and clerical, professors (not many, I hope), journalists, television and radio producers. Today most of them will have gone to some university. Make no mistake about it. History is not ancestral memory or collective tradition. It is what people learned from priests, schoolmasters, the writers of history books and the compilers of magazine articles and television programmes. It is very important for historians to remember their responsibility, which is, above all, to stand aside from the passions of identity politics – even if we feel them also. After all, we are human beings too.

How serious an affair this may be is shown in a recent article by the Israeli writer Amos Elon about the way in which the genocide of the Jews by Hitler has been turned into a legitimizing myth for the existence of the state of Israel. More than this: in the years of right-wing government it was turned into a sort of national ritual assertion of Israeli state identity and superiority and a central item of the official system of national beliefs, alongside God. Elon, who traces the evolution of this transformation of the concept of the 'Holocaust' argues, following the recent Minister of Education of the new Israeli Labour government, that history must now be separated from national myth, ritual and politics. As a non-Israeli, though a Jew, I express no views about this. However, as a historian I sadly note one observation by Elon. It is that the leading contributions to the scholarly historiography of the genocide, whether by Jews or non-Jews, were either not translated into Hebrew, like Hilberg's great work, or were translated only with considerable delay, and then sometimes with editorial disclaimers. The serious historiography of the genocide has not made it any less of an unspeakable tragedy. It was merely at variance with the legitimizing myth.

Yet this very story gives us ground for hope. For here we have mythological or nationalist history being criticized from within. I note that the history of the establishment of Israel ceased to be written in Israel essentially as national propaganda or Zionist polemic about forty years after the state came into being. I have noticed the same in Irish history. About half a century after most of Ireland won its independence, Irish historians no longer wrote the history of their island in terms of the mythology of the national liberation movement. Irish history, both in the Republic and in the North, is passing through a period of great brilliance because it has succeeded in so liberating itself. This is still a matter which has political implications and risks. The history that is written today breaks with the old tradition which stretches from the Fenians to the IRA, still fighting in the name of the old myths with guns and bombs. But the fact that a new generation has grown up which can stand back from the passions of the great traumatic and formative moments of their countries' history is a sign of hope for historians.

However, we cannot wait for the generations to pass. We must resist the *formation* of national, ethnic and other myths, as they are being formed. It will not make us popular. Thomas Masaryk, founder of the Czechoslovak Republic, was not popular when he entered politics as the man who proved, with regret but without hesitation, that the medieval manuscripts on which much of the Czech national myth was based were fakes. But it has to be done, and I hope those of you who are historians will do it.

That is all I wanted to say to you about the duty of historians. However, before I close, I want to remind you of one other thing. You, as students of this university, are privileged people. The odds are that, as alumni of a distinguished and prestigious institute you will, if you choose, have a good status in society, have better careers and earn more than other people, though not so much as successful businessmen. What I want to remind you of is something I was told when I began to teach in a university. 'The people for whom you are there,' said my own teacher, 'are not the brilliant students like yourself. They are the average students with boring minds who get uninteresting degrees in the lower range of the second class, and whose examination scripts all read the same. The first-class people will look after themselves, though you will enjoy teaching them. The others are the ones who need you.'

That applies not only to the university but to the world. Governments, the economy, schools, everything in society, is not for the benefit of the privileged minorities. We can look after ourselves. It is for the benefit of the ordinary run of people, who are not particularly clever or interesting (unless, of course, we fall in love with one of them), not highly educated, not successful or destined for success – in fact, are nothing very special. It is for the people who, throughout history, have entered history outside their neighbourhoods as individuals only in the records of their births, marriages and deaths. Any society worth living in is one designed for them, not for the rich, the clever, the exceptional, although any society worth living in must provide room and scope for such minorities. But the world is not made for our personal benefit, nor are we in the world for our personal benefit. A world that claims that this is its purpose is not a good, and ought not to be a lasting, world.

# 2

# *Nationalism in the Age of Revolution*

Every people has its special mission, which will
cooperate towards the fulfilment of the general
mission of humanity. That mission constitutes its
*nationality*. Nationality is sacred.

GIUSEPPE MAZZINI, 'Act of Brotherhood'
(*Patto di fratellazna*) from *Young Europe*, 1834

The day will come ... when sublime Germania shall
stand on the bronze pedestal of liberty and justice,
bearing in one hand the torch of enlightenment,
which shall throw the beam of civilization into the
remotest corners of the earth, and in the other the
arbiter's balance. The people will beg her to settle
their disputes; those very people who now show us
that might is right, and kick us with the jackboot of
scornful contempt.

PHILIPP JAKOB SIEBENPFEIFFER (1832)

I

After 1830 [ ... ] the general movement in favour of revolution
split. One product of this split deserves special attention: the
self-consciously nationalist movements.

The movements which best symbolize this development

15

are the 'Youth' movements founded or inspired by Giuseppe Mazzini shortly after the 1830 revolution: *Young Italy*, *Young Poland*, *Young Switzerland*, *Young Germany* and *Young France* (1831–6) and the analogous *Young Ireland* in the 1840s, the ancestor of the only lasting and successful revolutionary organization on the model of the early nineteenth-century brotherhoods, the Fenians or Irish Republican Brotherhood, better known through its executive arm of the Irish Republican Army. In themselves these movements were of no great importance; the mere presence of Mazzini would have been enough to ensure their total ineffectiveness. Symbolically they are of extreme importance, as is indicated by the adoption in subsequent nationalist movements of such labels as 'Young Czechs' or 'Young Turks'. They mark the disintegration of the European revolutionary movement into national segments. Doubtless each of these segments had much the same political programme, strategy and tactics as the others, and even much the same flag – almost invariably a tricolour of some kind. Its members saw no contradiction between their own demands and those of other nations, and indeed envisaged a brotherhood of all, simultaneously liberating themselves. On the other hand, each now tended to justify its primary concern with its own nation by adopting the role of a Messiah for all. Through Italy (according to Mazzini), through Poland (according to Mickiewicz) the suffering peoples of the world were to be led to freedom; an attitude readily adaptable to conservative or indeed imperialist policies, as witness the Russian Slavophiles with their championship of Holy Russia, the Third Rome, and the Germans who were subsequently to tell the world at some length that it would be healed by the German spirit. Admittedly this ambiguity of nationalism went back to the French Revolution. But in those days there had been only *one* great and revolutionary nation and it made sense (as indeed it still did) to regard it as the headquarters of all revolutions, and the necessary prime mover in the liberation of the world. To look to Paris was rational; to look to a vague 'Italy', 'Poland' or

'Germany' (represented in practice by a handful of conspirators and émigrés) made sense only for Italians, Poles and Germans.

If the new nationalism had been confined only to the membership of the national-revolutionary brotherhoods, it would not be worth much more attention. However, it also reflected much more powerful forces, which were emerging into political consciousness in the 1830s as the result of the double revolution. The most immediately powerful of these were the discontent of the lesser landowners or gentry and the emergence of a national middle and even lower middle class in numerous countries; the spokesmen for both being largely professional intellectuals.

The revolutionary role of the lesser gentry is perhaps best illustrated in Poland and Hungary. There, on the whole, the large landed magnates had long found it possible and desirable to make terms with absolutism and foreign rule. The Hungarian magnates were in general Catholic and had long been accepted as pillars of Viennese court society; very few of them were to join the revolution of 1848. The memory of the old *Rzeczpospolita* made even Polish magnates nationally minded; but the most influential of their quasi-national parties, the Czartoryski connection, now operating from the luxurious emigration of the Hotel Lambert in Paris, had always favoured the alliance with Russia and continued to prefer diplomacy to revolt. Economically they were wealthy enough to afford what they needed, short of really titanic dissipation, and even to invest enough in the improvement of their estates to benefit from the economic expansion of the age, if they chose to. Count Széchenyi, one of the few moderate liberals from this class and a champion of economic improvement, gave a year's income for the new Hungarian Academy of Sciences – some sixty thousand florins. There is no evidence that his standard of life suffered from such disinterested generosity. On the other hand, the numerous gentlemen who had little but their birth to distinguish them from other impoverished farmers – one in eight of the Hungarian population claimed gentlemanly status – had neither the money to make their holdings profitable nor the inclination to compete with Germans and Jews for middle-class wealth. If they could not live decently on their rents, and a degenerate age deprived them of a soldier's chances, then they might, if not too ignorant, consider the law, administration or some intellectual position; but no bourgeois activity. Such gentlemen had long been the stronghold of opposition to absolutism, foreigners and magnate rule in their respective countries, sheltering (as in Hungary) behind the dual buttress of Calvinism and county organization. It was natural that their opposition, discontent, and aspiration for more jobs for local gentlemen should now fuse with nationalism.

The national business classes which emerged in this period were, paradoxically, a rather less nationalist element. Admittedly in disunited Germany and Italy the advantages of a large unified national market made sense. The author of *Deutschland über Alles* apostrophized

> *Ham and scissors, boots and garters,*
> *Wool and soap and yarn and beer,*[1]

because they had achieved, what the spirit of nationality had been unable to, a genuine sense of national unity through customs union. However there is little evidence that, say, the shippers of Genoa (who were later to provide much of the financial backing for Garibaldi) preferred the possibilities of a national Italian market to the larger prosperity of trading all over the Mediterranean. And in the large multinational empires the industrial or trading nuclei which grew up in particular provinces might grumble about discrimination, but at bottom clearly preferred the great markets open to them now to the little ones of future national independence. The Polish industrialists, with all Russia at their feet, took little part as yet in Polish nationalism. When Palacky claimed on behalf of the Czechs that 'if Austria did not exist, it would have to be invented', he was not merely calling on the monarchy's support against the Germans, but also expressing the sound economic reasoning of the economically most advanced sector of a large and otherwise backward empire. Business interests were sometimes at the head of nationalism, as in Belgium, where a strong pioneer industrial community regarded itself, with doubtful reason, as disadvantaged under the rule of the powerful Dutch merchant community, to which it had been hitched in 1815. But this was an exceptional case.

The great proponents of middle-class nationalism at this stage were the lower and middle professional, administrative and intellectual strata, in other words the *educated* classes. (These are not, of course, distinct from the business classes, especially in backward countries where estate administrators, notaries, lawyers and the like are the key accumulators of rural wealth.) To be precise, the advance guard of middle-class nationalism fought its battle along the line which marked the educational progress of large numbers of 'new men' into areas hitherto occupied by a small elite. The progress of schools and universities measures that of nationalism, just as schools and especially universities became its most conscious champions: the conflict of Germany and Denmark over Schleswig-Holstein in 1848 and again in 1864 was anticipated by the conflict of Kiel and Copenhagen on this issue in the middle 1840s.

That progress was striking, though the total number of the 'educated' remains small. The number of pupils in the French state *lycées* doubled between 1809 and 1842, and increased with particular rapidity under the July monarchy, but even so in 1842 it was only just under nineteen thousand. (The total of all children receiving secondary education[2] then was about seventy thousand.) Russia, around 1850, had some twenty thousand secondary pupils out of a total population of sixty-eight million.[3] The number of university students was naturally even smaller, though it was rising. It is difficult to realize that the Prussian academic youth which was so stirred by the idea of liberation after 1806 consisted in 1805 of not much more than fifteen hundred young men all told; that the *Polytechnique*, the bane of the post-1815 Bourbons, trained a total of 1581 young men in the entire period from 1815 to 1830, i.e. an annual intake of about one hundred. The revolutionary prominence of the students in the 1848 period makes us forget that in the whole continent of Europe, including the unrevolutionary British Isles, there were probably not more than forty thousand university students in all.[4] Still their numbers rose. In Russia it rose from 1700 in 1825 to 4600 in 1848. And even if they did not, the transformation of society and the universities gave them a new consciousness of themselves as a social group. Nobody remembers that in 1789 there were something like six thousand students in the University of Paris, because they played no independent part in the Revolution.[5] But by 1830 nobody could possibly overlook such a number of young academics.

Small elites can operate in foreign languages; once the cadre of the educated becomes large enough, the national language imposes itself (as witness the struggle for linguistic recognition in the Indian states since the 1940s). Hence the moment when textbooks or newspapers in the national language are first written, or when that language is first used for some official purpose, measures a crucial step in national evolution. The 1830s saw this step taken over large areas of Europe. Thus the first major Czech works on astronomy, chemistry, anthropology, mineralogy and botany were written or completed in this decade; and so, in Romania, were the first school textbooks substituting Romanian for the previously current Greek. Hungarian was adopted instead of Latin as the official language of the Hungarian Diet in 1840, though Budapest University, controlled from Vienna, did not abandon Latin lectures until 1844. (However, the struggle for the use of Hungarian as an official language had gone on intermittently since 1790.) In Zagreb Gai published his *Croatian Gazette* (later *Illyrian National Gazette*) from 1835 in the first literary version of what had hitherto been merely a complex of dialects. In countries which had long possessed an official national language, the change cannot be so easily measured, though it is interesting that after 1830 the number of German books published in Germany (as against Latin and French titles) for the first time consistently exceeded 90 per cent, the number of French ones after 1820 fell below 4 per cent.[6] More generally the expansion of publishing gives us a comparable indication. Thus in Germany the number of books published remained much the same in 1821 as in 1800 – about four thousand titles a year; but by 1841 it had risen to twelve thousand titles.[7] In the early eighteenth century only about 60 per cent of all titles published in Germany were in the German language; since then the proportion had risen fairly steadily.

Of course the great mass of Europeans, and of non-Europeans, remained uneducated. Indeed, with the exception of the Germans, the Dutch, Scandinavians, Swiss and the citizens of the USA, no people can in 1840 be described as literate. Several can be described as totally illiterate, like the southern Slavs, who had less than 0.5 per cent literacy in 1827 (even much later only 1 per cent of Dalmatian recruits to the Austrian army could read and write) or the Russians who had 2 per cent (1840), and a great many as almost illiterate, like the Spaniards, the Portuguese (who appear to have had barely eight thousand children in all *at school* after the Peninsular War) and, except for the Lombards and Piedmontese, the Italians. Even Britain, France and Belgium were 40 to 50 per cent illiterate in the 1840s.[8] Illiteracy is no bar to political consciousness, but there is, in fact, no evidence that nationalism of the modern kind was a powerful mass force except in countries already transformed by the dual revolution: in France, in Britain, in the USA and – because it was an economic and political dependency of Britain – in Ireland.

To equate nationalism with the literate class is not to claim that the mass of, say, Russians, did not consider themselves 'Russian' when confronted with somebody or something that

was not. However, for the masses in general the test of nationality was still religion: the Spaniard was defined by being Catholic,
the Russian by being Orthodox. However, though such confrontations were becoming rather more frequent, they were still rare,
and certain kinds of national feeling such as the Italian were as
yet wholly alien to the great mass of the people, which did not
even speak the national literary language but mutually almost
incomprehensible *patois*. Even in Germany patriotic mythology
has greatly exaggerated the degree of national feeling against
Napoleon. France was extremely popular in western Germany,
especially among soldiers, whom it employed freely.[9] Populations
attached to the pope or the emperor might express resentment
against their enemies, who happened to be the French, but this
hardly implied any feelings of national consciousness, let alone
any desire for a national state. Moreover, the very fact that
nationalism was represented by middle class and gentry was
enough to make the poor man suspicious. The Polish radical-
democratic revolutionaries tried earnestly – as did the more
advanced of the South Italian Carbonari and other conspirators – to mobilize the peasantry even to the point of offering
agrarian reform. Their failure was almost total. The Galician
peasants in 1846 opposed the Polish revolutionaries even though
these actually proclaimed the abolition of serfdom, preferring to
massacre gentlemen and trust to the emperor's officials.

The uprooting of peoples, which is perhaps the most important single phenomenon of the nineteenth century, was to
break down this deep, age-old and localized traditionalism. Yet
over most of the world up to the 1820s hardly anybody as yet
migrated or emigrated, except under the compulsion of armies
and hunger, or in the traditionally migratory groups such as the
peasants from central France who did seasonal building jobs in
the north, or the travelling German artisans. Uprooting still
meant, not the mild form of homesickness which was to become
the characteristic psychological disease of the nineteenth century (reflected in innumerable sentimental popular songs), but

the acute, killing *mal de pays* or *mal de cœur* which had first been clinically described by doctors among the old Swiss mercenaries in foreign lands. The conscription of the Revolutionary Wars revealed it, notably among the Bretons. The pull of the remote northern forests was so strong, that it could lead an Estonian servant-girl to leave her excellent employers the Kügelgens in Saxony, where she was free, and return home to serfdom. Migration and emigration, of which the migration to the USA is the most convenient index, increased notably from the 1820s, though it did not reach anything like major proportions until the 1840s, when one and three-quarter million crossed the North Atlantic (a little less than three times the figure for the 1830s). Even so, the only major migratory nation outside the British Isles was as yet the German, long used to sending its sons as peasant settlers to eastern Europe and America, as travelling artisans across the continent and as mercenaries everywhere.

We can in fact speak of only one western national movement organized in a coherent form before 1848 which was genuinely based on the masses, and even this enjoyed the immense advantage of identification with the strongest carrier of tradition, the church. This was the Irish Repeal movement under Daniel O'Connell (1785–1847), a golden-voiced lawyer-demagogue of peasant stock, the first – and up to 1848 the only one – of those charismatic popular leaders who mark the awakening of political consciousness in hitherto backward masses. (The only comparable figures before 1848 were Feargus O'Connor (1794–1855), another Irishman, who symbolized Chartism in Britain, and perhaps Louis Kossuth (1802–94), who may have acquired some of his subsequent mass prestige before the 1848 revolution, though in fact his reputation in the 1840s was made as a champion of the gentry, and his later canonization by nationalist historians makes it difficult to see his early career at all clearly.) O'Connell's Catholic Association, which won its mass support and the not wholly justified confidence of the clergy in the successful struggle for Catholic Emancipation

(1829) was in no sense tied to the gentry, who were in any case Protestant and Anglo-Irish. It was a movement of peasants, and such elements of a native Irish lower-middle class as existed in that pauperized island. 'The Liberator' was borne into leadership by successive waves of a mass movement of agrarian revolt, the chief motive force of Irish politics throughout that appalling century. This was organized in secret terrorist societies which themselves helped to break down the parochialism of Irish life. However, his aim was neither revolution nor national independence, but a moderate middle-class Irish autonomy by agreement or negotiation with the British Whigs. He was, in fact, not a nationalist and still less a peasant revolutionary but a moderate middle-class autonomist. Indeed, the chief criticism which has been not unjustifiably raised against him by later Irish nationalists (much as the more radical Indian nationalists have criticized Gandhi, who occupied an analogous position in his country's history) was that he could have raised all Ireland against the British, and deliberately refused to do so. But this does not alter the fact that the movement he led was genuinely supported by the mass of the Irish nation.

## II

Outside the zone of the modern bourgeois world there were, however, movements of popular revolt against alien rule (i.e. normally understood as meaning rule by a different religion rather than a different nationality) which sometimes appear to anticipate later national movements. Such were the rebellions against the Turkish Empire, against the Russians in the Caucasus, and the fight against the encroaching British Raj in and on the confines of India. It is unwise to read too much modern nationalism into these, though in backward areas populated by armed and combative peasants and herdsmen, organized in clan groups and inspired by tribal chieftains, bandit-heroes and prophets, resistance to the foreign (or better, the unbelieving) ruler could take the form of veritable people's wars quite unlike the elite nationalist movements in less Homeric countries. In fact, however, the resistance of Mahrattas (a feudal-military Hindu group) and Sikhs (a militant religious sect) to the British in 1803–18 and 1845–9 respectively have little in connection with subsequent Indian nationalism and produced none of their own.[10] The Caucasian tribes, savage, heroic and feud-ridden, found in the puritan Islamic sect of Muridism a temporary bond of unity against the invading Russians and in Shamyl (1797–1871) a leader of major stature; but there is not to this day a Caucasian nation, but merely a congeries of small mountain peoples in small Soviet republics. (The Georgians and Armenians, who have formed nations in the modern sense, were not involved in the Shamyl movement.) The Bedouin, swept by puritan religious sects like the Wahhabi in Arabia and the Senussi in what is today Libya, fought for the simple faith of Allah and the simple life of the herdsman and raider against the corruption of taxes, pashas and cities; but what we now know as Arab nationalism – a product of the twentieth century – has come out of the cities, not the nomadic encampments.

Even the rebellions against the Turks in the Balkans, espe-cially among the rarely subdued mountain peoples of the south and west, should not be too readily interpreted in modern nationalist terms though the bards and braves of several – the two were often the same, as among the poet-warrior-bishops of Montenegro – recalled the glories of quasi-national heroes like the Albanian Skanderbeg and the tragedies like the Serbian defeat at Kosovo in the remote battles against the Turks. Nothing was more natural than to revolt, where necessary or desirable, against a local administration or a weakening Turkish Empire. However, little but a common economic backwardness untied what we now know about the Yugoslavs, even those in the Turkish Empire, and the very concept of Yugoslavia was the product of intellectuals in Austro-Hungary rather than those who actually fought for liberty.[11] The Orthodox Montenegrins, never subdued, fought the Turks; but with equal zest they fought the unbelieving Catholic Albanians and the unbelieving, but solidly Slav, Muslim Bosnians. The Bosnians revolted against the Turks, whose religion many of them shared, with as much readiness as the orthodox Serbs of the wooded Danube plain, and with more zest than the orthodox 'old Serbs' of the Albanian frontier area. The first of the Balkan peoples to rise in the nineteenth century were the Serbs under a heroic pig-dealer and brigand, Black George (1760–1817), but the initial phase of his rising (1804–7) did not even claim to be against Turkish local rule, but on the contrary for the sultan against the abuses of the local rulers. There is little in the early history of mountain rebellion in the western Balkans to suggest that the local Serbs, Albanians, Greeks and others would not in the early nineteenth century have been satisfied with the sort of non-national autonomous principality which a powerful satrap, Ali Pasha 'the Lion of Jannina' (1741–1822), for a time set up in Epirus.

In one and only one case did the perennial fight of the sheep-herding clansmen and bandit-heroes against *any* real government fuse with the ideas of middle-class nationalism and the French Revolution: in the Greek struggle for independence (1821–30). Not unnaturally Greece therefore became the myth and inspiration of nationalists and liberals everywhere. For in Greece alone did an entire people rise against the oppressor in a manner which could be plausibly identified with the cause of the European left; and in turn the support of the European left, headed by the poet Byron who died there, was of very considerable help in the winning of Greek independence.

Most Greeks were much like the other forgotten warrior-peasant countries and clans of the Balkan peninsula. A part, however, formed an international merchant and administrative class also settled in colonies or minority communities throughout the Turkish Empire and beyond, and the language and higher ranks of the entire Orthodox church, to which most Balkan peoples belonged, were Greek, headed by the Greek patriarch of Constantinople. Greek civil servants, transmuted into vassal princes, governed the Danubian principalities (the present Romania). In a sense the entire educated and mercantile classes of the Balkans, the Black Sea area and the Levant, whatever their national origins, were Hellenized by the very nature of their activities. During the eighteenth century this Hellenization proceeded more powerfully than before, largely because of the marked economic expansion which also extended the range and contacts of the Greek diaspora. The new and thriving Black Sea grain trade took it into Italian, French and British business centres and strengthened its links with Russia; the expansion of Balkan trade brought Greek or Grecized merchants into central Europe. The first Greek-language newspapers were published in Vienna (1784–1812). Periodic emigration and resettlement of peasant rebels further reinforced the exile communities. It was among this cosmopolitan diaspora that the ideas of the French Revolution – liberalism, nationalism and the methods of political organization by masonic secret societies – took root. Rhigas (1760–98), the leader of an early obscure and possibly pan-Balkanist revolutionary movement, spoke French and adapted the 'Marseillaise' to Hellenic conditions. The Philiké Hetairía, the secret patriotic society mainly responsible for the revolt of 1821, was founded in the great new Russian grain port of Odessa in 1814.

Their nationalism was to some extent comparable to the elite movements of the west. Nothing else explains the project of raising a rebellion for Greek independence in the Danube principalities under the leadership of local Greek magnates; for the only people who could be described as Greeks in these miserable serf-lands were lords, bishops, merchants and intellectuals. Naturally enough that rising failed miserably (1821). Fortunately, however, the Hetairía had also set out to enrol the anarchy of local brigand-heroes, outlaws and clan chieftains in the Greek mountains (especially in the Peloponnese), and with considerably greater success – at any rate after 1818 – than the

South Italian gentlemen Carbonari, who attempted a similar proselytization of their local banditti. It is doubtful whether anything like modern nationalism meant much to these 'klephts', though many of them had their 'clerks' – a respect for an interest in book-learning was a surviving relic of ancient Hellenism – who composed manifestos in the Jacobin terminology. If they stood for anything it was for the age-old ethos of a peninsula in which the role of man was to become a hero, and the outlaw who took to the mountains to resist any government and to right the peasant's wrongs was the universal political ideal. To the rebellions of men like Koloktrones, brigand and cattle-dealer, the nationalists of the western type gave leadership and a pan-Hellenic rather than a purely local scale. In turn they got from them that unique and awe-inspiring thing, the mass rising of an armed people.

The new Greek nationalism was enough to win independence, though the combination of middle-class leadership, klephtic disorganization and great power intervention produced one of those petty caricatures of the western liberal ideal which were to become so familiar in areas like Latin America. But it also had the paradoxical result of narrowing Hellenism to Hellas, and thus creating or intensifying the latent nationalism of the other Balkan peoples. While being Greek had been little more than the professional requirement of the Orthodox Balkan Christian, Hellenization had made progress. Once it meant the political support for Hellas, it receded, even among the assimilated Balkan literate classes. In this sense Greek independence was the essential preliminary condition for the evolution of the other Balkan nationalisms.

Outside Europe it is difficult to speak of nationalism at all. The numerous Latin American republics which replaced the broken Spanish and Portuguese Empires (to be accurate, Brazil became and remained an independent monarchy from 1816 to 1889), their frontiers often reflecting little more than the distribution of the estates of the grandees who had backed one rather than another of the local rebellions, began to acquired vested political interests and territorial aspirations. The original pan-American ideal of Simón Bolívar (1783–1830) of Venezuela and San Martín (1778–1850) of Argentina was impossible to realize, though it had persisted as a powerful revolutionary current throughout all the areas united by the Spanish language, just as pan-Balkanism, the heir of Orthodox unity against Islam, persisted and may still persist today. The vast extent and variety of the continent, the existence of independent foci of rebellion in Mexico (which determined Central America), Venezuela and Buenos Aires, and the special problem of the centre of Spanish colonialism in Peru, which was liberated from without, imposed automatic fragmentation. But the Latin American revolutions were the work of small groups of patricians, soldiers and Gallicized évolués, leaving the mass of the Catholic poor white population passive and the Indians indifferent or hostile. Only in Mexico was independence won by the initiative of a popular agrarian, i.e. Indian, movement marching under the banner of the Virgin of Guadalupe, and Mexico has consequently ever since followed a different and politically more advanced road from the remainder of continental Latin America. However, even among the tiny layer of the politically decisive Latin Americans it would be anachronistic in our period to speak of anything more than the embryo of Colombian, Venezuelan, Ecuadorian, etc. 'national consciousness'.

Something like a proto-nationalism, however, existed in various countries of eastern Europe, but paradoxically it took the direction of conservatism rather than national rebellion. The Slavs were oppressed everywhere, except in Russia and in a few wild Balkan strongholds; but in their immediate perspective the oppressors were, as we have seen, not the absolute monarchs, but the German or Magyar landlords and urban exploiters. Nor did the nationalism of these allow any place for Slav national existence: even so radical a programme as that of the German United States proposed by the republicans and democrats of

Baden (in south-west Germany) envisaged the inclusion of an Illyrian (i.e. Croat and Slovene) republic with its capital in Italian Trieste, a Moravian one with its capital in Olomouc, and a Bohemian one led by Prague.[12] Hence the immediate hope of the Slav nationalists lay in the emperors of Austria and Russia. Various versions of Slav solidarity expressed the Russian orientation, and attracted Slav rebels – even the anti-Russian Poles – especially in times of defeat and hopelessness as after the failure of the risings in 1846. 'Illyriansm' in Croatia and moderate Czech nationalism expressed the Austrian trend, and both received deliberate support from the Habsburg rulers, two of whose leading ministers – Kolowrat and the chief of the police system, Sedlnitzky – were themselves Czechs. Croatian cultural aspirations were protected in the 1830s, and by 1840 Kolowrat actually proposed what was later to prove so useful in the 1848 revolution, the appointment of a Croat military *ban* as chief of Croatia, and with control over the military frontier with Hungary, as a counterweight to the obstreperous Magyars.[13] To be a revolutionary in 1848 therefore came to be virtually identical with opposition to Slav national aspirations; and the tacit conflict between the 'progressive' and the 'reactionary' nations did much to doom the revolutions of 1848 to failure.

Nothing like nationalism is discoverable elsewhere, for the social conditions for it did not exist. In fact, if anything the forces which were later to produce nationalism were at this stage opposed to the alliance of tradition, religion and mass poverty which produced the most powerful resistance to the encroachment of western conquerors and exploiters. The elements of a local bourgeoisie which grew up in Asian countries did so in the shelter of the foreign exploiters whose agents, intermediaries and dependants they largely were: the Parsee community of Bombay is an example. Even if the educated and 'enlightened' Asian was not a *compradore* or a lesser official of some foreign ruler or firm (a situation not dissimilar to that of the Greek diaspora in Turkey), his first political task was to westernize – i.e. to introduce the ideas of the French Revolution and of scientific and technical modernization among his people against the united resistance of traditional rules and the traditionally ruled (a situation not dissimilar to that of the gentlemen-Jacobins of southern Italy). He was therefore doubly cut off from his people. Nationalist mythology has often obscured this divorce, partly by suppressing the link between colonialism and the early native middle classes, partly lending to earlier anti-foreign resistance the colours of a later nationalist movement. But in Asia, in the Islamic countries, and even more in Africa, the junction between the évolués and nationalism, and between both and the masses, was not made until the twentieth century.

Nationalism in the East was thus the eventual product of western influence and western conquest. This link is perhaps most evident in the one plainly oriental country in which the foundations of what was to become the first modern colonial nationalist movement (other than the Irish) were laid: in Egypt. Napoleon's conquest introduced western ideas, methods and techniques, whose value an able and ambitious local soldier, Mohammed Ali (Mehmet Ali), soon recognized. Having seized power and virtual independence from Turkey in the confused period which followed the withdrawal of the French, and with French support, Mohammed Ali set out to establish an efficient and westernizing despotism with foreign (mainly French) tech- nical aid. European left-wingers in the 1820s and 30s hailed this enlightened autocrat, and put their services at his disposal, when reaction in their own countries looked too dispiriting. The extraordinary sect of the Saint-Simonians, equally suspended between the advocacy of socialism and of industrial develop- ment by investment bankers and engineers, temporarily gave him their collective aid and prepared his plans of economic development. They thus also laid the foundation for the Suez Canal (built by the Saint-Simonian de Lesseps) and the fatal dependence of Egyptian rulers on vast loans negotiated by competing groups of European swindlers, which turned Egypt into a centre of imperialist rivalry and anti-imperialist rebellion later on. But Mohammed Ali was no more a nationalist than any other oriental despot. His westernization, not his or his people's aspirations, laid the foundations for later nationalism. If Egypt acquired the first nationalist movement in the Islamic world and Morocco was one of the last, it was because Mohammed Ali (for perfectly comprehensible geopolitical reasons) was in the main paths of westernization and the isolated self-sealed Sherifian Empire of the Muslim far west was not, and made no attempts to be. Nationalism, like so many other characteristics of the modern world, is the child of the dual revolution.

# Notes

1  Hoffmann v. Fallersleben, 'Der Deutsche Zollverein', in *Unpolitische Lieder* (1842), p. 46.

2  G. Weill, *L'Enseigement Sécondaire en France 1802–1920* (Paris, 1921), p. 72.

3  E. de Laveleye, *L'Instruction du Peuple* (1872), p. 278.

4  F. Paulsen, *Geschichte des Gelehrten Unterrichts*, vol. 2 (1897), p. 703; A. Daumard, 'Les élèves de l'Ecole Polytechnique 1815–48', *Revue d'Histoire Moderne et Contemporaine*, 5:3 (1958), pp. 226–34; the total number of Belgian and German students in an average semester in the early 1840s was about fourteen thousand. J. Conrad, 'Die Frequenzverhältnisse der Universitäten der haupstächlichen Kulturländer', *Jb. f. Nationalök. u. Statistik*, 56 (1895), pp. 376ff.

5  L. Liard, *L'Enseignement Supérieur en France 1789–1889* (1888), pp. 11ff.

6  *Geschichte des Gelehrten Unterrichts*, II, pp. 690–1.

7  *Handwörterbuch d. Staabwissenschaften* (2nd edn) art. Buchhandel.

8  *L'Instruction du Peuple*, p. 264.

9  W. Wachsmuth, *Europäische Sittengeschichte*, V, 2 (1839), pp. 807–8.

10  The Sikh movement has remained largely *sui generis* to this day. The tradition of combative Hindu resistance in Maharashtra made that area an early centre of Indian nationalism, and provided some of its earliest – and highly traditionalist – leaders, notably B. G. Tilak; but this was at best a regional, and far from dominant strain in the movement. Something like Mahratta nationalism may exist today, but its social basis is the resistance of large Mahratta working class and underprivileged lower middle class to the economically and until recently linguistically dominant Gujaratis.

11  It is significant that the post-war Yugoslav regime has broken up what used to be classed as the Serb nation into the much more realistic

sub-national republics and units of Serbia, Bosnia, Montenegro, Macedonia and Kosovo-Metohidja. By the linguistic standards of nineteenth-century nationalism most of these belonged to a single 'Serb' people, except the Macedonians, who are closer to the Bulgarians, and the Albanian minority in Kosmet. But, in fact, they have never developed a single Serb nationalism.

12  J. Sigmann, 'Les radicaux badois et l'idée nationale allemande en 1848', *Etudes d'Histoire Moderne et Comtemporaine*, 2 (1948), pp. 213–14.

13  J. Miskolczy, *Ungarn und die Habsburger-Monarchie* (Vienna-Munich, 1959), p. 85.

# 3

## Building Nations in the Age of Capital

But what ... is a nation? Why is Holland a nation,
while Hanover and the Grand Duchy of Parma are
not?

ERNEST RENAN, 'What is a Nation?'
lecture at the Sorbonne (1882)

What's national? When nobody understands a word
of the language you speak.

JOHANN NESTROY, *Häuptling Abendwind* (1862)

If a great people does not believe that the truth is to
be found in itself alone ... if it does not believe that
it alone is fit and destined to raise up and save all
the rest by its truth, it would at once sink into being
ethnographic material, and not a great people ... A
nation which loses this belief ceases to be a nation.

FYODOR DOSTOEVSKY, *The Demons* (1871–2)

## I

If international and domestic politics were closely bound up with
one another during this period, the bond which linked them most
obviously was what we call 'nationalism' but the mid-nineteenth

century still knew as 'the principle of nationality'. What were the international politics of the years from 1848 to the 1870s about? Traditional western historiography has very little doubt: it was about the creation of a Europe of nation-states. There might be considerable uncertainty about the relation between this facet of the age and others which were evidently connected with it, such as economic progress, liberalism, perhaps even democracy, but none about the central role of nationality.

And indeed, how could there be? Whatever else it was, 1848, the 'springtime of peoples', was clearly also, and in international terms primarily, an assertion of nationality, or rather of rival nationalities. Germans, Italians, Hungarians, Poles, Romanians and the rest asserted their right to be independent and unified states embracing all members of their nations against oppressive governments, as did Czechs, Croats, Danes and others, though with growing misgivings about the revolutionary aspirations of bigger nations which seemed excessively ready to sacrifice their own. France was already an independent national state, but none the less nationalist for that.

The revolutions failed, but the European politics of the next twenty-five years were dominated by the same aspirations. As we have seen, they were actually achieved, in one form or another, though by non-revolutionary or only marginally revolutionary means. France returned to a caricature of the 'great nation' under a caricature of the great Napoleon, Italy and Germany were united under the kingdoms of Savoy and Prussia, Hungary achieved virtual home rule by the Compromise of 1867, Romania became a state by the merger of the two 'Danubian principalities'. Only Poland, which had failed to take an adequate part in the 1848 revolution, also failed to win independence or autonomy by the insurrection of 1863.

In the extreme west, as in the extreme south-east, of Europe the 'national problem' obtruded itself. The Fenians in Ireland raised it in the form of radical insurrection, backed by the millions of their countrymen driven by famine and hatred of

Britain to the United States. The endemic crisis of the multinational Ottoman Empire took the form of revolts by the various Christian peoples it had so long ruled in the Balkans. Greece and Serbia were already independent, though still much smaller than they thought they ought to be. Romania won independence of a sort at the end of the 1850s. Popular insurrections in the early 1870s precipitated yet another internal and international Turkish crisis, which was to make Bulgaria independent at the end of the decade and accelerate the 'Balkanization' of the Balkans. The so-called 'Eastern Question', that permanent preoccupation of foreign ministers, now appeared primarily as the question of how to redraw the map of European Turkey among an uncertain number of new states of uncertain size which claimed and were believed to represent 'nations'. And a little further to the north the internal problems of the Habsburg Empire were even more patently those of its constituent nationalities, several of which – and potentially all of which – put forward demands ranging from a mild cultural autonomy to secession.

Even outside Europe the construction of nations was dramatically visible. What was the American Civil War, if not the attempt to maintain the unity of the American nation against disruption? What was the Meiji Restoration, if not the appearance of a new and proud 'nation' in Japan? It seemed hardly deniable that 'nation-making', as Walter Bagehot (1826–77) called it, was taking place all over the world and was a dominant characteristic of the age.

So obvious, that the nature of the phenomenon was hardly investigated. 'The nation' was taken for granted. As Bagehot put it: 'We cannot imagine those to whom it is a difficulty: "we know what it is when you do not ask us", but we cannot very quickly explain or define it.'[1] And few thought they needed to. Surely the Englishman knew what being English was, the Frenchman, German, Italian or Russian had no doubt about their collective identity? Perhaps not, but in the age of nation-building this was believed to imply the logical necessary, as well as desirable transformation of 'nations' into sovereign nation-states, with a coherent territory defined by the area settled by the members of a 'nation', which was in turn defined by its past history, its common culture, its ethnic composition and, increasingly, its *language*. But there is nothing logical about this implication. If the existence of differing groups of men, distinguishing themselves from other groups by a variety of criteria is both undeniable and as old as history, the fact that they imply what the nineteenth century regarded as 'nationhood' is not. Still less so is the fact that they are organized in territorial states of the nineteenth-century kind, let alone states coinciding with 'nations'. These were relatively recent historical phenomena, though some older territorial states – England, France, Spain, Portugal and perhaps even Russia – could have been defined as 'nation-states' without obvious absurdity. Even as a general programme, the aspiration to form nation-states out of non-nation-states was a product of the French Revolution. We must therefore distinguish rather clearly between the formation of nations and 'nationalism', in so far as this took place during our period, and the creation of nation-states.

The problem was not merely analytical but practical. For Europe, let alone the rest of the world, was evidently divided into 'nations' about whose states or aspirations to found states there was, rightly or wrongly, little doubt, and those about which there was a considerable amount of uncertainty. The safest guide to the first was political fact, institutional history or the cultural history of the literate. France, England, Spain, Russia were undeniably 'nations' because they had states identified with the French, English, etc. Hungary and Poland were nations because a Hungarian kingdom existed as a separate entity even within the Habsburg Empire and a Polish state had long existed until destroyed at the end of the eighteenth century. Germany was a nation both because its numerous principalities, though never united into a single territorial state, had long formed the so-called 'Holy Roman Empire of the German Nation' and still formed the Germanic Federation, and also because all educated Germans shared the same written language and literature. Italy, though never a political entity as such, had perhaps the oldest common literary culture of its elite.[2] And so on.

The 'historic' criterion of nationhood thus implied the decisive importance of the institutions and culture of the ruling classes or educated elites, supposing them to be identified, or not too obviously incompatible, with those of the common people. But the *ideological* argument for nationalism was very different and much more radical, democratic and revolutionary. It rested on the fact that, whatever history or culture said, the Irish were Irish and not English, the Czechs Czech and not German, the Finns were not Russian, and no people ought to be exploited and ruled by another. Historic arguments might be found or invented to back this claim – they can always be discovered – but essentially the Czech movement did not rest on the claim to restore the Crown of St Wenceslas, nor the Irish on the Repeal of the Union in 1801. The basis of this sense of separateness was not necessarily 'ethnic', in the sense of readily identifiable differences of physical appearance, or even linguistic. During our period the movements of the Irish (most of whom already spoke English), the Norwegians (whose literate language was not very distinct from Danish) or the Finns (whose nationalists were both Swedish- and Finnish-speaking), did not make a fundamentally linguistic case for themselves. If it was cultural, it rested not on 'high culture', of which several of the peoples concerned as yet had little, but rather on the oral culture – songs, ballads, epics, etc., the customs and ways of life of 'the folk' – the common people, i.e. for practical purposes the peasantry. The first stage of 'national revival' was invariably one of collecting, recovering and acquiring pride in this folk heritage. But in itself this was not political. Those who pioneered it were, as often as not, cultured members of the foreign ruling class or elite, such as the German Lutheran pastors or intellectually minded gentlemen in the Baltic who collected the folklore and antiquities of the Latvian or Estonian peasantry. The Irish were not nationalists because they believed in leprechauns.

Why there were nationalists and how far they were nationalists, we shall discuss below. The significant point here is that the typical 'un-historical' or 'semi-historical' nation was also a *small* nation, and this faced nineteenth-century nationalism with a dilemma which has rarely been recognized. For the champions of the 'nation-state' assumed not only that it must be national, but also that it must be 'progressive', i.e. capable of developing a viable economy, technology, state organization and military force, i.e. that it must be at least moderately large. It was to be, in fact, the 'natural' unit of the development of the modern, liberal, progressive and de facto bourgeois society. 'Unification' as much as 'independence' was its principle, and where no historical arguments for unification existed – as they did for example in Italy and Germany – it was, where feasible, formulated as a programme. There is no evidence whatever that the Balkan Slavs had ever considered themselves parts of the same nation, but the nationalist ideologues who emerged in the first half of the century thought in terms of an 'Illyria' hardly more real than Shakespeare's, a 'Yugoslav' state which was to unite Serbs, Croats, Slovenes, Bosnians, Macedonians and others who to this day demonstrate that their Yugoslav nationalism is, to put it mildly, in conflict with their sentiments as Croats, Slovenes, etc.

The most eloquent and typical champion of the 'Europe of nationalities', Giuseppe Mazzini (1805–72), proposed a map of his ideal Europe in 1857:[3] it consisted of a mere eleven unions of this kind. Clearly his idea of 'nation-states' was very different from that of the Woodrow Wilson who presided over the only systematic redrawing of the European map according to national principles at Versailles in 1919–20. His Europe consisted of twenty-six or (including Ireland) twenty-seven sovereign states, and by Wilsonian criteria a case could have been made out for a few more. What was to happen to the small nations? They must plainly be integrated, federally or otherwise, with or without some as yet undetermined autonomy, into the viable nation-states, though it appeared to escape the notice of Mazzini that a man who proposed uniting Switzerland with Savoy, German Tyrol, Carinthia and Slovenia was hardly in a position to criticize, say, the Habsburg Empire for trampling on the national principle.

The simplest argument for those who identified nation-states with progress was to deny the character of 'real' nations to the small and backward peoples, or to argue that progress must reduce them to mere provincial idiosyncrasy within the larger 'real' nations, or even lead to their actual disappearance by assimilation to some *Kulturvolk*. This did not seem unrealistic. After all, membership of Germany did not stop the Mecklenburgers from talking a dialect which was closer to Dutch than to High German and which no Bavarian could understand, or for that matter the Lusatian Slavs from accepting (as they still do) a basically German state. The existence of Bretons, and a part of the Basques, Catalans and Flemings, not to mention the speakers of Provençal and the Langue d'oc, appeared perfectly compatible with the French nation of which they formed a part, and the Alsatians created a problem only because another large nation-state – Germany – disputed their allegiance. Moreover, there were examples of such small linguistic groups whose educated elite looked forward without gloom to the disappearance of their language. Plenty of Welshmen in the mid-nineteenth century were resigned to it, and some welcomed it as a means of facilitating a penetration of progress into a backward region.

There was a strong element of inegalitarianism and perhaps a stronger one of special pleading in such arguments. Some nations – the large, the 'advanced', the established, including certainly the ideologist's own – were destined by history to prevail or (if the ideologist preferred Darwinian phraseology) to be victors in the struggle for existence; others were not. Yet this must not be interpreted simply as a conspiracy of some nations to oppress others, though spokesmen of the unrecognized nations could hardly be blamed for thinking so. For the argument was directed as much against the regional languages and cultures of the nation itself as against outsiders, and did not necessarily envisage their disappearance, but only their downgrading from the status of 'language' to that of 'dialect'. Cavour did not deny the right of Savoyards to talk their language (closer to French than Italian) in a united Italy: he spoke it himself for most domestic purposes. He, and other Italian nationalists, merely insisted that there should be only one official language and medium of instruction, namely Italian, and others should sink or swim as best they could. As it so happened at this stage, neither the Sicilians nor the Sardinians insisted on their separate nationhood, so their problem could be defined as, at best, 'regionalism'. It only became politically significant once a small people claimed nationhood, as the Czechs did in 1848 when their spokesmen refused the invitation of the German liberals to take part in the Frankfurt parliament. The Germans did not deny that there were Czechs. They merely assumed, quite correctly, that all educated Czechs read and wrote German, shared German high culture and (incorrectly) that they therefore were German. The fact that the Czech elite also spoke Czech and shared the culture of the local common people seemed to be politically irrelevant, like the attitudes of the common people in general and the peasantry in particular.

Faced with the national aspirations of small peoples, the ideologists of a 'national Europe' therefore had three choices: they could deny their legitimacy or their existence altogether, they could reduce them to movements for regional autonomy, and they could accept them as undeniable but unmanageable facts. Germans tended to do the first with such people as the Slovenes, Hungarians with the Slovaks.[4] Cavour and Mazzini took the second view about the Irish movement. Nothing is more paradoxical than their failure to fit into the nationalist pattern the one national movement about whose mass basis there could be no conceivable doubt. Politicians of all kinds were constrained to take the third view of the Czechs, whose national movement, though not then envisaging total independence, could no longer be argued away after 1848. Where possible, of course, they paid no attention to such movements at all. Hardly any foreigner bothered to note that several of the most old-established 'national' states were in fact multinational (e.g. Britain, France, Spain), for the Welsh, the Scots, the Bretons, the Catalans, etc., posed no international problem, and (with the possible exception of the Catalans) no significant problems in the domestic politics of their own countries.

## II

There was thus a fundamental difference between the movement to found nation-states and 'nationalism'. The one was a programme to construct a political artefact claiming to be based on the other. There is no doubt that many who thought of themselves as 'Germans' for some purposes did not believe that this implied a single German state, a German state of a specific type, let alone one which included all Germans living within the area bounded, as the national song had it, but the rivers Meuse in the west and Niemen in the east, the sea-straits of Denmark (the Belt) in the north and the river Adige in the south. Bismarck, for one, would have denied that his rejection of this 'Greater German' programme meant that he was not a German as well as a Prussian *Junker* and servant of the state. He was a German, but not a German nationalist, probably not even a 'Little German' nationalist by conviction, although he actually unified the country (excluding the areas of the Austrian Empire which had belonged to the Holy Roman Empire, but including the areas taken by Prussia from Poland, which had never been part of it). An extreme case of a divergence between nationalism and the nation-state was Italy, most of which was unified under the king of Savoy in 1859–60, 1866 and 1870.

There was no historic precedent later than ancient Rome for a single administration of the entire area from the Alps to Sicily, which Metternich had, quite correctly, described as 'a mere geographical expression'. At the moment of unification, in 1860, it has been estimated that not more than 2.5 per cent of its inhabitants actually spoke the Italian language for the ordinary purposes of life, the rest talking idioms so different that the schoolmasters sent by the Italian state into Sicily in the 1860s were mistaken for Englishmen.[5] Probably a much larger percentage, but still a modest minority, at the date would have thought of themselves primarily as Italians. No wonder Massimo d'Azeglio (1792–1866) exclaimed in 1860: 'We have made Italy; now we must make the Italians.'

Nevertheless, whatever their nature and programme, movements representing 'the national idea' grew and multiplied. They did not often – or even normally – represent what by the early twentieth century had become the standard (and extreme) version of the national programme, i.e. the necessity of a totally independent, territorially and linguistically homogeneous, secular – and probably republican/parliamentary – state for each 'people'.[6] However, they all implied some more or less ambitious political changes, and this is what made them 'nationalist'. These we must now try to look at, avoiding both the anachronism of hindsight and the temptation to confuse the ideas of the most vociferous nationalist leaders with those actually held by their followers.

Nor should we overlook the substantial difference between old and new nationalisms, the former including not only the 'historic' nations not yet possessing their own states, but those who had long done so. How British did the British feel? Not very, in spite of the virtual absence at this stage of any movements for Welsh and Scottish autonomy. There was English nationalism, but it was not shared by the smaller nations in the island. English emigrants to the United States were proud of their nationality, and therefore reluctant to become American citizens, but Welsh and Scottish immigrants had no such loyalty. They could remain as proudly Welsh and Scottish under American as under British citizenship, and naturalized themselves freely. How French did the members even of *la grande nation* feel? We do not know, but statistics of draft evasion earlier in the century suggest that certain regions in the west and south (not to mention the special case of the Corsicans) regarded compulsory military service as a disagreeable imposition rather than as a national duty of the French citizen. The Germans, as we know, had different views about the size, nature and structure of the future united German state, but how many of them cared about German unification at all? Not, by general agreement, the German peasants, even in the 1848 revolution, when the national question dominated politics. These were countries in which mass nationalism and patriotism can hardly be denied, and they demonstrate how unwise it is to take its universality and homogeneity for granted.

In most other nations, especially the emergent ones, only myth and propaganda would have taken it for granted in the mid-nineteenth century. There the 'national' movement tended to become political after its sentimental and folkloristic phase, with the emergence of more or less large groups of cadres dedicated to 'the national idea', publishing national journals and other literature, organizing national societies, attempting to establish educational and cultural institutions, and engaging in various more frankly political activities. But in general at this stage the movement still lacked any serious support among the mass of the population. It consisted primarily of the strata intermediate between the masses and what local bourgeoisie or aristocracy existed (if any), and especially of the literate: teachers, the lower levels of the clergy, some urban shopkeepers and artisans, and the sort of men who had risen about as far as it was possible for the sons of a subordinate peasant people in a hierarchical society. Eventually the students – from some nationally minded faculties, seminaries and high schools – provided them with a ready-made body of active militants. Of course in 'historic' nations, which required little except the removal of foreign rule to re-emerge as states, the local elite – gentry in Hungary and Poland, middle-class bureaucrats in Norway – provided a more immediately political cadre and sometimes a larger base for nationalism (see 'Nationalism in the Age of Revolution' in this collection). On the whole this phase of nationalism ends between 1848 and the 1860s in northern, western and central Europe, though many of the smaller Baltic and Slav people were only beginning to enter it.

For obvious reasons the most traditional, backward or poor sections of a people were the last to be involved in such movements: workers, servants and peasants, who followed the path traced by the 'educated' elite. The phase of a mass nationalism, which therefore normally came under the influence of organizations of the nationalist liberal-democratic middle strata – except when offset by independent labour and socialist parties – was to some extent correlated with economic and political development. In the Czech lands it began in the revolution of 1848, relapsed in the absolutist 1850s, but grew enormously during the rapid economic progress of the 1860s, when political conditions were also more favourable. A native Czech bourgeoisie had by now acquired sufficient wealth to found an effective Czech bank, and eventually such expensive institutions as a National Theatre in Prague (provisionally opened in 1862). More to our point, mass cultural organizations like the Sokol gymnastic clubs (1862) now covered the countryside and the political campaigns after the Austro-Hungarian Compromise were conducted through a series of vast open-air mass rallies – some 140 with an estimated participation of 1.5 million in 1868–71[7] – which, incidentally, illustrate both the novelty and the cultural 'internationalism' of the mass national movements. For, lacking a proper name for such activities, the Czechs initially borrowed the term 'meeting' for them from the Irish movement which they attempted to copy. The word 'meeting' was also to be borrowed for mass rallies of the working class by the French and the Spaniards, but probably

in this instance from English experience. Soon a suitably traditional name was devised by harking back to the Hussites of
the fifteenth century, a natural example for Czech national
militancy, the 'tabor'; and this in turn was to be adopted by the
Croat nationalists for their rallies, though the Hussites had no
historical relevance to them.

This kind of mass nationalism was new, and quite distinct
from the elite or middle-class nationalism of the Italian or
German movements. And yet another form of mass nationalism
had long existed: both more traditional, more revolutionary and
more independent of local middle classes, if only because these
were of no great economic and political consequence. But can
we call the rebellions of peasants and mountaineers against foreign rule 'nationalist', when united only by the consciousness of
oppression, by xenophobia and by an attachment to ancient tradition, the true faith and a vague sense of ethnic identity? Only
when they happened to be attached for one reason or another to
modern national movements. Whether they can be so attached
in south-eastern Europe, where such risings destroyed much of
the Turkish Empire, particularly in the 1870s (Bosnia, Bulgaria),
may be debated, though it is undeniable that they produced
independent states (Romania, Bulgaria) which claimed to be
national. At best we may speak of a proto-nationalism, as among
the Romanians, conscious of the difference of their language
from the surrounding and intermingled Slavs, Hungarians and
Germans, or the Slavs, conscious of a certain 'Slavness', which
intellectuals and politicians tried to develop into an ideology of
pan-Slavism in our period; and even among them it is probable
that the feeling of solidarity of Orthodox Christians with the
great Orthodox empire of Russia was the force which gave it
reality in this period. Pan-Slavism appealed both to the conservative and imperial politicians of Russia, whom it offered an
extension of Russian influence, and to those of the lesser Slavic
peoples of the Habsburg Empire, whom it offered a powerful ally
and perhaps also, more remotely, the hope of forming a 'proper'

large nation instead of a collection of small and apparently unviable ones. (The revolutionary and democratic pan-Slavism of the anarchist Bakunin may be neglected as utopian.) It was therefore strongly opposed by the left, which regarded Russia as the main stronghold of international reaction.

One movement, however, was unquestionably national: the Irish. The Irish Republican Brotherhood ('Fenians'), with its still surviving Irish Republican Army, was the lineal descendant of the secret revolutionary fraternities of the pre-1848 period, and the longest-lived organization of its kind. Mass rural support for nationalist politicians was not in itself new, for the Irish combination of foreign conquest, poverty, oppression and largely Anglo-Protestant landlord class imposed on an Irish-Catholic peasantry mobilized the least political. In the first half of the century the leaders of these mass movements had belonged to the (small) Irish middle class and their aim – supported by the only effective national organization, the church – had been a moderate accommodation with the English. The novelty of the Fenians, who first appeared as such in the late 1850s, was that they were entirely independent of the middle-class moderates, that their support came entirely from among the popular masses – even, in spite of the open hostility of the church, parts of the peasantry – and that they were the first to put forward a programme of total independence from England, to be achieved by armed insurrection. In spite of their name, derived from the heroic mythology of ancient Ireland, their ideology was quite non-traditional, though its secular, even anti-clerical nationalism cannot conceal that for the mass of the Fenian Irish the criterion of nationality was (and still is) the Catholic faith. Their wholehearted concentration on an Irish Republic won by armed struggle replaced a social and economic, even a domestic political programme, and their heroic legend of rebel gunmen and martyrs has up to the present been too strong for those who wanted to formulate one. This is the 'Republican tradition' which survives into the 1970s and has re-emerged in the Ulster civil war, in the 'Provisional' IRA. The readiness of the Fenians to ally themselves with socialist revolutionaries, and of these to recognize the revolutionary character of Fenianism, should not encourage illusions about this.

But neither should we underestimate the novelty, and the historic significance, of a movement whose financial support came from the masses of Irish labourers in the United States, whose recruits came from Irish emigrant proletarians in America and England – there were hardly any industrial workers in what is now the Irish Republic – and from young peasants and farm workers in the ancient strongholds of Irish 'agrarian terrorism'; whose cadres were men such as these and the lowest strata of revolutionary urban white-collar workers, and whose leaders dedicated their lives to insurrection. It anticipates the revolutionary national movements of underdeveloped countries in the twentieth century. It lacked the core of socialist labour organization, or perhaps merely the inspiration of socialist ideology, which was to turn the combination of national liberation and social transformation into such a formidable force in this country. There was no socialism anywhere, let alone socialist organization in Ireland, and the Fenians who were also social revolutionaries, notably Michael Davitt (1846–1906), succeeded merely in making explicit in the Land League the always implicit relation between mass nationalism and mass agrarian discontent; and even this not until after the end of our period, during the great Agrarian Depression of the 1870s and 1880s. Fenianism was mass nationalism in the epoch of triumphant liberalism. It could do little except reject England and demand total independence through revolution for an oppressed people, hoping that somehow this would solve all problems of poverty and exploitation. It did not do even this very effectively, for in spite of the self-abnegation and heroism of the Fenians, the scattered insurrections (1867) and invasions (e.g. of Canada from the United States) were conducted with notable inefficiency, and their dramatic coups achieved, as usual in such operations, little more than temporary publicity; occasionally bad publicity. They generated the force which was to win independence for most of Catholic Ireland but, since they generated nothing else, they left the future of that Ireland to the middle-class moderates, the rich farmers and small-town tradesmen of a small agrarian country who were to take over their heritage.

Though the Irish case was still unique, there is no denying that in our period nationalism increasingly became a mass force, at least in countries populated by whites. Even though the *Communist Manifesto* was less unrealistic than is often supposed in stating that 'the workers have no country', it probably advanced among the working-class *pari passu* with political consciousness, if only because the tradition of revolution itself was national (as in France) and because the leaders and ideologists of the new labour movements were themselves deeply involved in the national question (as almost everywhere in 1848). The alternative to a 'national' political consciousness was not, in practice, 'working-class internationalism' but a sub-political consciousness which still operated on a scale much smaller than, or irrelevant to, that of the nation-state. The men and women on the political left who chose clearly between national and supranational loyalties, such as the cause of the international proletariat, were few. The 'internationalism' of the left in practice meant solidarity and support for those who fought the same cause in other nations and, in the case of political refugees, the readiness to participate in the struggle wherever they found themselves. But, as the examples of Garibaldi, Gustave Cluseret of the Paris Commune (who helped the Fenians in America) and numerous Polish fighters prove, this was not incompatible with passionately nationalist beliefs.

It might also mean a refusal to accept the definitions of the 'national interest' put forward by governments and others. Yet the German and French socialists who in 1870 joined in protesting against the 'fratricidal' Franco-Prussian War were not insensible to nationalism as *they* saw it. The Paris Commune derived its support from the Jacobin patriotism of Paris as much as from the slogans of social emancipation, and the Marxist German Social Democrats of Liebknecht and Bebel derived much of theirs from their appeal to the radical-democratic nationalism of 1848 against the Prussian version of the national programme. What German workers resented was reaction rather than German patriotism; and one of the most unacceptable aspects of reaction was that it called Social Democrats *vaterlandslose Gesellen* (fellows without a fatherland), thus denying them the right to be not only workers but good Germans. And, of course, it was almost impossible for political consciousness not to be in some way or another nationally defined. The proletariat, like the bourgeoisie, existed only conceptually as an international fact. In reality it existed as an aggregate of groups defined by their national state of ethnic/linguistic difference: British, French or, in multinational states, German, Hungarian or Slav. And, in so far as 'state' and 'nation' were supposed to coincide in the ideology of those who established institutions and dominated civil society, politics in terms of the state implied politics in terms of the nation.

## III

And yet, however powerful national feelings and (as nations turned into states or the other way round) allegiances, the 'nation' was not a spontaneous growth but an artefact. It was not merely historically novel, though embodying the things members of some very ancient human groups had in common or thought they had in common as against 'foreigners'. It had actually to be constructed. Hence the crucial importance of the institutions which could *impose* national uniformity, which meant primarily the state, especially state education, state employment and conscription (such as in France, Germany, Italy, Belgium and Austro-Hungary). The educational systems of developed countries expanded substantially during this period, at all levels.

The number of university students remained unusually modest by modern standards. Omitting theology students, Germany led the field at the end of the 1870s with almost seventeen thousand, followed a long way after by Italy and France with nine to ten thousand each and Austria with some eight thousand.[8] It did not grow much except under nationalist pressure and in the United States, where institutions dedicated to higher education were in the process of multiplying. Secondary education grew with the middle classes, though (like the superior bourgeoisie for whom they were destined) they remained very much elite institutions, except once again in the United States, where the public 'high school' began its career of democratic triumph. (In 1850 there had only been a hundred of them in the entire nation.) In France, the proportion of those undergoing a secondary education rose from one in thirty-five (1842) to one in twenty (1864): but secondary graduates – they averaged about five and a half thousand per annum in the first half of the 1860s – formed only one in fifty-five or sixty of the conscript class, though this was better than in the 1840s when they had formed only one in ninety-three. Most countries were situated somewhere between the totally pre-educational or the totally restrictive countries such as Britain with its twenty-five thousand boys in 225 purely private establishments miscalled 'public schools' and the education-hungry Germans whose *gymnasia* contained perhaps a quarter of a million pupils in the 1880s.

But the major advance occurred in the primary schools, whose purpose was by general consent not only to teach the rudiments of literacy and arithmetic but, perhaps even more, to impose the values of society (morals, patriotism, etc.) on their inmates. This was the sector of education which had previously been neglected by the secular state, and its growth was closely linked with the advance of the masses into politics; as witness the setting-up of the state primary education system in Britain three years after the Reform Act of 1867 and the vast expansion of the system in the first decade of the Third Republic in France.

Progress was indeed striking: between 1840 and the 1880s the population of Europe rose by 33 per cent, but the number of its children attending school by 145 per cent. Even in well-schooled Prussia the number of primary schools increased by over 50 per cent between 1843 and 1871. But it was not due merely to the educational backwardness of Italy that the fastest increase in the school population in our period occurred there: 460 per cent. In the fifteen years following unification the number of primary-school children doubled.

In fact, for new nation-states these institutions were of crucial importance, for through them alone the 'national language' (generally constructed earlier by private efforts) could actually become the written and spoken language of the people, at least for some purposes. Hence also the crucial importance of struggling national movements of the fight to win 'cultural autonomy', i.e. to control the relevant part of state institutions, e.g. to achieve school instruction in and administrative use for their language. The issue was not one which affected the illiterate, who learned their dialect from their mothers anyway, nor the minority peoples who assimilated *en bloc* to the prevailing language of the ruling class. The European Jews were content to retain their native languages – the Yiddish derived from medieval German and the Ladino derived from medieval Spanish – as a *Mame-Loschen* (mother-tongue) for domestic use, communicating with their gentile neighbours in whatever idiom was required and, if they became bourgeois, abandoning their old language for that of their surrounding aristocracy and middle class, English, French, Polish, Russian, Hungarian, but especially German. But the Jews at that stage were not nationalist, and their failure to attach importance to a 'national' language, as well as their failure to possess a national territory, led many to doubt that they could be a 'nation'. A movement to develop both Yiddish and Ladino into standard literary languages developed [...] and was later to be taken up by the Jewish revolutionary (Marxist) movements, *not* by Jewish nationalism (Zionism). On the other hand, the issue was vital for the middle class and educated elites emerging from backward or subaltern peoples. It was they who specially resented the privileged access to important and prestigious posts which native speakers of the 'official' language had; even when (as was the case with the Czechs), their own compulsory bilingualism actually gave them a career advantage of the monoglot Germans in Bohemia. Why should a Croat have to learn Italian, the language of a small minority, to become an officer in the Austrian navy?

And yet, as nation-states were formed, as the public posts and professions of progressive civilization multiplied, as school education became more general, above all as migration urbanized rural peoples, these resentments found an increasingly general resonance. For schools and institutions, in imposing one language of instruction, also imposed a culture, a nationality. In areas of homogeneous settlement this did not matter: the Austrian constitution of 1867 recognized elementary education in the 'language of the country'. But why should Slovenes or Czechs, migrating into hitherto German cities, be compelled to become Germans as a price of becoming literate? They demanded the right to their own schools even when they were minorities. And why should the Czechs and Slovenes of Prague or Ljubljana (Laibach), having reduced the Germans from a majority to a smallish minority, have to confront street names and municipal regulations in a foreign tongue? The politics of the Austrian half of the Habsburg Empire were complex enough for the government to have to think multinationally. But what if other governments used schooling, that most powerful weapon for forming the nations upon which they purported to rest, to Magyarize, Germanize or Italianize systematically? The paradox of nationalism was that in forming its own nation it automatically created the counter-nationalism of those whom it now forced into the choice between assimilation and inferiority.

The age of liberalism did not grasp this paradox. Indeed, it did not understand that 'principle of nationality' which it approved, considered itself to embody, and in suitable cases actively supported. Contemporary observers were no doubt right in supposing, or acting as if, nations and nationalism were as yet largely unformed and malleable. The American nation, for instance, was based on the assumption that in migrating across the ocean many millions of Europeans would lightly and quickly abandon any political loyalties to their homeland and any claims to official status for their native languages and cultures. The United States (or Brazil, or Argentina) would not be multinational, but absorb the immigrants into its own nation. And in our period this is what happened, even though the immigrant communities did not lose their identity in the 'melting pot' of the new world, but remained or even became consciously and proudly Irish, German, Swedish, Italian, etc. The communities of immigrants might be important national forces in their countries of origin, as the American Irish were in the politics of Ireland; but in the United States itself they were of major significance chiefly to candidates for municipal elections. Germans in Prague by their very existence raised the most far-reaching political problems for the Habsburg Empire; not so Germans in Cincinnati or Milwaukee for the United States.

Nationalism therefore still seemed readily manageable within the framework of a bourgeois liberalism, and compatible with it. A world of nations would, it was believed, be a liberal world, and a liberal world would consist of nations. The future was to show that the relationship between the two was not as simple as this.

## Notes

1 Walter Bagehot, *Physics and Politics* (London, 1873), pp. 20–1.
2 No modern Englishman, German or Frenchman can read the works of fourteenth-century literature written in their countries without learning what amounts to a different language, but all educated Italians today can read Dante with less difficulty than modern English-speakers can read Shakespeare.
3 Cited in Denis Mack Smith, *Il Risorgimento Italiano* (Bari, 1968), p. 422.

4   This attitude must be distinguished from that of social revolutionaries who did not – at least in our period – assign any major significance to nationalism at all, and therefore took a purely operational view of it. For Marx, Hungarian and Polish nationalism in 1848 was good, because mobilized on the side of the revolution, Czech and Croat nationalism bad, because objectively on the side of counter-revolution. But we cannot deny that there was an element of great-nation nationalism in such views, very obviously among the highly chauvinist French revolutionaries (notably the Blanquists), and not easily to be denied even in Frederick Engels.

5   Tullio de Mauro, *Storia linguistica dell'Italia unita* (Bari, 1963).

6   Zionism, by the very extremism of its claims, illustrates this clearly, for it implied taking a territory, inventing a language and secularizing the political structures of a people whose historic unity had consisted exclusively in the practice of a common religion.

7   Jiri Kořalka, 'Social problems in the Czech and Slovak national movements', in Commission Internationale d'Histoire des Mouvements Sociaux et des Structures Sociales, *Mouvements Nationaux d'Indépendance et Classes Populaires*, vol. 1 (Paris, 1971), p. 62.

8   Johannes Conrad, 'Die Frequenzverhältnisse der Universitäten der hauptsächlichsten Kulturländer', in *Jahrbücher für Natinonalökonomie und Statistik* (1891) 3rd ser. 1, pp. 376ff.

# 4

# *Waving Flags in the Age of Empire*

'*Scappa, che arriva la patria*' (Run away, the fatherland
is coming).

Italian peasant woman to her son

Their language has become complex, because
now they read. They read books – or at any rate
they learn to read out of books ... The word and
the idiom of the literary language tend and the
pronunciation suggested by its spelling tends to
prevail over the local usage.

H. G. WELLS, *Anticipations* (1901)

Nationalism ... attacks democracy, demolishes anti-
clericalism, fights socialism and undermines pacifism,
humanitarianism and internationalism ... It declares
the programme of liberalism finished.

ALFREDO ROCCO, *Che cosa è il nazionalismo
e che cosa vogliono i nazionalisti* (1914)

## I

If the rise of working-class parties was one major by-product of
the politics of democratization, the rise of nationalism in politics
was another. In itself it was plainly not new. Yet in the period

from 1880 to 1914 nationalism took a dramatic leap forward, and its ideological and political content was transformed. Its very vocabulary indicates the significance of these years. For the word 'nationalism' itself appeared at the end of the nineteenth century to describe groups of right-wing ideologists in France and Italy, keen to brandish the national flag against foreigners, liberals and socialists and in favour of that aggressive expansion of their own state which was to become so characteristic of such movements. This was also the period when 'Deutschland über Alles' (Germany above all others) replaced rival compositions to become the actual national anthem of Germany. Though it originally described only a right-wing version of the phenomenon, the word 'nationalism' proved to be more convenient than the clumsy 'principle of nationality' which had been part of the vocabulary of European politics since about 1830, and so it came to be used also for all movements to whom the 'national cause' was paramount in politics: that is to say for all demanding the right to self-determination, i.e. in the last analysis to form an independent state, for some nationally defined group. For the number of such movements, or at least of leaders claiming to speak for such movements, and their political significance, increased strikingly in our period.

The basis of 'nationalism' of all kinds was the same: the readiness of people to identify themselves emotionally with 'their' nation and to be politically mobilized as Czechs, Germans, Italians or whatever, a readiness which could be politically exploited. The democratization of politics, and especially elections, provided ample opportunities for mobilizing them. When states did so they called it 'patriotism', and the essence of the original 'right-wing' nationalism, which emerged in already established nation-states, was to claim a monopoly of patriotism for the extreme political right, and thereby brand everyone else as some sort of traitor. This was a new phenomenon, for during most of the nineteenth century nationalism had been rather identified with liberal and radical movements and with the tradition of the French Revolution. But elsewhere nationalism had no necessary identification with any colour in the political spectrum. Among the national movements still lacking their own states we shall encounter those identifying with the right or the left, or indifferent to either. And indeed, as we have suggested, there were movements, and not the least powerful, which mobilized men and women on a national basis, but, as it were, by accident, since their primary appeal was for social liberation. For while in this period national identification clearly was or became a major factor in the politics of states, it is quite mistaken to see the national appeal as incompatible with any other. Nationalist politicians and their opponents naturally liked to suggest that one kind of appeal excluded another at the same time. But, as a matter of history, and observation, this is not so. In our period it was perfectly possible to become simultaneously a class-conscious Marxian revolutionary and an Irish patriot, like James Connolly, who was to be executed in 1916 for leading the Easter Rising in Dublin.

But of course, insofar as parties in the countries of mass politics competed for the same body of supporters, these had to make mutually exclusive choices.

The new working-class movements, appealing to their potential constituency on grounds of class identification, soon realized this, insofar as they found themselves competing, as was usually the case in multinational regions, against parties which asked proletarians and potential socialists to support them as Czechs, Poles or Slovenes. Hence their preoccupation as soon as they actually became mass movements, with 'the national question'. That virtually every Marxist theorist of importance, from Kautsky and Rosa Luxemburg, via the Austro-Marxists, to Lenin and the young Stalin, took part in the impassioned debates on this subject during this period, suggests the urgency and centrality of this problem.[1]

Where national identification became a political force, it therefore formed a sort of general substratum of politics. This makes its multifarious expressions extremely difficult to define, even when they claimed to be specifically nationalist or patriotic. As we shall see, national identification almost certainly became more widespread in our period, and the significance of the national appeal in politics grew. However, what was almost certainly more important was a major set of mutations within political nationalism, which was to have profound consequences for the twentieth century.

Four aspects of this mutation must be mentioned. The first [...] is the emergence of nationalism and patriotism as an ideology taken over by the political right. This was to find its extreme expression between the wars in fascism, whose ideological ancestors are to be found here. The second is the assumption, quite foreign to the liberal phase of national movements, that national self-determination up to and including the formation of independent sovereign states applied not just to some nations which could demonstrate economic, political and cultural viability, but to any and all groups which claimed to be a 'nation'. The difference between the old and the new assumption is illustrated by the difference between the twelve rather large entities envisaged as constituting 'the Europe of nations' by Giuseppe Mazzini, the great prophet of nineteenth-century nationalism, in 1857 (see 'Building Nations in the Age of Capital' in this collection), and the twenty-six states – twenty-seven if we include Ireland – which emerged from President Wilson's principle of national self-determination at the end of the First World War. The third was the growing tendency to assume that 'national self-determination' could not be satisfied by any form of autonomy less than full state independence. For most of the nineteenth century, the majority of demands for autonomy had not envisaged this. Finally, there was the novel tendency to define a nation in terms of ethnicity and especially in terms of language.

Before the middle 1870s there had been states, mainly in the western half of Europe, which saw themselves as representing 'nations' (e.g. France, Britain or the new Germany and Italy), and states which, though based on some other political principle, were regarded as representing the main body of their inhabitants on grounds which could be thought of as something like national (this was true of the tsars, who certainly enjoyed the loyalty of the Great Russian people as both Russian and Orthodox rulers). Outside the Habsburg Empire and perhaps the Ottoman Empire, the numerous nationalists within the established states did not constitute much of a political problem, especially once a German and an Italian state had been established. There were, of course, the Poles, divided between Russia, Germany and Austria but never losing sight of the restoration of an independent Poland. There were, within the United Kingdom, the Irish. There were various chunks of nationalities which, for one reason or another, found themselves outside the frontiers of the relevant nation-state to which they would much have preferred to belong, though only some created political problems, e.g. the inhabitants of Alsace-Lorraine, annexed by Germany in 1871. (Nice and Savoy, handed over by what was to become Italy to France in 1860, showed no marked signs of discontent.)

There is no doubt that the number of nationalist movements increased considerably in Europe from the 1870s, though in fact much fewer new national states were established in Europe in the last forty years before the First World War than in the forty years preceding the formation of the German Empire, and those established were not very significant: Bulgaria (1878), Norway (1907), Albania (1913). The states established or internationally recognized in 1830–71 included Germany, Italy, Belgium, France, Greece, Serbia and Romania. The so-called 'Compromise' of 1867 also amounted to the grant of very far-reaching autonomy by the Habsburg Empire to Hungary.

There were now 'national movements' not only among peoples hitherto considered 'unhistorical' (i.e. who had never previously possessed an independent state, ruling class or cultural elite), such as Finns and Slovaks, but among peoples about whom hardly anybody except folklore enthusiasts had previously thought about at all, such as Estonians and Macedonians. And within long-established nation-states regional populations now began to mobilize politically as 'nations'; this happened in Wales, where a Young Wales movement was organized in the 1890s under the leadership of a local lawyer of whom much more was to be heard in future, David Lloyd George, and in Spain, where a Basque National Party was formed in 1894. And about the same time Theodor Herzl launched Zionism among the Jews, to whom the sort of nationalism it represented had hitherto been unknown and meaningless.

Many of these movements did not yet have much support among the people for whom they claimed to speak, though mass emigration now gave many more members of backward communities the powerful incentive of nostalgia to identify with what they had left behind, and opened their minds to new political ideas. Nevertheless, mass identification with a 'nation' almost certainly grew, and the political problem of nationalism probably became more difficult to manage for both states and non-nationalist competitors. Probably most observers of the European scene in the 1870s felt that, after the period of Italian and German unification and the Austro-Hungarian compromise, the 'principle of nationality' was likely to be less explosive than it had been. Even the Austrian authorities, asked to include a question on language in their censuses (a step recommended by the International Statistical Congress of 1873), though unenthusiastic, did not say no. However, they thought, one had to give time for the hot national tempers of the past ten years to cool down. They thought they could safely assume that this would have happened by the census of 1880. They could not have been more spectacularly mistaken.[2]

However, what proved to be significant in the long run was not so much the degree of support for the national cause achieved at the time among this or that people, as the transformation of the definition and programme of nationalism. We are now so used to an ethnic–linguistic definition of nations that we forget that this was, essentially, invented in the later nineteenth century. Without going at length into the matter, it is enough to recall that the ideologists of the Irish movement did not begin to tie the cause of the Irish nation to the defence of the Gaelic language until some time after the foundation of the Gaelic League in 1893; that the Basques did not base their national claims on their language (as distinct from their historic *fueros* or constitutional privileges) until the same period; that the impassioned debates about whether Macedonian is more like Bulgarian than it is like Serbo-Croat were among the last arguments used to decide which of those two people they should unite with. As for the Zionist Jews, they went one better by identifying the Jewish nation with Hebrew, a language which no Jews had used for ordinary purposes since the days of the Babylonian captivity, if then. It had just (1880) been invented as a language for everyday use – as distinct from a sacred and ritual tongue or a learned lingua franca – by a man who began the process of providing it with a suitable vocabulary by inventing a Hebrew term for 'nationalism', and it was learned as a badge of Zionist commitment rather than as a means of communication.

This does not mean that language had previously been unimportant as a national issue. It was one criterion of nationality among several others; and, in general, the less prominent it was, the stronger was the identification of the masses of a people with its collectivity. Language was not an ideological battleground for those who merely talked it, if only because the exercise of control over what language mothers talked with children, husbands with wives, and neighbours with each other, was virtually impossible. The language which most Jews actually spoke, namely Yiddish, had virtually no ideological dimension until the non-Zionist left took it up, nor did most Jews who spoke it mind that many authorities (including those of the Habsburg Empire) refused even to accept it as a separate language. Millions chose to become members of the American nation, which obviously had not single ethnic basis, and learned English as a matter of necessity or convenience, without reading any essential element of a national soul or a national continuity into their efforts to speak the language. Linguistic nationalism was the creation of people who wrote and read, not of people who spoke. And the 'national languages' in which they discovered the essential character of their nations were, more often than not, artefacts, since they had to be compiled, standardized, homogenized and modernized for contemporary and literary use, out of the jigsaw puzzle of local or regional dialects which constituted non-literary languages as actually spoken. The major written national languages of old nation-states or literate cultures had gone through this phase of compilation and 'correction' long since: German and Russian in the eighteenth century, French and English in the seventeenth, Italian and Castilian even earlier. For most languages of smaller linguistic groups the nineteenth century was the period of the great 'authorities' who established the vocabulary and 'correct' usage of their idiom. For several – Catalan, Basque, the Baltic languages – it was the turn of the nineteenth and twentieth centuries.

Written languages are closely, though not necessarily, linked with territories and institutions. The nationalism which established itself as the standard version of the national ideology and programme was essentially territorial, since its basic model was the territorial state of the French Revolution, or at any rate the nearest thing to complete political control over a clearly defined territory and its inhabitants which was available in practice. Once again Zionism provides the extreme example, just because it was so clearly a borrowed programme which had no precedent in, or organic connection with, the actual tradition which had given the Jewish people permanence, cohesion and indestructible identity for some millennia. It asked them to acquire a territory (inhabited by other people) – for Herzl it was not even necessary that the territory should have any historical

63

connection with the Jews – as well as a language they had not spoken for millennia.

The identification of nations with an exclusive territory created such problems over large areas of the world of mass migration, and even of the non-migratory world, that an alternative definition of nationality was developed, notably in the Habsburg Empire and among the Jewish diaspora. It was here seen as inherent, not in a particular piece of the map to which a body of inhabitants were attached, but in the members of such bodies of men and women as considered themselves to belong to a nationality, wherever they happened to live. As such members, they would enjoy 'cultural autonomy'. Supporters of the geographical and human theories of 'the nation' were locked in embittered argument, notably in the international socialist movement and between Zionism and Bundists among the Jews. Neither theory was particularly satisfactory, though the human theory was more harmless. At all events it did not lead its supporters to create a territory first and squeeze its inhabitants into the right national shape afterwards; or, in the words of Piłsudski, the leader of the newly independent Poland after 1918: 'It is the state which makes the nation and not the nation the state.'[3]

As a matter of sociology, the non-territorialists were almost certainly right. Not that men and women – give or take a few nomadic or diaspora peoples – were not deeply attached to some piece of land they called 'home'; especially considering that for most of history the great majority of them belonged to that most rooted part of humanity, those who live by agriculture. But that 'home territory' was no more like the territory of the modern nation than the word 'father' in the more modern term 'fatherland' was like a real parent. The 'homeland' was the locus of a *real* community of human beings with real social relations with each other, not the imaginary community which creates some sort of bond between members of a population of tens – today even of hundreds – of millions. Vocabulary itself proves this. In Spanish *patria* did not become coterminous with Spain until late in the nineteenth century. In the eighteenth it still meant simply the place or town where a person was born. *Paese* in Italian ('country') and *pueblo* in Spanish ('people') can and do still mean a village as well as the national territory or its inhabitants. Nationalism and the state took over the associations of kin, neighbours and home ground, for territories and populations of a size and scale which turned them into metaphors.

But, of course, with the decline of the real communities to which people had been used – village and kin, parish and *barrio*, guild, confraternity or whatever – a decline which occurred because they clearly no longer encompassed, as they once had done, most contingencies of people's lives, their members felt a need for something to take their place. The imaginary community of 'the nation' could fill this void.

It found itself attached, and inevitably so, to that characteristic phenomenon of the nineteenth century, the 'nation-state'. For as a matter of politics, Piłsudski was right. The state not only made the nation, but *needed* to make the nation. Governments now reached down directly to each citizen on their territory in everyday life, through modest but omnipresent agents, from postmen and policemen to teachers and (in many countries) railway employees. They might require his, and eventually even her, active personal commitment to the state: in fact, their 'patriotism'. Authorities in an increasingly democratic age, who could no longer rely on the social orders submitting spontaneously to their social superiors in the traditional manner, or on traditional religion as an effective guarantee of social obedience, needed a way of welding together the state's subjects against subversion and dissidence. 'The nation' was the new civic religion of states. It provided a cement which bonded all citizens to their state, a way to bring the nation-state directly to each citizen, and a counterweight to those who appealed to other loyalties over state loyalty – to religion, to nationality or ethnicity not identified with the state, perhaps above all to class. In constitutional states, the more the masses were drawn into politics by elections, the more scope there was for such appeals to be heard.

Moreover, even non-constitutional states now learned to appreciate the political force of being able to appeal to their subjects on grounds of nationality (a sort of democratic appeal without the dangers of democracy), as well as on grounds of their duty to obey the authorities sanctioned by God. In the 1880s even the Russian tsar, faced with revolutionary agitations, began to apply the policy vainly suggested to his grandfather in the 1830s, namely to base his rule not only on the principles of autocracy and orthodoxy, but also on nationality: i.e. on appealing to Russians as Russians.[4] Of course in one sense practically all nineteenth-century monarchs had to put on national fancy dress, since hardly any of them were natives of the countries they ruled. The (mostly) German princes and princesses who became rulers or rulers' consorts of Britain, Greece, Romania, Russia, Bulgaria, or whatever other country needed crowned heads, paid their respect to the principle of nationality by turning themselves into Britons (like Queen Victoria) or Greeks (like Otto of Bavaria) or learning some other language which they spoke with an accent, even though they had far more in common with the other members of the international princes' trade union – or rather family, since they were all related – than with their own subjects.

What made state nationalism even more essential was that both the economy of a technological era and the nature of its public and private administration required mass elementary education, or at least literacy. The nineteenth century was the era when oral communication broke down, as the distance between authorities and subjects increased, and mass migration put days or weeks of travel between even mothers and sons, bridegrooms and brides. From the state's point of view, the school had a further and essential advantage: it could teach all children how to be good subjects and citizens. Until the triumph of television, there was no medium of secular propaganda to compare with the classroom.

Hence, in educational terms, the era from 1870 to 1914 was above all, in most European countries, the age of the primary school. Even in notoriously well-schooled countries the number of primary school teachers multiplied. It trebled in Sweden and rose almost as much in Norway. Relatively backward countries caught up. The number of primary-school children in the Netherlands doubled; in the United Kingdom (which had no public educational system before 1870) it trebled; in Finland it increased thirteenfold. Even in the illiterate Balkans the number of children in elementary schools quadrupled and the number of teachers almost trebled. But a national, i.e. an overwhelmingly state-organized and state-supervised, education system required a national language of instruction. Education joined the law courts and bureaucracy as a force which made language into the primary condition of nationality.

States therefore created 'nations', i.e. national patriotism and, at least for certain purposes, linguistically and administratively homogenized citizens, with particular urgency and zeal. The French republic turned peasants into Frenchmen. The Italian kingdom, following d'Azeglio's slogan, did its best, with mixed success, to 'make Italians' through school and military service, after having 'made Italy'. The USA made a knowledge of English a condition for American citizenship and, from the end of the 1880s on, began to introduce actual worship under the new civic religion – the only one permitted under an agnostic constitution – in the form of a daily ritual of homage to the flag in every American school. The Hungarian state did its best to turn all its multinational inhabitants into Magyars; the Russian state pressed the Russification of its lesser nationalities – i.e. it tried to give Russian the monopoly of education. And where multinationality was sufficiently recognized to permit elementary or even secondary education in some other vernacular (as in the Habsburg Empire), the state language inevitably enjoyed a decisive advantage at the highest levels of the system. Hence the significance, for non-state nationalities, of the struggle for a university of their own, as in Bohemia, Wales or Flanders.

For state nationalism, real or (as in the case of the monarchs) invented for convenience, was a double-edged strategy. As it mobilized some inhabitants, it alienated others – those who did not belong, or wish to belong, to the nation identified with the state. In short, it helped to define the nationalities excluded from the official nationality by separating out those communities which, for whatever reason, resisted the official public language and ideology.

## II

But why should some have resisted, where so many others did not? After all, there were quite substantial advantages for peasants – and even more for their children – in becoming Frenchmen, or indeed for anyone who acquired a major language of culture and professional advancement in addition to their own dialect or vernacular. In 1910 70 per cent of German immigrants to the USA, who arrived there, on average after 1900, with $41 in their pockets, had become English-speaking American citizens, though they had plainly no intention of ceasing to speak and feel German.[5] (To be fair, few states really tried to stop the private life of a minority language and culture, so long as it did not challenge the public supremacy of the official state-nation.) It might well be that the unofficial language could not effectively compete with the official one, except for purposes of religion, poetry and community or family sentiment. Hard though it may be to believe today, there were passionately national Welshmen who accepted a lesser place for their ancient Celtic tongue in the century of progress, and some who envisaged an eventual natural euthanasia for it. There were, indeed, many who chose to migrate not from one territory but from one class to another; a voyage which was apt to mean a change of nation or at least a change of language. Central Europe became full of German nationalists with obviously Slav names, and Magyars whose names were literal translations of German or adaptations of Slovak ones. The American nation and English language were not the only ones which, in the era of liberalism and mobility, issued a more or less open invitation for membership. And there were plenty who were happy to accept such invitations, all the more so when they were not actually expected to deny their origins by doing so. 'Assimilation' for most of the nineteenth century was far from a bad word: it was what vast numbers of people hoped to achieve, especially among those who wanted to join the middle classes.

One obvious reason why members of some nationalities refused to 'assimilate' was because they were not allowed to become full members of the official nation. The extreme case is that of the native elites in European colonies, educated in the language and culture of their masters so that they could administer the colonials on the Europeans' behalf, but patently not treated as their equals. Here a conflict was bound to erupt sooner or later, all the more so since western education actually provided a specific language for articulating their claims. Why, wrote an Indonesian intellectual in 1913 (in Dutch), should Indonesians be expected to celebrate the centenary of the liberation of the Netherlands from Napoleon? If he were a Dutchman, 'I would not organise an independence celebration in a country where the independence of the people had been stolen.'[6]

Colonial peoples were an extreme case, since it was clear from the outset that, given the pervasive racism of bourgeois society, no amount of assimilation would turn men with dark skins into 'real' Englishmen, Belgians or Dutchmen, even if they had as much money and noble blood and as much taste for sports as the European nobility – as was the case with many an Indian rajah educated in Britain. And yet, even within the zone of white skins, there was a striking contradiction between the offer of unlimited assimilation to anyone who proved his or her willingness and ability to join the state-nation and the rejection of some groups in practice. This was particularly dramatic for those who had hitherto assumed, on highly plausible grounds, that there were no limits to what assimilation could achieve: the middle-class, westernized, cultivated Jews. That is why the Dreyfus case in France, the victimization of a single French staff officer for being Jewish, produced so disproportionate a reaction of horror – not only among Jews but among all liberals – and led directly to the establishment of Zionism, a territorial state nationalism for Jews.

The half-century before 1914 was a classic era of xenophobia, and therefore of nationalist reaction to it, because – even leaving aside global colonialism – it was an era of massive mobility and migration and, especially during the Depression decades, of open or concealed social tension. To take a single example: by 1914 something like 3.6 million (or almost 15 per cent of the population) had permanently left the territory of inter-war Poland, not counting another half-million *a year* of seasonal migrants.[7] The consequent xenophobia did not only come from below. Its most unexpected manifestations, which reflected the crisis of bourgeois liberalism, came from the established middle classes, who were not likely actually ever to meet the sort of people who settled on New York's Lower East Side or who lived in the harvest labourers' barracks in Saxony. Max Weber, glory of open-minded German bourgeois scholarship, developed so passionate an animus against the Poles (whom he, correctly, accused German landowners of importing en masse as cheap labour) that he actually joined the ultra-nationalist Pan-German League in the 1890s.[8] The real systematization of race-prejudice against 'Slavs, Mediterraneans and Semites' in the USA is to be found among the native white, preferably Protestant anglophone-born middle and upper classes, which even, in this period, invented their own heroic nativist myth of the white Anglo-Saxon (and fortunately non-unionized) cowboy of the wide open spaces, so different from the dangerous ant-heaps of the swelling great cities.[9] Those members of the north-eastern elite chiefly responsible for this myth (which, incidentally, excluded the people chiefly responsible for the cowboy culture and vocabulary, the Mexicans) were Owen Wister (author of *The Virginian*, 1902), the painter Frederick Remington (1861–1909) and the later president, Theodore Roosevelt.

For this bourgeoisie the influx of the alien poor dramatized and symbolized the problems raised by the expanding urban proletariat, combining as they did the characteristics of internal and external 'barbarians', which threatened to swamp civilization as respectable men knew it. They also dramatized, nowhere more than in the USA, the apparent inability of society to cope with the problems of headlong change, and the unpardonable failure of the new masses to accept the superior position of the old elites. It was in Boston, the centre of the traditional white, Anglo-Saxon, Protestant bourgeoisie, both educated and wealthy, that the Immigration Restriction League was founded in 1893. Politically the xenophobia of the middle classes was almost certainly more effective than the xenophobia of the labouring classes, which reflected cultural frictions between neighbours and the fear of low-wage competition for jobs. Except in one respect. It was sectional working-class pressure which actually excluded foreigners from labour markets, since for employers the incentive to import cheap labour was almost irresistible. Where exclusion kept the stranger out entirely, as did the bans on non-white immigrants in California and Australia, which triumphed in the 1880s and 1890s, this produced no national or communal friction, but where it discriminated against a group already on the spot, such as Africans in white South Africa or Catholics in Northern Ireland, it was naturally apt to do so. However, working-class xenophobia was rarely very effective before 1914. All things considered, the greatest international migration of people in history produced surprisingly little by way of anti-foreign labour agitations even in the USA, and sometimes virtually none, as in Argentina and Brazil.

Nevertheless, bodies of immigrants into foreign countries were very likely to discover national sentiments, whether or not they were met by local xenophobia. Poles and Slovaks would become conscious of themselves as such, not only because once they left their home villages they could no longer take themselves for granted as people who did not require any definition, and not only because the states they moved to imposed some new definition on them, classifying people who had hitherto thought of themselves as Sicilians or Neapolitans, or even as natives of Lucca or Salerno, as 'Italians' on arrival in the USA. They needed their community for mutual aid. From whom could migrants into new, strange, unknown lives expect help except kin and friends, people from the old country? (Even regional migrants within the same country would usually stick together.) Who could even understand him or, more to the point, her – for women's domestic sphere left them more monoglot than men? Who could give them shape as a community rather than a mere heap of foreigners, except, in the first instance, some body like their church which, even though in theory universal, was in practice national, because its priests came from the same people as their congregations and Slovak priests had to talk Slovak to them, whatever the language in which they celebrated the mass? In this manner 'nationality' became a real network of personal relations rather than a merely imaginary community, simply because, far from home, every Slovene actually had a potential personal connection with every other Slovene when they met.

Moreover, if such populations were to be organized in any manner for the purpose of the new societies in which they found themselves, it had to be done in ways which allowed communication. Labour and socialist movements, as we have seen, were internationalist, and even dreamed, as liberals had done, of a future in which all would talk a single world language – a dream still surviving in small groups of Esperantists. Eventually, as Kautsky still hoped in 1908, the entire body of educated humanity would be fused into a single language and nationality.[10] Yet in the meantime they faced the problem of the Tower of Babel: unions in Hungarian factories might have to issue strike calls in four different languages.[11] They soon discovered that nationally mixed branches did not work well, unless members were already bilingual. International movements of labouring people *had to be* combinations of national or linguistic units. In the USA the party which in effect became the workers' mass party, the Democrats, necessarily developed as an 'ethnic' coalition.

The greater the migration of peoples and the more rapid the development of cities and industry which threw uprooted masses against each other, the greater the bias for national consciousness among the uprooted. Hence, in the case of new national movements, exile was often their main place of incubation. When the future President Masaryk signed the agreement which was to create a state uniting Czechs and Slovaks (Czechoslovakia) he did so in Pittsburgh, for the mass basis of an organized Slovak nationalism was to be found in Pennsylvania rather than Slovakia. As for the backward mountain peoples of the Carpathians known in Austria as Ruthenes, who were also to be joined to Czechoslovakia from 1918 to 1945, their nationalism had no organized expression whatever except among emigrants to the USA.

The mutual aid and protection of emigrants may have contributed to the growth of nationalism in their nations, but is not enough to explain it. However, insofar as it rested on an ambiguous and double-edged nostalgia for the old ways emigrants had left behind, it had something in common with a force which undoubtedly fostered nationalism at home, especially in the smaller nations. This was neo-traditionalism, a defensive or conservative reaction against the disruption of the old social order by the advancing epidemic of modernity, capitalism, cities and industry, not forgetting the proletarian socialism which was their logical outcome.

The traditionalist element is obvious enough in the support of the Catholic church for such movements as Basque and

Flemish nationalism, or indeed many nationalisms of small peoples which were, almost by definition, rejected by liberal nationalism as incapable of forming viable nation-states. The right-wing ideologues who now multiplied also tended to develop a taste for traditionally rooted cultural regionalism such as the Provençal *félibrige*. In fact, the ideological ancestors of most of the separatist–regionalist movements in late-twentieth-century western Europe (Breton, Welsh, Occitan, etc.) are to be found on the pre-1914 intellectual right. Conversely, among these small peoples neither the bourgeoisies nor the new proletariat usually found mininationalism to their taste. In Wales the rise of Labour undermined the Young Wales nationalism which had threatened to take over the Liberal Party. As for the new industrial bourgeoisie, it could be expected to prefer the market of a large nation or world to the provincial constriction of a small country or region. Neither in Russian Poland nor in the Basque country, two disproportionately industrialized regions of larger states, did indigenous capitalists show enthusiasm for the national cause, and the demonstratively Franco-centred bourgeoisie of Ghent was a permanent provocation to Flemish nationalists. Though this lack of interest was not quite universal, it was strong enough to mislead Rosa Luxemburg into supposing that there was no bourgeois base for Polish nationalism.

But, even more frustrating to traditionalist nationalists, the most traditionalist of all classes, the peasantry, also showed only a faint interest in nationalism. The Basque-speaking peasants showed little enthusiasm for the Basque National Party, founded in 1894 to defend all that was ancient against the incursion of Spaniards and godless workers. Like most other such movements, it was primarily an urban middle- and lower-middle-class body.[12]

In fact, the advance of nationalism in our period was largely a phenomenon carried by these middle strata of society. Hence there is much point to the contemporary socialists who called it 'petty-bourgeois'. And its connection with these strata helps to explain the three novel characteristics we have already observed: its shifts to linguistic militancy, to a demand for independent states rather than lesser kinds of autonomy, and to the political right and ultra-right.

For the lower middle classes rising from a popular background, career and vernacular language were inseparably welded together. From the moment that society rested on mass literacy, a spoken language had to be in some sense official – a medium of bureaucracy and instruction – if it was not to sink into the half-world of purely oral communication occasionally dignified with the status of an exhibit in a folklore museum. *Mass*, i.e. primary, education was the crucial development, since it was possible only in a language which the bulk of the population could be expected to understand. The prohibition of the use of Welsh, or some local language or patois in the classroom, which left such traumatic traces in the memories of local scholars and intellectuals, was due not to some kind of totalitarian claims by the dominant state-nation, but almost certainly to the sincere belief that no adequate education was possible except in the state language, and that the person who remained a monoglot would inevitably be handicapped as a citizen and in his or her professional prospects. Education in a totally foreign language, alive or dead, is possible only for a select and sometimes exiguous minority which can afford the considerable time, expense and effort to acquire sufficient command of it. Bureaucracy, again, was a crucial element, both because it decided the official status of a language and because, in most countries, it provided the largest body of employment requiring literacy. Hence the endless petty struggles which disrupted the politics of the Habsburg Empire from the 1890s, about the language in which street signs were to be written in areas of mixed nationality, and about such matters as the nationality of particular assistant postmasters or railway station masters.

But only political power could transform the status of lesser languages or dialects (which, as everyone knows, are just languages without an army and police force). Hence the pressures and counter-pressures behind the elaborate linguistic censuses of the period (e.g. most notably, those of Belgium and Austria in 1910), on which the political claims of this or that idiom depended. And hence, at least in part, the political mobilization of nationalists for language at the very moment when, as in Belgium, the number of bilingual Flemings grew very strikingly or, as in the Basque country, the use of the Basque language was virtually dying out in the rapidly growing cities.[13] For political pressure alone could win a place for what were in practice 'uncompetitive' languages as a medium of education or written public communication. This, and this alone, made Belgium officially bilingual (1870) and Flemish a compulsory subject in the secondary schools of Flanders (as late as 1883). But once the unofficial language had thus won official standing it automatically created a substantial political constituency of vernacular literates for itself. The 4.8 million pupils in the primary and secondary schools of Habsburg Austria in 1912 obviously contained a great many more potential and actual nationalists than the 2.2 million of 1874, not to mention the hundred thousand or so extra teachers who now instructed them in various rival languages.

And yet in multilingual societies those educated in the vernacular, and able to use this education for professional advancement, probably still felt themselves to be inferior and unprivileged. For while they were in practice at an advantage in competing for the lesser jobs, because they were much more likely to be bilingual than the snobs of the elite language, they might justifiably feel that they were at a disadvantage in the search for the top jobs. Hence the pressure to extend vernacular teaching from primary to secondary education, and eventually to the crown of a full educational system, the vernacular university. In both Wales and Flanders the demand for such a university was intensely, and exclusively, political for this reason. In fact, in Wales the national university (1893) actually became for a while the first and *only* national institution of a people whose small country had no administrative or other existence distinct from England. Those whose first language was an unofficial vernacular would almost certainly still be excluded from the higher ranges of culture and private or public affairs, unless as speakers of the official and superior idiom in which they would certainly be conducted. In short, the very fact that new lower middle and even middle classes had been educated in Slovene or Flemish emphasized that the major prizes and the top status still went to those who spoke French or German, even if they did not bother to learn the lesser language.

Yet more political pressure was needed to overcome this built-in handicap. In fact, what was needed was political *power*. To put it bluntly, people had to be compelled to use the vernacular for purposes for which they would normally have found it preferable to use another language. Hungary insisted on Magyarized schooling, even though every educated Hungarian, then as now, knew perfectly well that a knowledge of at least one internationally current language was essential for all except the most subaltern functions in Hungarian society. Compulsion, or government pressure amounting to it, was the price paid for turning Magyar into a literary language which could serve all modern purposes in its own territory, even if nobody could understand a word of it outside. Political power alone – in the last analysis state power – could hope to achieve such results. Nationalists, especially those whose livelihood and career prospects were tied up with their language, were unlikely to ask whether there were other ways in which languages might develop and flourish.

To this extent linguistic nationalism had a built-in bias towards secession. And, conversely, the call for an independent state territory seemed increasingly inseparable from language, so that we find the official commitment to Gaelic entering Irish nationalism (in the 1890s) even though – perhaps actually because – most of the Irish were satisfied to speak only English, and Zionism invented Hebrew as an everyday language, because no other language of the Jews committed them to the construction of a territorial state. There is room for interesting reflections about the varied fate of such essentially political efforts at linguistic engineering, for some were to fail (like the reconversion of the Irish to Gaelic) or half-fail (like the construction of a more Norwegian Norwegian – Nynorsk), while others were to succeed. However, before 1914 they generally lacked the required state power. In 1916 the number of actual everyday speakers of Hebrew was no more than sixteen thousand.

But nationalism was linked to the middle strata in another way, which gave both it and them a twist towards the political right. Xenophobia appealed readily to traders, independent craftsmen and some farmers threatened by the progress of the industrial economy, especially, once again, during the hard-pressed years of the Depression. The foreigner came to symbolize the disruption of old ways and the capitalist system we have observed spreading across the western world from the 1880s had little to do with the actual number of Jews against whom it was directed: it was as effective in France, where there were sixty thousand among forty million, in Germany where there were half a million among sixty-five million, as in Vienna where they formed 15 per cent of the population. (It was not a political factor in Budapest, where they formed a quarter of it.) This anti-Semitism took aim rather against the bankers, entrepreneurs and others who were identified with the ravages of capitalism among the 'little men'. The typical cartoon image of the capitalist in the *belle époque* was not just a fat man in a top hat smoking a cigar, but one with a Jewish nose – because the fields of enterprise in which Jews were prominent competed with small shopkeepers and gave or refused credit to farmers and small artisans.

Anti-Semitism, the German socialist leader August Bebel therefore felt, was 'the socialism of idiots'. Yet what strikes us about the rise of political anti-Semitism at the end of the century is not so much the equation 'Jew = capitalist', which was not implausible in large parts of east-central Europe, but its association with *right-wing* nationalism. This was not only due to the rise of socialist movements which systematically combated the latent or overt xenophobia of their supporters, so that a deeply rooted dislike of foreigners and Jews in those quarters tended to be rather more shamefaced than in the past. It marked a distinct shift of the nationalist ideology to the right in the major states, especially in the 1890s, when we can see, for instance, the old mass organizations of German nationalism, the *Turner* (gymnastic associations), veer from the liberalism inherited from the 1848 revolution to an aggressive, militarist and anti-Semitic posture. This is when the banners of patriotism become so much a property of the political right that the left found trouble in grasping them, even where patriotism was as firmly identified with revolution and the case of the people as was the French tricolour. To brandish the national name and flag, they felt, risked contamination from the ultra-right. Not until the days of Hitler did the French left recover the full use of Jacobin patriotism.

Patriotism shifted to the political right, not only because its former ideological stablemate, bourgeois liberalism, was in disarray, but because the international situation which had apparently made liberalism and nationalism compatible no longer held good. Up to the 1870s – perhaps even up to the Congress of Berlin of 1878 – it could be claimed that one nation-state's gain was not necessarily another's loss. Indeed, the map of Europe had been transformed by the creation of two major new nation-states (Germany and Italy) and the formation of several minor ones in the Balkans, without either war or intolerable disruption of the international state system. Until the Great Depression something very like global free trade, while perhaps benefiting Britain rather more than others, had been in the interest of all. Yet from the 1870s on such claims ceased to ring true, and as a global conflict came, once more, to be considered as a serious, if not an impending possibility, the sort of nationalism which saw other nations frankly as menace or victims gained ground.

It both bred and was encouraged by the movements of the political right which emerged out of the crisis of liberalism. Indeed the men who first called themselves by the novel name of 'nationalists' were frequently stimulated into political action by the experience of their state's defeat in war, like Maurice Barrès (1862–1923) and Paul Déroulède (1846–1914) after the German victory over France in 1870–1, and Enrico Corradini (1865–1931) after Italy's even more galling defeat at the hands of Ethiopia in 1896. And the movements they founded, which brought the word 'nationalism' into the general dictionaries, were quite deliberately set up 'in reaction against the democracy then in government', i.e. against parliamentary politics.[14] The French movements of this kind remained marginal, like the Action Française (est. 1898) which lost itself in a politically irrelevant monarchism and in vituperative prose. The Italian ones eventually merged with fascism after the First World War. They were characteristic of a new breed of political movements built on chauvinism, xenophobia and, increasingly, the idealization of national expansion, conquest and the very act of war.

Such nationalism lent itself exceptionally well to expressing the collective resentments of people who could not explain their discontents precisely. It was the foreigners' fault. The Dreyfus case gave French anti-Semitism a special edge, not only because the accused was a Jew (what business had an alien in the French general staff?) but because his alleged crime was espionage on behalf of Germany. Conversely, the blood of 'good' Germans curdled at the thought that their country was being systematically 'encircled' by the alliance of its enemies, as their leaders frequently reminded them. Meanwhile the English were getting ready to celebrate the outbreak of the world war (like other belligerent peoples) by an outburst of anti-alien hysteria which made it advisable to change the German family name of the royal dynasty to the Anglo-Saxon 'Windsor'. No doubt every native citizen, apart from a minority of internationalist socialists, a few intellectuals, cosmopolitan businessmen and members of the international club of aristocrats and royals, felt the appeal of chauvinism to some extent. No doubt almost all, including even many socialists and intellectuals, were so deeply imbued with the fundamental racism of nineteenth-century civilization that they were also indirectly vulnerable to the temptations which come from believing one's own class or people to have a built-in natural superiority over others. Imperialism could not but reinforce these temptations among members of imperial states. Yet there is little doubt that those who responded most eagerly to the nationalist bugles were to be found somewhere between the established upper classes of society and the peasants and proletarians at the bottom.

For this widening body of middle strata, nationalism also had a wider and less instrumental appeal. It provided them with a collective identity as the 'true defenders' of the nation which eluded them as a class, or as aspirants to the full bourgeois status they so much coveted. Patriotism compensated for social inferiority. Thus in Britain, where there was no compulsory military service, the curve of volunteer recruitment of working-class soldiers in the imperialist South African War (1899–1902) simply reflects the economic situation. It rose and fell with unemployment. But the curve of recruitment for lower-middle-class and white-collar youths clearly reflected the appeals of patriotic propaganda. And, in a sense, patriotism in uniform could bring its social rewards. In Germany it provided the potential status as reserve officer for boys who had undergone secondary education to the age of sixteen, even if they went no further. In Britain, as the war was to show, even clerks and salesmen in the service of the nation could become officers and – in the brutally frank terminology of the British upper class – 'temporary gentlemen'.

## III

Yet, nationalism between the 1870s and 1914 cannot be confined to the kind of ideology which appealed to the frustrated middle

On Nationalism

classes or the anti-liberal (and anti-socialist) ancestors of fascism. For it is beyond question that in this period governments and parties or movements which could make, or imply, a national appeal were likely to enjoy an extra advantage; and conversely those which could not or would not were to some extent handicapped. It is quite undeniable that the outbreak of war in 1914 produced genuine, if sometimes short-lived, outbursts of mass patriotism in the main belligerent countries. And in multinational states working-class movements organized on an all-state basis fought and lost a rearguard action against disintegration into separate movements based on the workers of each nationality. The labour and socialist movement of the Habsburg Empire thus fell apart before the empire itself did.

Nevertheless, there is a major difference between nationalism as an ideology of nationalist movements and flag-waving governments, and the broader appeal of nationality. The first did not look beyond the establishment or aggrandizement of 'the nation'. Its programme was to resist, expel, defeat, conquer, subject or eliminate 'the foreigner'. Anything else was unimportant. It was enough to assert the Irishness, Germanness or Croatiannesss of the Irish, German or Croatian people in an independent state of their own, belonging exclusively to them, to announce its glorious future and to make every sacrifice to achieve it.

It was this which, in practice, limited its appeal to a cadre of impassioned ideologists and militants, to shapeless middle classes searching for cohesion and self-justification, for such groups (again mainly among the struggling 'little men') as could ascribe all their discontents to the damned foreigners – and, of course, to governments which welcomed an ideology which told citizens that patriotism was enough.

But for most people nationalism alone was not enough. This is, paradoxically, most evident in the actual movements of nationalities which had not yet achieved self-determination. The national movements which gained genuine mass support in

82

our period – and by no means all which wanted it had achieved it – were almost invariably those which combined the appeal of nationality and language with some more powerful interest or mobilizing force, ancient or modern. Religion was one. Without the Catholic church the Flemish and Basque movements would have been politically negligible, and nobody doubts that Catholicism gave consistency and mass strength to the nationalism of Irish and Poles ruled by rulers of a different faith. In fact, during this period the nationalism of Irish Fenians, originally a secular, indeed anti-clerical, movement appealing to Irishmen across confessional frontiers, became a major political force precisely by letting Irish nationalism identify itself essentially with the Catholic Irish.

More surprisingly, as we have already suggested, parties whose original and primary object was international class and social liberation found themselves becoming the vehicles of national liberation also. The re-establishment of an independent Poland was achieved, not under the leadership of any of the numerous nineteenth-century parties devoted exclusively to independence, but under leadership coming from the Second International's Polish Socialist Party. Armenian nationalism shows the same pattern, as indeed does Jewish territorial nationalism. What made Israel was not Herzl or Weizmann, but (Russian-inspired) labour Zionism. And while some such parties were, justifiably, criticized within international socialism because they put nationalism a long way before social liberation, this cannot be said of other socialist, or even Marxist, parties which found themselves to their surprise to be the representative of particular nations: the Finnish Socialist Party, the Mensheviks in Georgia, the Jewish Bund in large areas of eastern Europe – in fact, even the rigidly non-nationalist Bolsheviks in Latvia. Conversely, nationalist movements became aware of the desirability of spelling out, if not a specific social programme, then at least a concern with economic and social questions. Characteristically it was in industrialized Bohemia, torn between Czechs and

Germans both drawn to labour movements, that movements specifically describing themselves as 'national socialist' emerged. The Czech national socialists eventually became the characteristic party of independent Czechoslovakia, and provided its last president (Edvard Beneš). The German national socialists inspired a young Austrian who took their name and their combination of anti-Semitic ultra-nationalism with a vague populist social demagogy into post-war Germany: Adolf Hitler.

Nationalism therefore became genuinely popular essentially when it was drunk as a cocktail. Its attraction was not just its own flavour, but its combination with some other component or components which, it was hoped, would slake the consumers' spiritual and material thirst. But such nationalism, though genuine enough, was neither as militant nor as single minded, and certainly not as reactionary, as the flag-waving right would have wanted it to be.

The Habsburg Empire, about to disintegrate under the various national pressures, paradoxically illustrates the limitations of nationalism. For though most of its people were, by the early 1900s, unquestionably conscious of belonging to some nationality or other, few of them thought that this was incompatible with support for the Habsburg monarchy. Even after the outbreak of war national independence was not a major issue, and a decided hostility to the state was to be found in only four of the Habsburg nations, three of which could identify with national states beyond their borders (the Italians, the Romanians, the Serbs and the Czechs). Most of the nationalities did not visibly wish to break out of what middle- and lower-middle-class zealots like to call 'the prison of peoples'. And when, in the course of the war, discontent and revolutionary feelings really mounted, it took the form, in the first instance, not of movements for national independence but for social revolution.[15]

As for the western belligerents, in the course of the war anti-war feeling and social discontent increasingly overlaid, but without destroying, the patriotism of mass armies. The extraordinary international impact of the Russian revolutions of 1917 is comprehensible only if we bear in mind that those who had gone to war willingly, even enthusiastically, in 1914 were moved by the idea of patriotism which could not be confined within nationalist slogans: for it included a sense of what was due to citizens. These armies had not gone to war out of a taste for fighting, for violence and heroism, or to pursue the unconditional national egoism and expansionism of the nationalism of the right. And still less out of hostility to liberalism and democracy.

On the contrary. The domestic propaganda of all belligerents with mass politics demonstrates, in 1914, that the point to stress was not glory and conquest, but that 'we' were the victims of aggression, or of a policy of aggression, that 'they' represented a mortal threat to the values of freedom and civilization which 'we' embodied. What is more, men and women would not be successfully mobilized for the war unless they felt that the war was more than a plain armed combat: that in some sense the world would be better for 'our' victory and 'our' country would be – to use Lloyd George's phrase – 'a land fit for heroes to live in'. The British and French governments thus claimed to defend democracy and freedom against monarchical power, militaries and barbarism ('the Huns'), while the German government claimed to defend the values of order, law and culture against Russian autocracy and barbarism. The prospects of conquest and imperial aggrandizement could be advertised in colonial wars, but not in the major conflicts – even if they occupied foreign ministries behind the scenes.

The German, French and British masses who marched to war in 1914 did so, not as warriors or adventurers, but as citizens and civilians. Yet this very fact demonstrates both the necessity of patriotism for governments operating in democratic societies and its force. For only the sense that the cause of the state was genuinely their own could mobilize the masses effectively: and in 1914 the British, French and Germans had it. They were so mobilized, until three years of unparalleled massacre and the

example of revolution in Russian taught them that they had
been mistaken.

## Notes

1   See Georges Haupt, Michel Lowy and Claudie Weill, *Les Marxistes et la question nationale 1848–1914: études et textes* (Paris, 1974).
2   Emil Brix, *Die Umgangssprachen in Altösterreich zwischen Agitation und Assimilation: Die Sprachenstatistik in den zisleithanischen Volkszählungen 1880–1910* (Vienna, Cologne and Graz, 1982), p. 97.
3   Hans Roos, *A History of Modern Poland* (London, 1966), p. 48.
4   Hugh Seton-Watson, *Nations and States* (London, 1977), p. 85.
5   'Naturalization and Citizenship', in Thernstrom et al. (eds), *Harvard Encyclopedia of American Ethnic Groups* (Cambridge, Mass., 1980), p. 747.
6   Benedict Anderson, *Imagined Communities: Reflections on the Origins and Spread of Nationalism* (London, 1983), pp. 107–8.
7   Celina Bobińska and Andrzej Pilch (eds), *Employment-Seeking Emigrations of the Poles World-Wide: XIX and XX C.* (Cracow, 1975), pp. 124–6.
8   Wolfgang J. Mommsen, *Max Weber and German Politics 1890–1920* (Chicago, 1984), pp. 54ff.
9   Lonn Taylor and Ingrid Maar, *The American Cowboy* (Washington DC, 1983), pp. 96–8.
10  Hans Mommsen, *Nationalitätenfrage und Arbeiterbewegung* (Trier, 1971), pp. 18–19.
11  *History of the Hungarian Labour Movement. Guide to the Permanent Exhibition of the Museum of the Hungarian Labour Movement* (Budapest, 1983), pp. 31ff.
12  Marianne Heiberg, 'Insiders/Outsiders; Basque Nationalism', *Archives Européennes de Sociologie*, XVI (1975), pp. 169–93.
13  Aristide Zolberg, 'The Making of Flemings and Walloons: Belgium 1830–1914', *Journal of Interdisciplinary History*, V (1974), pp. 179–235; Hans-Jürgen Puhle, 'Baskischer Nationalismus im spanischen Kontext' in Heinrich August Winkler (ed.), *Nationalismum in der Welt von Heute* (Göttingen, 1982), especially pp. 60–5.
14  *Enciclopedia Italiana*, 'Nazionalismo'.
15  Peter Hanak, 'Die Volksmeinung während den letzten Kriegsjahren in Österreich-Ungarn', in R. G. Plaschka and K. H. Mack (eds), *Die Auflösung des Habsburgerreiches: Zusammenbruch und Neuorientierung im Donauraum* (Vienna, 1970), pp. 58–67.

# 5

# *Do Workers Have a Country?*

If it is wrong to assume that workers have no country, it is equally misleading to assume that they have only one, and that we know what it is. We talk of the French, German or Italian working classes, and in doing so we indicate, quite rightly, that much of the most important forces defining any particular working class are those of the national economy of the state in which a worker lives, and the laws, institutions, practices and official culture of that state. An Irish labourer migrating to Boston, his brother who settled in Glasgow, and a third brother who went to Sydney would remain Irish, but become part of three very different working classes with different histories. At the same time, and as this example suggests, it is also wrong to assume that the members of such national working classes are or ever were homogeneous bodies of Frenchmen, Britons, Italians, or, even when they saw themselves as such, that they are not divided by other communal demarcations, or that they are exclusively identified with the state which defines their effective existence as a class and an organized movement. It is equally wrong to assume that such an identification is eternal and unchanging. These assumptions are based on the myths of modern nationalism, a nineteenth-century invention. Though they are not entirely fictitious, they are not much more realistic than the opposite assumption that national or communal identity are irrelevant to the proletariat.

No doubt it is possible to discover countries in which the working class is nationally homogeneous in this sense [ ... ] but for practical purposes such cases may be neglected. All national working classes tend to be heterogeneous, and with multiple identifications, though for certain purposes and at certain times some may loom larger than others. An Indian shop steward in Slough may see himself for one purpose as a member of the British working class (as distinct from his brother who remained in India), for another as a coloured person (as distinct from the whites), for another as an Indian (as distinct from the British or Pakistanis), for yet another as a Sikh (as distinct from Christians, Hindus or Muslim), as a Punjabi (as distinct from a Gujarati), probably also as someone from a particular area and village in the Punjab, and certainly as a member of a particular network of kinship. Of course some of these identifications, however important for everyday purposes (e.g. in arranging the marriage of sons and daughters), are politically rather subordinate.

Moreover, one identification does not exclude the others. The Andalusians, Basques and Catalans who fought Napoleon did so as Spaniards, without in the least losing the sense of the differences which separated them from each other. What is more, such identifications change over time, as well as with the context of action. Sicilian and Calabrian labourers went to America and became Americans, but in doing so they also came to see themselves – as they probably had not done before – as Italians who belonged, to some extent, not only to the old country but also to a nation whose members were scattered across the world from Argentina and Brazil to Australia. Conversely, workers who once saw themselves primarily as Belgians, in spite of talking two quite different and mutually incomprehensible languages, today identify themselves primarily as Flemings and French-speaking Walloons.

These multiple identities give rise to something like a 'national' problem within working classes only when they seriously get in each other's way. So far as one can tell there was no serious national problem before 1914 in the mines of South Wales where English immigrants, English- and Welsh-speaking Welshmen, a handful of Spaniards and doubtless a few other minorities worked together, joining the South Wales Miners' Federation and supporting Labour. There was in the Ruhr, where a mass of immigrant Polish miners, separated from the Germans by language and from the freethinking Social Democratic Party by Catholicism, showed a marked reluctance to support the party of their class. Again, to take the extreme case of the United States, where the working class consisted largely of immigrants incapable initially of understanding the language of the country or of other groups of immigrants: their national and linguistic differences undoubtedly made the formation of a working-class consciousness more difficult, though they did not entirely inhibit it, and certainly did not prevent the formation of a general political consciousness of the immigrant poor – the 'ethnic Americans' who, much as they fought with each other collectively, formed the basis of the Democratic Party in the big cities. But they certainly created no major political problems for the country which officially welcomed them and was neutral about their religions. The very same people who in their home states – as Irishmen in the United Kingdom, as Poles in Russia and Germany, as Czechs in Austria – constituted a 'national problem' which threatened the political unity or even the existence of these states were of little more significance across the ocean than in the choice of candidates for municipal elections.

Indeed, the example of the Irish in Britain illustrates the same point. Most of them were both workers and, very consciously, Catholic and Irish. Until the twenty-six counties separated from the United Kingdom, most of them found a formula which combined national and class identification by supporting, or allying with, parties and movements which claimed to be in favour of both, or at any rate hostile to both. (Few Irish Nationalist candidates stood in Britain, and outside the Scotland division of Liverpool, none was elected.) Unions with a strong Irish tinge – the National Union of Dock Labourers was commonly known as 'the Irish union' – behaved much like other unions. No doubt this was facilitated by the fact that the movement which claimed to stand for 'the people' or the working class – Liberals, Labour and Socialists – opposed the oppression of Ireland, joined in protests against it, and indeed supported the Irish nationalist demand for Home Rule for a united Ireland. After Irish separation had been achieved, the bulk of the Catholic Irish in Britain, insofar as they organized and voted at all, undoubtedly gravitated to the parties of their class. Nor did the fact that they enjoyed dual political rights seem to create any major difficulties: even today Irishmen who vote Labour in Britain will not necessarily feel obliged to vote for a Labour or working-class party when they return to the Republic of Ireland.

The relatively smooth integration is all the more striking when we recall that at the grassroots anti-Catholic and anti-Irish sentiments were powerful and sometimes savage in Britain – and by no means only in Liverpool and Glasgow. Moreover, in the case of Ulster or British Orange workers, Protestant identification unquestionably cut across both class and national identification. Nevertheless, for the majority group among the Irish, perhaps just because they were so evidently a majority, the double identification as Irish and (when in Britain) British workers seems to have been relatively unproblematic.

Thus practically all so-called 'national' working classes consist of a jigsaw of heterogeneous groups. On the one hand, historical development has tended to weld these together into more or less nation-wide blocks, so that differences between Kerrymen and Tipperary men are subordinated to a general Irishness (except, perhaps, for purposes of sporting contests), or between Catholic and Lutheran Germans into a general Germanness (except for purposes of electoral identification). Such nation-wide 'national consciousness' is historically recent, though some examples (perhaps 'Englishness') date back rather longer. But on the other hand, the mobility and the shifting of people in contemporary society, which may be essentially described as a world on the move, create new bonds and new frictions breaking up these blocks.

Thus mass migration into the mines of South Wales, mainly from England, created a strongly Welsh working class, but one which ceased to speak Welsh, thus intensifying the silent tensions between the English-speaking majority of the Welsh and the regionally concentrated and diminishing Welsh-speaking minority. A much smaller migration into North Wales – but one not absorbed into the fabric of the local social structure – has, as we know, produced considerable friction between the Welsh and the English in that region, and, in some parts, a transfer of political loyalties from the all-British Labour Party (inheritor of the all-British Liberal Party) to Plaid Cymru. Similarly, even without migration, changes in the economy, in society and in politics may disturb the established stable pattern of relations between different groups, with unpredictable and sometimes catastrophic results. We have seen this happen in Cyprus, where Greeks and Turks had long coexisted, and in the Lebanon, a notorious jigsaw puzzle of Maronite, Orthodox and variously Catholic Christians, Sunni and Shiite Muslim, Arabs, Armenians, Druzes and various others. Still, the major disturbances have almost certainly come from mass mobility, our economic and social transformations implying mass migration within and between states. Neither capitalist nor socialist industrialization is conceivable without it and this produces the special problems of 'strangers' or 'foreigners' – a problem already created in many regions by pre-capitalist patterns of settlement and colonization. This clearly affects the working class very directly.

There are two aspects to the intermingling of different communities, of which the relation between 'natives' and immigrants is a particularly clear example.

First, there is the fourfold pattern of the balance between the two. We may neglect case (a), a country without working-class emigration or immigration as too rare to be significant. Case (b), a country with little emigration but significant immigration, is comparatively rare, though France might fit the bill. The French, while receiving masses of foreign workers since industrialization, have never moved outside their frontiers themselves. Case (c) is rather more common: countries with little immigration but a good detail of emigration: in the nineteenth century Norway and the territory of the present Republic of Ireland were obvious examples. Case (d), which is probably the most common in industrial Europe, consists of countries with both substantial emigration and immigration – as in nineteenth-century Britain and Germany. Both immigration and emigration have a bearing on the history of national working classes for, as every Irishman knows, emigration does not snap the links between the exiles and the home country, not least in the history of its labour movement. Martin Tranmæl, the leader of the Norwegian labour movement during and after the First World War, had been in the Industrial Workers of the World in the United States, whither the Norwegians migrated. Tom Mann migrated to Australia and returned to Britain. As for the Irish movement, its history is filled with returned emigrants: Michael Davitt, James Larkin, James Connolly.

The second aspect concerns the complexity of the pattern of migration and the distribution of migrant groups. Emigrants from one state or national group may either flow in a single stream to one region and nowhere else, as the peasant from the Creuse in central France moved as building labourers to Paris, or they may fan out to produce a temporary or permanent diaspora which may be worldwide. Wherever there was hard-rock mining on the globe in the nineteenth century, groups of

Cornishmen were to be found. The converse of this phenomenon is even more relevant for our purposes.

In some regions or countries, the game of 'foreigners' has only two players: Poles and Germans in the Ruhr, Basques and Spaniards in the Basque country. More commonly the working class contains an immigrant sector composed of a variety of 'strangers' of different kinds, divided among themselves as well as separated from the natives, and in the extreme case the working class is predominantly composed of immigrants, as in the United States, Argentina and Brazil during the major period of mass migration before 1914. Yet, while the number of players in the game is greater or smaller, the pattern which usually develops is one of occupational specialization, or a sort of national stratification.

Thus in 1914 there were a few mines in the Ruhr which did not have a majority of Polish miners, and even today everyone in Britain expects construction sites to be full of Irishmen. What tends to set one national or religious or racial group of workers against another, is not so much occupational specialization in itself, as the tendency for one group to occupy, and seek to monopolize, the most highly skilled, better paid and more desirable jobs. Such divisions and stratifications occur even in nationally homogeneous working classes, but it is certain that they are enormously exacerbated when they coincide with differences of language, colour, religion or nationality. Belfast is an unhappy and obvious case in point.

Yet communal differences alone have not prevented labour movements from organizing workers successfully across such divisions. A powerful Social Democratic Party in Vienna united Czech and German workers. Before 1914 the differences between Flemish and Walloon workers in Belgium were politically so insignificant that a standard work on socialism in Belgium by two leaders of the Labour Party there did not bother to so much as mention the 'Flemish question'. Today, when all Belgian parties are linguistically divided, the motto 'Workers of all Lands, Unite' incised in Flemish on the Labour Hall in Ghent remains as a melancholy reminder of this lost unity. Highly unified working classes with a powerful class consciousness have been forged out of a mixture of natives and various immigrant groups, as in Argentina. Single working-class movements have even been created, as in India, out of a conglomerate of mutually hostile and linguistically incomprehensible castes, language groups and religions. For that matter, even in Ulster men who feared for their lives from Catholic or Protestant proletarians outside the shipyard or dock gates were – and perhaps still are – prepared to act together inside them for purposes of industrial disputes. The historical as well as practical problem is to discover under what circumstances such class unity can come into being, work, or cease to work.

Three circumstances may be suggested, in which natural or communal divisions may fatally disrupt working classes. Such disruption may arise from the influence of nationalist or other political movements outside the working class; from rapid and major changes in the composition of that class (or more generally, in society) which established patterns cannot absorb; and from the attempt to maintain disproportionately favourable conditions by strict limitations of entry into the working class.

The last case is probably the least common, for while the tendency to form 'labour aristocracies' is fairly general, blanket exclusion is rather uncommon, except on the grounds of colour and sex, two barriers which, because of their visibility, are very difficult to cross. Still, where such blanket exclusion operates or has operated, as in the White Australia policy, the Chinese Exclusion laws in the United States and the anti-black discrimination in South African industry, it has certainly come primarily from within the unusually favoured local working class, afraid of losing its exceptionally advantageous conditions. Where exclusion is totally successful, there is no split in the working class, since the excluded are kept out altogether. Where the favoured and the unprivileged coexist, as in South Africa, in practice two parallel and perhaps mutually hostile working classes tend to develop. However, in capitalist and probably also socialist industrialization it is rare for labour to be consistently so favoured or so strong as to impose permanent blanket exclusiveness. Consequently even labour movements based on the attempt to create congeries of labour aristocracies, as in mid-nineteenth-century Britain, aimed at labour movements which were inclusive, that is they recognized that they ought ideally to achieve the organization of all workers, and certainly of all who were likely to penetrate into the enclosure they reserved for their trade or occupation. Within such a comprehensive movement, the special advantages of labour aristocracy ought, of course, to be safeguarded.

Changes in the social composition of the working class may be divisive, insofar as they disturb established social patterns and allow rivalries within the class to be nationally or communally coloured, or class lines to coincide with national or communal lines. This has been the danger in regions like Catalonia and, even more, the Basque country, where industrial development leads to a mass influx of Spanish workers, slow to learn to speak Catalan and even slower to learn Basque, and rather despised by native Catalans or feared by native Basques. Nobody acquainted with the problems of the coloured minorities in Britain would want to under-estimate the consequent sense of mutual hostility and even fear between different groups of workers. This is all the more dramatic, since traditionally organized labour movements have actively discouraged national, racial or religious prejudices. At the same time one may doubt whether these frictions, by themselves, are of decisive significance. It is chiefly when the state and its institutions are involved, as by demands for a linguistic monopoly, or for legal equality, or for autonomy or separatism, that they become explosive – as they unfortunately have in Ulster. In fact, traditionally national and regional minority groups in states, especially when composed of workers, have, other things being equal, tended to support the mass party on the progressive wing of the majority nation's politics as being the most likely to defend their minority interests. Even today American blacks and white ethnics, between whom no love is lost, both tend to vote for the Democratic Party, while in Britain Asian and West Indian workers tend to vote Labour in spite of the racialism of many white working-class Labour voters.

However, the most powerful divisive forces, in the form of political parties and movements such as those inspired by nationalism, come from outside the working classes. Historically such movements have hardly ever originated within them, though they have often sought to appeal to them. They were divisive, not only because they naturally accentuated the linguistic, religious, physical and other distinctions between 'their' sector of a heterogeneous working class and the rest, but also because their objects were by definition at odds with those of class consciousness. They sought to substitute the dividing line between 'the nation' (including both its exploiters and exploited) and 'the foreigners' (including all workers classifiable as such) for class lines. Moreover, in the early stages of nationalist movements, nationalists either took little interest in the issues which preoccupied workers as workers – organized or unorganized – or regarded the solution of such problems as conditional on the prior achievement of the nationalist objectives. The discovery that national and social liberation must go together was not usually made by the pioneers of nationalist movements, which is why some of the most effective nationalist parties and organizations emerged out of socialist agitations (e.g. the Polish Socialist Party whose leader, Piłsudski, became the head of independent Poland after the First World War, and labour Zionism, which became the real architect of Israel). Even when the discovery was made within nationalist movements, activists who gave too high a priority to social liberation were difficult to digest. The nationalist reputation of Michael Davitt has suffered accordingly.

Historically it has proved difficult to deny and prevent class consciousness, since it arises naturally and logically out of the proletarian condition, at least in the elementary form of 'trade-union consciousness', that is to say the recognition of works as such need to organize collectively against employers in order to defend and improve their conditions as hired hands. Thus Catholic trade unions were formed not because most 'social Catholics' at the end of the nineteenth century favoured them – they regarded them, in Albert de Mun's words, as 'the specific organization of the war of one group against another' and preferred mixed associations of employers and workers – but because the latter did not meet the trade union needs of Catholic workers. In France 'social Catholics' accepted them, with more or less reluctance, between 1897 and 1912. Again, even in countries with strong national loyalties among workers, trade unionism tended to resist the fragmentation of unions along national lines. Czech workers certainly did not think of themselves as the same as German workers, but while they were inclined to vote for Czech political parties rather than non-Czech or all-Austrian ones, the pressure to split the Austrian trade union movement along national lines did not come from within the labour movement. It arose some time after the split into national sections of the Social Democratic Party had become effective, and was resisted more strongly by the all-Austrian unions. Indeed, even after the split had taken place, the majority of Czech unionists remained in the all-Austrian organizations, where, of course, they were entitled to form their own Czech branches and had their own Bohemian leadership. Similarly, today, while the parties of the left in Spain have split along national or regional lines, there has been no comparable tendency to divide the all-Spanish trade union movements. The reasons are obvious. The unity of all workers is an evident asset when they go on strike for economic reasons, and even though for other purposes they may think of themselves chiefly as Catholics or Protestants, black or white, Poles or Mexicans, it is advisable to put these distinctions aside for such purposes as asking for higher wages.

Nevertheless, it is equally clear that if class consciousness cannot be eliminated, it certainly neither excludes nor,
usually, dominates national sentiments. The collapse of the
Second International in 1914 into socialist parties and trade
union movements – most of which supported their belligerent
governments – is familiar. What is less familiar, since the internationalism of labour historians has not insisted on it, is the
strong current of chauvinism which is found in some politically
radical working classes. Thomas Wright, the 'Journeyman
Engineer' who reported on the English working class of the
1860s, notes specifically that the older, radical and Chartist
generation of workers combined a passionate distrust of all who
were not workers with a John-Bullish patriotism. In itself, strong
national sentiment may not be of great political consequence.
English and French workers, who almost certainly did not like
what they thought they knew about one another's country, have
never since 1815 been expected to fight against their neighbours
across the Channel. At times social-revolutionary or anti-war
sentiment may override patriotism, as in the last years of the
First World War. Even at such times patriotism may not be
negligible. It has been suggested that in France (unlike Britain)
the growth of mass working-class support for the Russian
Revolution was distinctly slow until it became clear it would not
jeopardize the chances of victory in the west. A similar phenomenon may be observable in the Habsburg Empire. While the
famous wave of anti-war strikes in January 1918, which began
in the armaments works near Vienna, rapidly spread throughout the engineering factories of ethnic Austria and Hungary,
it did not spread to the Czech areas of Bohemia. It has been
suggested that anti-war mobilization was inhibited here by the
policy of the nationalist movement (by this time echoed among
many Czech workers), which relied on an Allied victory for the
achievement of its aim – the independence of what was shortly
to become Czechoslovakia.

In certain circumstances the appeal of nationalism or

patriotism to workers was likely to be particularly effective. One of these occurred when they could identify with an existing nation-state as citizens rather than mere passive subjects, i.e. where their integration into the political and hegemonic system of their rules was under way, not least through that major agent of conscious socialization from above, a public system of elementary education. Class and private discontent did not prevent most English, French or German workers from seeing Britain, France and Germany as in some sense 'their country', as, say, Austrian ones in 1914 did not (because there was no nation-state), or Italian workers and peasants did not, since few even spoke and even fewer could read Italian, and hardly any of them had enjoyed the right to vote for more than a year. Another occurred, where nationalist agitation, often building memories of a former political state or autonomy, or organizations embodying the separateness of a nationality (e.g. the Catholicism of the dependent people as against the Protestantism or Orthodoxy of the ruling state) were in existence before an industrial working class developed. This was the case among people like the Irish, the Poles and the Czechs. However, as already suggested, what made national sentiments explosive and capable of destroying the cross-national unity of the working class was that they were intertwined with issues directly affecting the state and its institutions. Thus linguistic nationalism becomes explosive when language ceases to be merely a medium of communication between people, but one language or dialect rather than another becomes 'official' – e.g. the language of law courts, schools and public notices.

All this implies that working-class consciousness, however inevitable and essential, is probably politically secondary to other kinds of consciousness. As we know, where it has come into conflict in our century with national, or religious, or racial consciousness, it has usually yielded and retreated. It is clear that, for certain limited purposes, working-class consciousness and the labour movements it generates – at all events at the elementary 'trade-unionist' level – are very strong indeed. They are not indestructible, for sheer force has frequently destroyed such movements, but even these are potentially permanent and revivable. We have recently seen such consciousness and such movements revive in the very different circumstances of two rapidly industrializing countries, Brazil and Poland. They may well be the decisive lever for major political changes, as looked likely in 1980–1 in Poland. But historians must note that it is equally clear that working-class consciousness alone coexists with other forms of collective identification and neither eliminates nor replaces them. And, as Lenin rightly observed, while it will spontaneously and everywhere generate 'trade-unionist' practices and (where it is allowed to) organizations or other movements for corporate pressure and self-defence, it does not automatically generate mass parties with a socialist consciousness.

That such parties were generated almost as a matter of course during a certain historical period, mainly between the 1880s and 1930s, is significant, but requires more historical explanation than it has generally received. These parties, or their lineal successors, are still in being and often influential, but where they did not already exist, or the influence of socialists/communists were significant in labour movements before the Second World War, hardly any such parties have emerged out of the working classes since then, notably in the so-called 'Third World'. This may have implications for traditional socialist expectations about the role of the working class and working-class parties in bringing about socialism, which need not be discussed here.

What bearing has all this on the making of the Irish working class? The major fact which requires explanation, at least for outsiders, is why labour as an independent political force has in the past been relatively negligible in Ireland, compared with the countries of the United Kingdom. Neither in North or South have class movements of the workers made a more than marginal political mark. This is not adequately explained by the lack, until recently, of much industrialization in Ulster. Moreover from the days when Dublin was a stronghold of trade societies to the period before the First World War, when both Belfast and Dublin were the scene of some of the largest and most dramatic industrial disputes in the United Kingdom, Ireland has been familiar with labour battles. The most obvious explanation is that – except at moments or for rather limited trade unionist purposes – the potential Irish constituency for such working-class movements have identified themselves in politics as Catholic nationalists or Protestant unionists rather than as 'labour'. It is difficult to think of any other country in western Europe in which this has been so marked and persistent a characteristic of the working class.

Without pushing the analogy too far, a comparison of Ireland with Belgium, a more recently partitioned country and working class, may be instructive. As north-east Ulster and the rest of Ireland followed their divergent economic evolution, so did Wallonia and Flanders. Wallonia industrialized heavily, while Flanders, though containing a major port (Antwerp) and a significant industrial centre (Ghent), remained predominantly agrarian and saw itself as underprivileged. As old-fashioned nineteenth-century basic industries lost their firm footing in Ulster and Wallonia, so Flanders and to some extent the Republic of Ireland have become more industrialized and prosperous; but not, like the old zones, as part of the British or – de facto – the French industrial economies, but within a European and transnational framework. As Catholics and Protestants are inseparable in Belfast, so Flemings and French-speakers are inseparable in Brussels.

Yet Belgium, though occupied from time to time, has long been independent of its immediate neighbours (France and the Netherlands) and, since 1830, it has been an independent state, whereas the connection with Britain clearly dominated Irish affairs throughout, and still dominates those of Ulster. In the Belgian working class the two groups hardly mixed, since the language border is rather clearly marked. Where they did mix as in Brussels, the city grew slowly enough – from say 6 per cent of the population in the early nineteenth century to about 9 per cent in 1911 – for Flemish immigrants to be assimilated, as it seemed they were willing to be, facing little real resistance. On the other hand, Belfast grew from very little to about a third of the population of the six counties during the century, at first by a mass influx of Ulster Catholics which, around the middle of the century, looked as though it might swamp the Protestants, later by a mass growth of Ulster Protestants, which reduced the Catholics to a permanent and embittered minority. By 1911 Belfast was disproportionately more Protestant than the rest of the province, and Catholics were far more systematically excluded from the city's skilled trade than they had been in 1870.

The Belgian labour movement grew up from the 1880s as a strong, single and unified body operating across language lines, and largely engaged, before 1914, in the struggle for universal male suffrage, which minimized internal divergences within the working class. It was not so seriously split linguistically until after the Second World War. Not so in Ireland, where the official commitment to a single all-Irish labour movement often concealed an essentially nationalist orientation struggling against the trade union movement of skilled workers who were quite content with the usual autonomy within an all-UK organization. Moreover, the established dominance of the national issue (Home Rule or independence from Britain) deprived labour of a unifying issue of political mobilization, such as the fight for electoral democracy provided in Belgium.

The paradox of the Irish situation in the period when a major labour movement might have been expected to emerge – from the end of the 1880s to 1914, the era of 'new unionism' and 'labour unrest' – is that three factors converged to tie Catholic workers to Fenian nationalism. Mass nationalist mobilization and Orange resistance equated political Irishness with

# Do Workers Have a Country?

Catholicism. The old craft unionism of skilled workers (concentrated in industrial Ulster) would in any case not have been much use to unskilled workers, but the increasingly systematic exclusion of Catholics from skilled Ulster trades intensified the tensions between the two sectors of the working class. Finally, the very radicalism, or even the socialist and revolutionary convictions, of the 'new' union leaders and organizers, who wanted to break with the caution and 'reformism' of the old unions, had political implications in Ireland which it did not have in Britain; for in Ulster, at least, organized skilled workers were not only 'old' unionists but also tended to be Orangemen. In short, both political mobilization (National and Unionist) and the class mobilization of hitherto unorganized and unorganizable workers, united to divide the working class. A labour movement which was both political and industrial and which united Protestant and Catholic, Orange and Green, skilled and unskilled, became impossible. It would have been possible only if divisions between sections of workers had not coincided with divisions between Catholic and Protestant (which increasingly implied between Green and Orange), as they did in Belfast, the test of any united Irish labour movement. In any case, such a movement would have been possible only by overlooking the separation from Britain, i.e. by regarding the uses around which Irish politics revolved as irrelevant to Labour as such. It is not impossible to conceive of this, but the prospect hardly seemed realistic between 1880 and 1921. The most that could be expected of a political labour movement neutral as between Orange and Green, but many of whose members were far from neutral as individuals, would have been a pressure group for the specific interests of trade unionists, or for legislation of specific interest to wage-workers: in fact, something like an all-Irish Labour Representation Committee. Yet even in Britain itself, the Labour Representation Committee, though in theory operating outside the field of political dispute between Liberals and Conservatives, which was distinctly less impassioned than that between Nationalist and Unionists, actually had great difficulty until after the First World War in emancipating itself from the political loyalties of so many organized workers to one of the two parties, and the suspicion of those who supported the other.

This, then, was the dilemma of Irish labour leaders. It was independent of their personal convictions. A case can be made for James Connolly's choice of the 'Green' option, on the grounds that most Irishmen were Catholics, and that in any case the dour and respectable 'old unionist' (and Unionists) of Protestant Belfast hardly looked like promising material for social revolution. Yet if the Catholic labouring masses seemed to offer better prospects for revolutionaries – after all, even James Larkin who was not an Irish nationalist in the sense Connolly was, or became, had his greatest triumphs among them – the Green option automatically excluded that united movement of all Irish workers of which Connolly dreamed. But Connolly's decision for an Irish labour movement which would not merely appeal essentially to Southerners and Catholics in practice, but was nationalist in aspiration, had even more serious consequences. It meant the subordination of Southern Irish labour to nationalism. Marxist parties have sometimes succeeded in transforming their societies after taking the lead of movements of national liberation, but hardly ever, if at all, in competition with previously established and strong national movements under other leadership. In spite of Connolly's efforts and his leadership in 1916 it was the IRA and not the Citizens' Army which took over the Green flag. Connolly lives on in official memory as a Fenian martyr rather than as a Marxist revolutionary. Perhaps this was inevitable. One cannot confidently say otherwise. Nevertheless, it meant that a strong and independent political movement of labour developed neither in the north nor in the south, though it is possible that today the conditions for such a movement are better in the south, because partition is de facto no longer a significant issue in the Republic. In the north, as we know, it still is.

## Do Workers Have a Country?

Does this mean that Ireland contained not one but two working classes or even, as some enthusiasts hold, not one but two nations? In the literal sense this is obviously not so. Catholics and Protestants in Ulster no more formed separate working classes in any economic or operational sense than they did on Clydeside. Such questions arise chiefly because it is often assumed, without much thought, that working classes, or any other large classes, do not 'exist' except as monolithic blocks, as it is assumed that a nation is not 'real' unless each member, living on its territory, who is not a certified foreigner or a defined 'minority', is uniformly coloured right through with whatever is considered the accepted national dye. Today this is usually language, though the Irish have learned the hard way that this dye does not always take. In a few European countries and many more Afro-Asian ones it is still religion. Right-wing Americans think it is a set of conventional practices and beliefs, lacking which a person is 'un-American'. This is not so. The unity of classes and nations is defined by what they have in common as against other groups, and not by their internal homogeneity. There is no state which does not contain regional, sectional, or other differences among its population, and these are potentially disruptive, as the recent rise of separatist movements in western Europe proves. The only difference in principle between Ireland and Bavaria is that the Catholic–Protestant difference in Ireland has proved disruptive, whereas the attempt to prove that the Protestant minority in the northern part of Bavaria (Franconia) is oppressed by the Catholic majority is at present confined to a lunatic fringe of ultra-left ex-students. Similarly, all working classes contain internal conflicts, though usually they remain subordinate.

On the other hand, the course of history can both merge and split societies, and therefore the classes within them. It has divided Ireland. Given that there now exist separate political units and economies in north and south, it becomes impossible any longer to speak of a single Irish working class any more than a single Bengali or German working class, to name but two other partitioned nations. Separate states are powerful definers of economy and society. This does not mean that the two Irelands cease to have much in common as have the two Germanies – not least kinfolk and culture. We may speculate about what might happen if both were united – given the widening divergences it is increasingly difficult to say 're-united' – but in both cases the question is at present academic. To this extent history has up to the present led to the making of two Irish working classes.

Of these, the Ulster working class suffers particularly, indeed one is tempted to say uniquely, acute divisions. The only parallel one can readily think of is the Hindu–Muslim communal tension on the Indian subcontinent. For these reasons no general conclusions about working class and nation can be drawn from Ulster. Ireland remains resolutely unique in this respect. So, no doubt, does every other country or nation, once historians concentrate their attention sufficiently upon it. However, unfortunately the uniqueness of Irish historical development has manifested itself – so far – largely at the expense of the making of its working class and its labour movement.

# 6

## Inventing National Traditions

Nothing appears more ancient, and lined to an immemorial past, than the pageantry which surrounds the British monarchy in its public ceremonial manifestations. Yet, in its modern form it is the product of the late nineteenth and twentieth centuries. 'Traditions' which appear or claim to be old are often quite recent in origin and sometimes invented. Anyone familiar with the colleges of ancient British universities will be able to think of the institution of such 'traditions' on a local scale, though some – like the annual Festival of Nine Lessons and Carols in the chapel of King's College, Cambridge, on Christmas Eve – may become generalized through the modern mass medium of radio.

The term 'invented tradition' is used in a broad, but not imprecise, sense. It includes both 'traditions' actually invented, constructed and formally instituted and those emerging in a less easily traceable manner within a brief and dateable period – a matter of a few years perhaps – and establishing themselves with great rapidity. The royal Christmas broadcast in Britain (instituted in 1932) is an example of the first; the appearance and development of the practices associated with the Cup Final in British Association Football, of the second. It is evident that not all of them are equally permanent, but it is their appearance and establishment rather than their chances of survival which are our primary concern.

'Invented tradition' is taken to mean a set of practices, normally governed by overtly or tacitly accepted rules and of a ritual symbolic nature, which seek to inculcate certain values and norms of behaviour by repetition, which automatically implies continuity with the past. In fact, where possible, they normally attempt to establish continuity with a suitable historic past. A striking example is the deliberate choice of a Gothic style for the nineteenth-century rebuilding of the British parliament, and the equally deliberate decision after the Second World War to rebuild the parliamentary chamber on exactly the same basic plan as before. The historic past into which the new tradition is inserted need not be lengthy, stretching back into the assumed mists of time. Revolutions and 'progressive movements' which break with the past, by definition, have their own relevant past, though it may be cut off at a certain date, such as 1789. However, insofar as there is such reference to a historic past, the peculiarity of 'invented' traditions is that the continuity with it is largely factitious. In short, they are responses to novel situations which take the form of reference to old situations, or which establish their own past by quasi-obligatory repetition. It is the contrast between the constant change and innovation of the modern world, and the attempt to structure at least some parts of social life within it as unchanging and invariant, that makes the 'invention of tradition' so interesting for historians of the past two centuries.

'Tradition' in this sense must be distinguished clearly from 'custom' which dominates so-called 'traditional' societies. The object and characteristic of 'traditions', including invented ones, is invariance. The past, real or invented, to which they refer imposes fixed (normally formalized) practices, such as repetition. 'Custom' in traditional societies has the double function of motor and flywheel. It does not preclude innovation and change up to a point, though evidently the requirement that it must appear compatible or even identical with precedent imposes substantial limitations on it. What it does is to give any desired change (or resistance to innovation) the sanction of precedent, social continuity and natural law as expressed in history. Students of peasant movements know that a village's claim to some common land or right 'by custom from time immemorial' often expresses not a historical fact, but the balance of forces in the constant struggle of village against lords or against other villages. Students of the British labour movement know that 'the custom of the trade' or of the shop may represent not ancient tradition, but whatever right the workers have established in practice, however recently, and which they now attempt to extend or defend by giving it the sanction of perpetuity. 'Custom' cannot afford to be invariant, because even in 'traditional' societies life is not so. Customary or common law still shows this combination of flexibility in substance and formal adherence to precedent. The difference between 'tradition' and 'custom' in our sense is indeed well illustrated here. 'Custom' is what judges do; 'tradition' (in this instance invented tradition) is the wig, robe and other formal paraphernalia and ritualized practices surrounding their substantial action. The decline of 'custom' inevitably changes the 'tradition' with which it is habitually intertwined.

A second, less important, distinction that must be made is between 'tradition' in our sense and convention or routine, which has no significant ritual or symbolic function as such, though it may acquire it incidentally. It is evident that any social practice that needs to be carried out repeatedly will tend, for convenience and efficiency, to develop a set of such conventions and routines, which may be de facto or de jure formalized for the purposes of imparting the practice to new practitioners. This applies to unprecedented practices (such as the work of an aircraft pilot) as much as to long-familiar ones. Societies since the Industrial Revolution have naturally been obliged to invent, institute or develop new networks of such convention or routine more frequently than previous ones. Insofar as they function best when turned into habit, automatic procedure or even reflex action, they require invariance, which may get in the way of the other necessary requirement of practice, the capacity to deal with unforeseen or inhabitual contingencies. This is a well-known weakness of routinization or bureaucratization, particularly at the subaltern levels where invariant performance is generally considered the most efficient.

Such networks of convention and routine are not 'invented traditions' since their functions, and therefore their justifications, are technical rather than ideological (in Marxian terms they belong to 'base' rather than 'superstructure'). They are designed to facilitate readily definable practical operations, and are readily modified or abandoned to meet changing practical needs, always allowing for the inertia which any practice acquires with time and the emotional resistance to any innovation by people who have become attached to it. The same applies to the recognized 'rules' of games or other patterns of social interaction, where these exist, or to any other pragmatically based norms. Where these exist in combination with 'tradition', the difference is readily observable. Wearing hard hats when riding makes practical sense, like wearing crash helmets for motorcyclists or steel helmets for soldiers; wearing a particular type of hard hat in combination with hunting pink makes an entirely different kind of sense. If this were not so, it would be as easy to change the 'traditional' costume of fox-hunters as it is to substitute a differently shaped helmet in armies – rather conservative institutions – if it can be shown to provide more effective protection. Indeed, it may be suggested that 'traditions' and pragmatic conventions or routines are inversely related. 'Tradition' shows weakness when, as among liberal Jews, dietary prohibitions are justified pragmatically, as by arguing that the ancient Hebrews banned pork on grounds of hygiene. Conversely, objects or practices are liberated for full symbolic and ritual use when no longer fettered by practical use. The spurs of Cavalry officers' dress uniforms are more important for 'tradition' when there are no horses, the umbrellas of Guards officers in civilian dress lose their significance when not carried tightly furled (that is, useless), the wigs of lawyers could hardly acquire their modern significance until other people stopped wearing wigs.

Inventing traditions, it is assumed here, is essentially a process of formalization and ritualization, characterized by reference to the past, if only by imposing repetition. The actual process of creating such ritual and symbolic complexes has not been adequately studied by historians. Much of it is still rather obscure. It is presumably most clearly exemplified where a 'tradition' is deliberately invented and constructed by a single initiator, as for the Boy Scouts by Baden-Powell. Perhaps it is almost as easily traced in the case of officially instituted and planned ceremonials, since they are likely to be well documented, as in the case of the construction of Nazi symbolism and the Nuremberg party rallies. It is probably most difficult to trace where such traditions are partly invented, partly evolved in private groups (where the process is less likely to be bureaucratically recorded), or informally over a period of time as, say, in parliament and the legal profession. The difficulty is not only one of sources but also of techniques, though there are available both esoteric disciplines specializing in symbolism and ritual, such as heraldry and the study of liturgy, as well as Warburgian historic disciplines for the study of such subjects. Unfortunately neither are usually familiar to historians of the industrial era.

There is probably no time and place with which historians are concerned which has not seen the 'invention' of tradition in this sense. However, we should expect it to occur more frequently when a rapid transformation of society weakens or destroys the social patterns for which 'old' traditions had been designed, producing new ones to which they were not applicable, or when such old traditions and their institutional carriers and promulgators no longer prove sufficiently adaptable and flexible, or are otherwise eliminated: in short, when there are sufficiently large and rapid changes on the demand or the supply side. Such changes have been particularly significant in the past two hundred years, and it is therefore reasonable to expect these instant formalizations of new traditions to cluster during this period. This implies, incidentally, against both nineteenth-century liberalism and more recent 'modernization' theory that such formalizations are not confined to so-called 'traditional' societies, but also have their place, in one form or another, in 'modern' ones. Broadly speaking this is so, but one must beware of making the further assumptions, firstly that older forms of community and authority structure, and consequently the traditions associated with them, were unadaptable and became rapidly unviable, and secondly that 'new' traditions simply resulted from the inability to use or adapt old ones.

Adaptation took place for old uses in new conditions and by using old models for new purposes. Old institutions with established functions, references to the past and ritual idioms and practices might need to adapt in this way: the Catholic church faced with new political and ideological challenges and major changes in the composition of the faithful (such as the notable feminization both of lay piety and of clerical personnel);[1] professional armies faced with conscription; ancient institutions such as law courts now operating in a changed context and sometimes with changed functions in new contexts. So were institutions enjoying nominal continuity, but in fact turning into something very, very different, such as universities. Thus Karsten Bahnson[2] has analysed the sudden decline, after 1848, of the traditional practice of mass student exodus from German universities (for reasons of conflict or demonstration) in terms of the changed academic character of universities, the rising age of the student population, its embourgeoisement which diminished town/ gown tensions and student riotousness, the new institution of free mobility between universities, the consequent change in student associations and other factors.[3] In all such cases novelty is no less novel for being able to dress up easily as antiquity.

More interesting, from our point of view, is the use of ancient materials to construct invented traditions of a novel type for quite novel purposes. A large store of such materials is accumulated in the past of any society, and an elaborate language of symbolic practice and communication is always available. Sometimes new traditions could be readily grafted on old ones, sometimes they could be devised from borrowing from the well-supplied warehouses of official ritual, symbolism and moral exhortation – religion and princely pomp, folklore and freemasonry (itself an earlier invented tradition of great symbolic force). Thus the development of Swiss nationalism, concomitant with the formation of the modern federal state in the nineteenth century, has been brilliantly studied by Rudolf Braun,[4] who has the advantage of training in a discipline ('*Volkskunde*') which lends itself to such studies, and in a country where its modernization has not been set back by association with Nazi abuses. Existing customary traditional practices – folksong, physical contests, marksmanship – were modified, ritualized and institutionalized for the new national purposes. Traditional folksongs were supplemented by new songs in the same idiom, often composed by schoolmasters, transferred to a choral repertoire whose content was patriotic–progressive ('Nation, Nation, wie voll klingt der Ton'), though it also embodied ritually powerful elements from religious hymnology. (The formation of such new song repertoires, especially for schools, is well worth study.) The statutes of the Federal Song Festival – are we not reminded of the eisteddfodau? – declare its object to be 'the development and improvement of the people's singing, the awakening of more elevated sentiments for God, Freedom and Country, union and fraternization of the friends of Art and the Fatherland'. (The word 'improvement' introduces the characteristic note of nineteenth-century progress.)

A powerful ritual complex formed round these occasions: festival pavilions, structures for the display of flags, temples for offerings, processions, bell-ringing, tableaux, gun salutes, government delegations in honour of the festival, dinners, toasts and oratory. Old materials were again adapted for this:

> The echoes of baroque forms of celebration, display and pomp are unmistakable in this new festival architecture. And as, in the baroque celebration, state and church merge on a higher plane, so an alloy of religious and patriotic elements emerges from these new forms of choral, shooting and gymnastic activity.[5]

How far new traditions can thus use new materials, how far they may be forced to invent new languages or devices, or extend the old symbolic vocabulary beyond its established limits, cannot be discussed here. It is clear that plenty of political institutions, ideological movements and groups – not least in nationalism – were so unprecedented that even historic continuity had to be invented, for example by creating an ancient past beyond effective historical continuity, either by semi-fiction (Boadicea, Vercingetorix, Arminius the Cheruscan) or by forgery (Ossian, the Czech medieval manuscripts). It is also clear that entirely new symbols and devices came into existence as part of national movements and states, such as the national anthem (of which the British in 1740 seems to be the earliest), the national flag (still largely a variation on the French revolutionary tricolour, evolved 1790–4), or the personification of 'the nation' in symbol or image, either official, as with Marianne and Germania, or unofficial, as in the cartoon stereotypes of John Bull, the lean Yankee Uncle Sam and the 'German Michel'.

Nor should we overlook the break in continuity which is sometimes clear even in traditional topoi of genuine antiquity. If we follow Lloyd,[6] English Christmas folk carols ceased to be created in the seventeenth century, to be replaced by hymn-book carols of the Watts–Wesley kind, though a demotic modification of these in largely rural religions like Primitive Methodism may be observed. Yet carols were the first kind of folksong to be revived by middle-class collectors to take their place 'in novel surroundings of church, guild and women's institute' and thence to spread in a new urban popular setting 'by street-corner singers or by hoarse boys chanting on doorsteps in the ancient hope of reward'. In this sense 'God Rest Ye Merry, Gentlemen' is not old but new. Such a break is visible even in movements deliberately describing themselves as 'traditionalist', and appealing to groups which were, by common consent, regarded as the repositories of historic continuity and tradition, such as peasants.[7] Indeed, the very appearance of movements for the defence or revival of traditions, 'traditionalist' or otherwise, indicates such a break. Such movements, common among intellectuals since the Romantics, can never develop or even preserve a living past (except conceivably by setting up human natural sanctuaries for isolated corners of archaic life), but must become 'invented tradition'. On the other hand, the strength and adaptability of genuine traditions is not to be confused with the 'invention of tradition'. Where the old ways are alive, traditions need to be neither revived nor invented.

Yet it may be suggested that where they are invented, it is often not because old ways are no longer available or viable, but because they are deliberately not used or adapted. Thus, in consciously setting itself against tradition and for radical innovation, the nineteenth-century liberal ideology of social change systematically failed to provide for the social and authority ties taken for granted in earlier societies, and created voids which might have to be filled by invented practices. The success of nineteenth-century Tory factory masters in Lancashire (as distinct from Liberal ones) in using such old ties to advantage shows that they were still there to be used – even in the unprecedented environment of the industrial town.[8] The long-term inadaptability of pre-industrial ways to a society revolutionized beyond a certain point is not to be denied, but is not to be confused with the problems arising out of the rejection of old ways in the short term by those who regarded them as obstacles to progress or, even worse, as its militant adversaries.

This did not prevent innovators from generating their own invented traditions – the practices of freemasonry are a case in point. Nevertheless, a general hostility to irrationalism, superstition and customary practices reminiscent of the dark past, if not actually descended from it, made impassioned believers in the verities of the Enlightenment, such as liberals, socialists and communists, unreceptive to traditions old or novel. Socialists, as we shall see below, found themselves acquiring an annual May Day without quite knowing how; National Socialists exploited such occasions with liturgical sophistication and zeal and a conscious manipulation of symbols.[9] The liberal era in Britain at best tolerated such practices, insofar as neither ideology nor economic efficiency were at issue, sometimes as a reluctant concession to the irrationalism of the lower orders. Its attitude to the sociable and ritual activities of Friendly Societies was a combination of hostility ('unnecessary expenses' such as 'payments for anniversaries, processions, bands, regalia' were legally forbidden) and toleration of events such as annual feasts on the grounds that 'the importance of this attraction, especially as respects the country population, cannot be denied'.[10] But a rigorous individualist rationalism dominated not only as an economic calculus but as a social ideal.

We may conclude with some general observations about the invented traditions of the period since the Industrial Revolution.

They seem to belong to three overlapping types:

(a) Those establishing or symbolizing social cohesion or the membership of groups, real or artificial communities.

(b) Those establishing or legitimizing institutions, status or relations of authority.

(c) Those whose main purpose was socialization, the inculcation of beliefs, value systems and conventions of behaviour.

Inventing National Traditions

While traditions of types (b) and (c) were certainly devised (as in those symbolizing submission to authority in British India), it may be tentatively suggested that type (a) was prevalent, the other functions being regarded as implicit in or flowing from a sense of identification with a 'community' and/or the institutions representing, expressing or symbolizing it such as a 'nation'.

One difficulty was that such larger social entities were plainly not *Gemeinschaften* or even systems of accepted ranks. Social mobility, the facts of class conflict and the prevalent ideology made traditions combining community and marked inequality in formal hierarchies (as in armies) difficult to apply universally. This did not much affect traditions of type (c) since general socialization inculcated the same values in every citizen, member of the nation and subject of the crown, and the functionally specific socializations of different social groups (such as public school pupils as distinct from others) did not usually get in each other's way. On the other hand, insofar as invented traditions reintroduced, as it were, status into a world of contract, superior and inferior into a world of legal equals, they could not do so directly. They could be smuggled in by formal symbolic assent to a social organization which was de facto unequal, as by the restyling of the British coronation ceremony.[11] More commonly they might foster the corporate sense of *superiority* of elites – particularly when these had to be recruited from those who did not already possess it by birth or ascription – rather than by inculcating a sense of obedience in inferiors. Some were encouraged to feel more equal than others. This might be done by assimilating elites to pre-bourgeois ruling groups or authorities, whether in the militarist/bureaucratic form characteristic of Germany (as with the duelling student corps), or the non-militarized 'moralized gentry' model of the British public schools. Alternatively, perhaps the *esprit de corps*, self-confidence and leadership of elites could be developed by more esoteric 'traditions' marking the cohesiveness of a senior official mandarinate (as in France or among whites in the colonies).

117

Granted that 'communitarian' invented traditions were the basic type, their nature remains to be studied. Anthropology may help to elucidate the differences, if any, between invented and old traditional practices. Here we may merely note that while rites of passage are normally marked in the traditions of particular groups (initiation, promotion, retirement, death), this was not usually the case in those designed for all-embracing pseudo-communities (nations, countries), presumably because these underlined their eternal and unchanging character – at least since the community's foundation. However, both new political regimes and innovatory movements might seek to find their own equivalents for the traditional rites of passage associated with religion (civil marriage, funerals).

One marked difference between old and invented practices may be observed. The former were specific and strongly binding social practices, the latter tended to be quite unspecific and vague as to the nature of the values, rights and obligations of the group membership they inculcate: 'patriotism', 'loyalty', 'duty', 'playing the game', 'the school spirit' and the like. But if the content of British patriotism or 'Americanism' was notably ill defined, though usually specified in commentaries associated with ritual occasions, the *practices* symbolizing it were virtually compulsory – as in standing up for the singing of the national anthem in Britain, the flag ritual in American schools. The crucial element seems to have been the invention of emotionally and symbolically charged signs of club membership rather than the statutes and objects of the club. Their significance lay precisely in their undefined universality:

> The National Flag, the National Anthem and the National Emblem are the three symbols through which an independent country proclaims its identity and sovereignty, and as such they command instantaneous respect and loyalty. In themselves they reflect the entire background, thought and culture of a nation.[12]

In this sense, as an observer noted in 1880, 'soldiers and policemen wear badges for us now', though he failed to predict their revival as adjuncts to individual citizens in the era of mass movements which was about to begin.[13]

The second observation is that it seems clear that, in spite of much invention, new traditions have not filled more than a small part of the space left by the secular decline of both old tradition and custom; as might indeed be expected in societies in which the past becomes increasingly less relevant as a model or precedent for most forms of human behaviour. In the private lives of most people, and in the self-contained lives of small sub-cultural groups, even the invented traditions of the nineteenth and twentieth centuries occupied or occupy a much smaller place than the old traditions do in, say, old agrarian societies.[14] 'What is done' structures the days, seasons and life cycles of twentieth-century western men and women very much less than it did their ancestors', and very much less than the external compulsions of the economy, technology, bureaucratic state organization, political decision and other forces which neither rely or nor develop 'tradition' in our sense.

However, this generalization does not apply in the field of what might be called the public life of the citizen (including to some extent public forms of socialization, such as schools, as distinct from private ones such as the mass media). There is no real sign of weakening in the neo-traditional practices associated either with bodies of men in the public service (armed forces, the law, perhaps even public servants) or in practices associated with the citizens' membership of states. Indeed most of the occasions when people become conscious of citizenship as such remain associated with symbols and semi-ritual practices (for instance, elections), most of which are historically novel and largely invented: flags, images, ceremonies and music. Insofar as the invented traditions of the era since the Industrial and French revolutions have filled a permanent gap – at all events up to the present – it would seem to be in this field.

Why, it may be asked finally, should historians devote their attention to such phenomena? The question is in one sense unnecessary, since a growing number of them plainly do. So it is better rephrased. What benefit can historians derive from the study of the invention of tradition?

First and foremost, it may be suggested that they are important symptoms and therefore indicators of problems which might not otherwise be recognized, and developments which are otherwise difficult to identify and to date. They are evidence. The transformation of German nationalism from its old liberal to its new imperialist-expansionist pattern is more exactly illuminated by the rapid replacement of the old black–red–gold colours by the new black–white–red ones (especially by the 1890s) among the German gymnastic movement, than by official statements of authorities or spokesmen for organizations. The history of the British football cup finals tells us something about the development of an urban working-class culture which more conventional data and sources do not. By the same token, the study of invented traditions cannot be separated from the wider study of the history of society, nor can it expect to advance much beyond the mere discovery of such practices unless it is integrated into a wider study.

Second, it throws a considerable light on the human relation to the past, and therefore on the historian's own subject and craft. For all invented traditions, so far as possible, use history as a legitimator of action and cement of group cohesion. Frequently it becomes the actual symbol of struggle, as in the battles over the monuments to Walther von der Vogelweide and Dante in South Tyrol in 1889 and 1896.[15] Even revolutionary movements back their innovations by reference to a 'people's past' (Saxons versus Normans, '*nos ancêtres les Gaulois*' against the Franks, Spartacus), to traditions of revolution ('The German people are by no means lacking in revolutionary tradition', as Engels claimed in the first words of his *Peasant War in Germany*)[16] and to its own heroes and martyrs. James Connolly's *Labour in*

## Inventing National Traditions

*Irish History* exemplifies this union of themes excellently. The element of invention is particularly clear here, since the history which became part of the fund of knowledge or the ideology of the nation, state or movement is not what has actually been preserved in popular memory, but what has been selected, written, pictured, popularized and institutionalized by those whose function it is to do so. Oral historians have frequently observed how in the actual memories of the old the General Strike of 1926 plays a more modest and less dramatic part than interviewers anticipated.[17] The formation of such an image of the French Revolution in and by the Third Republic has been analysed.[18] Yet all historians, whatever else their objectives, are engaged in this process inasmuch as they contribute, consciously or not, to the creation, dismantling and restructuring of images of the past which belong not only to the world of specialist investigation but to the public sphere of man as a political being. They might as well be aware of this dimension of their activities.

In this connection, one specific interest of 'invented traditions' for, at all events, modern and contemporary historians ought to be singled out. They are highly relevant to that comparatively recent historical innovation, the 'nation', with its associated phenomena: nationalism, the nation-state, national symbols, histories and the rest. All these rest on exercises in social engineering which are often deliberately and always innovative, if only because historical novelty implies innovation. Israeli and Palestinian nationalism or nations must be novel, whatever the historic continuities of Jews or Middle Eastern Muslims, since the very concept of territorial states of the currently standard type in their regions was barely thought of a century ago, and hardly became a serious prospect before the end of the First World War. Standard national languages, to be learned in schools and written, let alone spoken, by more than a smallish elite, are largely constructs of varying, but often brief, age. As a French historian of Flemish language observed, quite correctly, the Flemish taught in Belgium today is not the language which the mothers and grandmothers of Flanders spoke to their children: in short, it is only metaphorically but not literally a 'mother-tongue'. We should not be misled by a curious, but understandable, paradox: modern nations and all their impedimenta generally claim to be the opposite of novel, namely rooted in the remotest antiquity, and the opposite of constructed, namely human communities so 'natural' as to require no definition other than self-assertion. Whatever the historic or other continuities embedded in the modern concept of 'France' and 'the French' – and which nobody would seek to deny – these very concepts themselves must include a constructed or 'invented' component. And just because so much of what subjectively makes up the modern 'nation' consists of such constructs and is associated with appropriate and, in general, fairly recent symbols or suitably tailored discourse (such as 'national history'), the national phenomenon cannot be adequately investigated without careful attention to the 'invention of tradition'.

Finally, the study of the invention of tradition is interdisciplinary. It is a field of study which brings together historians, social anthropologists and a variety of other workers in the human sciences, and cannot adequately be pursued without such collaboration.

# Notes

1  See for instance André Tihon, 'Les religieuses en Belgique du XVIIIe au XXe siècle: Approche Statistique', *Belgisch Tijdschrift v. Nieuwste Geschiedenis/Revue Belge d'Histoire Contemporaine*, 7 (1976), pp. 1–54.

2  Karsten Bahnson, *Akademische Auszüge aus deutschen Universitäts und Hochschulorten* (Saarbrücken, 1973).

3  Seventeen such exoduses are recorded in the eighteenth century, fifty in 1800–48, but only six from 1848 to 1973.

4  Rudolf Braun, *Sozialer und kultureller Wandel in einem ländlichen Industriegebiet im 19. Und 20. Jahrhundert* (Erlenbach-Zürich, 1965), ch. 6.

5  Ibid., pp. 336–7.

6  A. L. Lloyd, *Folk Song in England* (London, 1969), pp. 134–8.

7  This is to be distinguished from the revival of tradition for purposes which actually demonstrated its decline. 'The farmers' revival (around

1900) of their old regional dress, folk dances and similar rituals for festive occasions was *neither* a bourgeois *nor* a traditionalistic feature. On the surface it could be viewed as a nostalgic longing for the old-time culture which was so rapidly disappearing, but in reality it was a demonstration of class identity by which prosperous farmers could distance themselves horizontally relative to the townspeople and vertically from the cottars, craftsmen and labourers.' Palle Ove Christiansen, 'Peasant Adaptations to Bourgeois Culture? Class Formation and Cultural Redefinition in the Danish Countryside?', *Ethnologica Scandinavica* (1978), p. 128. See also Gavin Lewis, 'The Peasantry, Rural Change and Conservative Agrariansim: Lower Austria at the Turn of the Century', *Past & Present*, 81 (1978), pp. 119–43.

8   Patrick Joyce, 'The Factory Politics of Lancashire in the Later Nineteenth Century', *Historical Journal*, 18 (1975), pp. 525–53.

9   Helmut Hartwig, 'Plaketten zum 1. Mai 1934–39', *Aesthetik und Kommunikation*, 7: 26 (1976), pp. 56–9.

10  P. H. J. H. Gosden, *The Friendly Societies in England, 1815–1875* (Manchester, 1961), pp. 123, 119.

11  J. E. C. Bodley, *The Coronation of Edward VIIth: A Chapter of European and Imperial History* (London, 1903), pp. 201, 204.

12  Official Indian government commentary, quoted in Raymond Firth, *Symbols, Public and Private* (London, 1973), p. 341.

13  Frederick Marshall, *Curiosities of Ceremonials, Titles, Decorations and Forms of International Vanities* (London, 1880), p. 20.

14  Not to mention the transformation of long-lasting rituals and signs of uniformity and cohesion into rapidly changing fashions – in costume, language, social practice etc., as in the youth cultures of industrialized countries.

15  John W. Cole and Eric Wolf, *The Hidden Frontier: Ecology and Ethnicity in an Alpine Valley* (New York and London, 1974), p. 55.

16  For the popularity of books on this and other militant historical subjects in German workers' libraries, see Hans-Josef Steinberg, *Sozialismus und deutsche Sozialdemokratie. Zur Ideologie der Partei vor dem ersten Weltkrieg* (Hanover, 1967), pp. 131–3.

17  There are perfectly sound reasons why participants at the bottom do not usually see historic events they live through as top people or historians do. One might call this (after the hero of Stendhal's *Chartreuse de Parme*) the 'Fabrice syndrome'.

18  E.g. Alice Gérard, *La Révolution Française: Mythes et Interprétations, 1789–1970* (Paris, 1970).

# 7

# *The Production of 'National' Traditions*

Once we are aware how commonly traditions are invented, it can easily be discovered that one period which saw them spring up with particular assiduity was in the thirty or forty years before the First World War. One hesitates to say 'with greater assiduity' than at other times, since there is no way of making realistic quantitative comparisons. Nevertheless, the creation of traditions was enthusiastically practised in numerous countries [ . . . ] It was both practised officially and unofficially, the former – we may loosely call it 'political' – primarily in or by states or organized social and political movements, the latter – we may loosely call it 'social' – mainly by social groups not formally organized as such, or those whose objects were not specifically or consciously polit-ical, such as clubs and fraternities, whether or not these also had political functions. The distinction is one of convenience rather than principle. It is designed to draw attention to two main forms of the creation of tradition in the nineteenth century, both of which reflect the profound and rapid social transformations of the period. Quite new, or old but dramatically transformed, social groups, environments and social contexts called for new devices to ensure or express social cohesion and identity and to structure social relations. At the same time a changing society made the traditional forms of ruling by states and social or political hierarchies more difficult or even impracticable. This required new methods of ruling or establishing bonds of loyalty. In the nature of things, the consequent invention of 'political' traditions was more conscious and deliberate, since it was largely undertaken by institutions with political purposes in mind. Yet we may as well note immediately that conscious invention succeeded mainly in proportion to its success in broadcasting on a wavelength to which the public was ready to tune in. Official new public holidays, ceremonies, heroes or symbols, which commanded the growing armies of the state's employees and the growing captive public of schoolchildren, might still fail to mobilize the citizen volunteers if they lacked genuine popular resonance. The German Empire did not succeed in its efforts to turn the Emperor William I into a popularly accepted founding father of a united Germany, nor in turning his birthday into a genuine national anniversary. (Who, by the way, now remembers the attempt to call him 'William the Great'?) Official encouragement did secure the building of 327 monuments to him by 1902, but within *one* year of Bismarck's death in 1898, 470 municipalities had decided to erect 'Bismarck columns'.[1]

Nevertheless, the state linked both formal and informal, official and unofficial, political and social inventions of tradition, at least in those countries where the need for it arose. Seen from below, the state increasingly defied the largest stage on which the crucial activities determining human lives as subjects and citizens were played out. Indeed, it increasingly defined as well as registered their civil existence (*état civil*). It may not have been the only such stage, but its existence, frontiers and increasingly regular and probing interventions in the citizen's life were in the last analysis decisive. In developed countries the 'national economy', its area defined by the territory of some state or its subdivisions, was the basic unit of economic development. A change in the frontiers of the state or in its policy had substantial and continuous material consequences for its citizens. The standardization of administration and law within it, and, in particular state education, transformed people into citizens of a specific country: 'peasants into Frenchmen'.[2] The state was the framework of the citizens' collective actions, insofar as these were officially recognized. To influence or change the government of the state, or its policy, was plainly the main objective of domestic politics, and the common man was increasingly entitled to take part in it. Indeed, politics in the new nineteenth-century sense was essentially nation-wide politics. In short, for practical purposes, society ('civil society') and the state within which it operated became increasingly inseparable.

It was thus natural that the classes within society, and in particular the working class, should tend to identify themselves through nationwide political movements or organizations ('parties'), and equally natural that de facto these should operate essentially within the confines of the nation.[3] Nor is it surprising that movements seeking to represent an entire society or 'people' should envisage its existence essentially in terms of that of an independent or at least an autonomous state. State, nation and society converged.

For the same reason, the state, seen from above in the perspective of its former rules or dominant groups, raised unprecedented problems of how to maintain or even establish the obedience, loyalty and cooperation of its subjects or members, or its own legitimacy in their eyes. The very fact that its direct and increasingly intrusive and regular relations with the subjects and citizens as individuals (or at most, heads of families) became increasingly central to its operations, tended to weaken the older devices by means of which social subordination had largely been maintained: relatively autonomous collectivities or corporations under the ruler, but controlling their own members, pyramids of authority linked to higher authorities at their apexes, stratified social hierarchies in which each stratum recognized its place, and so on. In any case social transformations such as those which replaced ranks by classes undermined them. The problems of states and rulers were evidently much more acute where their subjects had become citizens, that is people whose political activities were institutionally recognized as something that had to be taken note of – if only in the form of elections. They became even more acute when the political movements of citizens as masses deliberately challenged the legitimacy of the systems of political or social rule, and or threatened to prove incompatible with the state's order by setting the obligations to some other human collectivity – most usually class, church or nationality – above it.

The problem appeared to be most manageable where social structure had changed least, where men's fates appeared to be subject to no other forces than those which an inscrutable divinity had always unleashed among the human race, and where the ancient ways of hierarchical superiority and stratified, multiform and relatively autonomous subordination remained in force. If anything could mobilize the peasantry of south Italy beyond their localities, it was church and king. And indeed the traditionalism of peasants (which must not be confused with passivity, though there are not many cases where they challenged the actual existence of the lords, so long as these belonged to the same faith and people) was constantly praised by nineteenth-century conservatives as the ideal model of the subject's political comportment. Unfortunately, the states in which this model worked were by definition 'backward' and therefore feeble, and any attempt to 'modernize' them was likely to make it less workable. A 'modernization' which maintained the old ordering of social subordination (possibly with some well-judged invention of tradition) was not theoretically inconceivable, but apart from Japan it is difficult to think of an example of practical success. And it may be suggested that such attempts to update the social bonds of a traditional order implied a demotion of social hierarchy, a strengthening of the subject's direct bonds to the central rule who, whether this was intended to or not, increasingly came to represent a new kind of state. 'God save the King' was increasingly (if sometimes symbolically) a more effective political injunction than 'God bless the squire and his relations and keep us in our proper stations'.

[...]

The problem was most intractable in states which were completely new, where the rulers were unable to make effective use of already existing bonds of political obedience and loyalty, and in states whose legitimacy (or that of the social order they represented) was effectively no longer accepted. In the period 1870–1914 there were, as it happens, unusually few 'new states'. Most European states, as well as the American republics, had by then acquired the basic official institutions, symbols and practices which Mongolia, establishing a sort of independence from China in 1912, quite rightly regarded as novel and necessary. They had capitals, flags, national anthems, military uniforms and similar paraphernalia, based largely on the model of the British, whose national anthem (datable *c.* 1740) is probably the first, and of the French, whose tricolour flag was very generally imitated. Several new states and regimes could either, like the French Third Republic, reach back into the store of earlier empire, combine appeals to an earlier German Empire, with the myths and symbols of a liberal nationalism popular among the middle classes, and the dynastic continuity of the Prussian monarchy, of which by the 1860s half of the inhabitants of Bismarckian Germany were subjects. Among the major states only Italy had to start from scratch in solving the problem summarized by d'Azeglio in the phrase: 'We have made Italy: now we must make Italians'. The tradition of the kingdom of Savoy was no political asset outside the north-western corner of the country, and the church opposed the new Italian state. It is perhaps not surprising that the new kingdom of Italy, however enthusiastic about 'making Italians', was notably unenthusiastic about giving the vote to more than 1 or 2 per cent of them until this seemed quite unavoidable.

Yet if the establishment of the legitimacy of new states and regimes was relatively uncommon, its assertion against the challenge of popular politics was not. As noted above, that challenge was chiefly represented, singly or in combination, by the sometimes linked, sometimes competing, political mobilization of masses through religion (mainly Roman Catholicism), class consciousness (social democracy), and nationalism, or at least xenophobia. Politically these challenges found their most visible expression in the vote, and were at this period inextricably linked either with the existence of, or struggle for, mass suffrage, waged against opponents who were mainly by now resigned to fighting a delaying rearguard action. By 1914 some form of extensive if not universal manhood suffrage was operating in Australia (1901), Austria (1907), Belgium (1894), Italy (1913), Norway (1898), Sweden (1907), Switzerland (1848–79), the United Kingdom (1867–84) and the USA, though it was still only occasionally combined with political democracy. Yet even where constitutions were not democratic, the very existence of a mass electorate dramatized the problem of maintaining its loyalty. The unbroken rise of the Social Democratic vote in imperial Germany was no less worrying to its rulers because the Reichstag in fact had very little power.

The widespread progress of electoral democracy and the consequent emergence of mass politics therefore dominated the invention of official traditions in the period 1870–1914. What made it particularly urgent was the dominance both of the model of liberal constitutional institutions and of liberal ideology. The former provide no theoretical, but only at best empirical, barriers against electoral democracy. Indeed, it was difficult for the liberal not to expect an extension of civic rights to all citizens – or at least to male ones – sooner or later. The latter had achieved its most spectacular economic triumphs and social transformations by systematically opting for the individual against the institutionalized collectivity, for market transactions (the 'cash nexus') against human ties, for class against rank hierarchy, for *Gesellschaft* against *Gemeinschaft*. It had thus systematically failed to provide for those social bonds and ties of authority taken for granted in earlier societies, and had indeed set out to and succeeded in weakening them. So long as the masses remained outside politics, or were prepared to follow the liberal bourgeoisie, this created no major political difficulties. Yet from the 1870s onwards it became increasingly obvious that the masses were becoming involved in politics and could not be relied upon to follow their masters.

After the 1870s, therefore, and almost certainly in connection with the emergence of mass politics, rulers and middle-class observers rediscovered the importance of 'irrational' elements in the maintenance of the social fabric and the social order. As Graham Wallas was to observe in *Human Nature in Politics* (1908): 'Whoever sets himself to base his political thinking on a re-examination of the working of human nature, must begin by trying to overcome his own tendency to exaggerate the intellectuality of mankind'.[4] A new generation of thinkers had no difficulty in overcoming this tendency. They rediscovered irrational elements in the individual psyche (Freud), in social psychology (Le Bon), through anthropology in primitive peoples whose practices no longer seemed to preserve merely the childhood traits of modern humanity (did not Durkheim see the elements of all religion in the rites of the Australian aborigines?[5]), even in that quintessential fortress of ideal human reason, classical Hellenism (James Frazer, Francis Cornford).[6] The intellectual study of politics and society was transformed by the recognition that whatever held human collectivities together it was not the rational calculation of their individual members.

[ . . . ]

An alternative 'civic religion' had to be constructed. The need for it was the core of Durkheim's sociology, the work of a devoted non-socialist republican. Yet it had to be instituted by less eminent thinkers, if more practical politicians.

It would be foolish to suggest that the men who ruled the

Third Republic relied mainly on inventing new traditions in order to achieve social stability. Rather, they relied on the hard political fact that the right was in a permanent electoral minority, that the social-revolutionary proletariat and the inflammable Parisians could be permanently outvoted by the over-represented villages and small towns, and that the Republican rural voters' genuine passion for the French Revolution and hatred of the moneyed interest could usually be assuaged by roads suitably distributed around the arrondissements, by the defence of high farm prices and, almost certainly, by keeping taxes low. The Radical Socialist grandee knew what he was about when he worked his electoral address, through appeals to the spirit of 1789 – nay 1793 – and a hymn to the Republic to the climax in which he pledged his loyalty to the interests of the *viticulteurs* of his Languedoc constituency.[7]

Nevertheless, the invention of tradition played an essential role in maintaining the Republic, if only by safeguarding it against both socialism and the right. By deliberately annexing the revolutionary tradition, the Third Republic either domesticated social revolutionaries (like most socialists) or isolated them (like the anarcho-syndicalists). In turn, it was now able to mobilize even a majority of its potential adversaries on the left in defence of a republic and a past revolution, in a common front of the classes which reduced the right to a permanent minority in the nation. Indeed, as that textbook of Third Republican politics, *Clochemerle* (1934), makes clear, the main function of the right was to provide something for good Republicans to mobilize against. The Socialist labour movement resisted its co-option by the bourgeois Republic to some extent; hence the establishment of the annual commemoration of the Paris Commune at the Mur des Fédérés (1880) against the institutionalization of the Republic; hence also the substitution of the new 'Internationale' for the traditional, but now official, 'Marseillaise' as its anthem, during the Dreyfus affair, and especially during the controversies on socialist participation in bourgeois governments.

Again, the radical Jacobin Republicans continued, within the official symbolism, to mark their separation from the moderate and dominant ones. Maurice Agulhon, who has studied the characteristic mania for putting up monuments, notably of the Republic itself, during the period 1875 to 1914, acutely notes that in the more radical municipalities Marianne (the personification of revolutionary France) bared at least one breast, while in the more moderate ones she was decently clothed.[8] Yet the basic fact was that those who controlled the imagery, the symbolism, the traditions of the Republic were the men of the centre masquerading as men of the extreme left: the Radical Socialists, proverbially 'like the radish, red outside, white inside, and always on the side the bread is buttered'. Once they ceased to control the Republic's fortunes – from the days of the Popular Front onwards – the days of the Third Republic were numbered.

There is considerable evidence that the moderate Republican bourgeoisie recognized the nature of its main political problem ('no enemies on the left') from the late 1860s onwards, and set about solving it as soon as the Republic was firmly in power.[9] In terms of the invention of tradition, three major innovations are particularly relevant. The first was the development of a secular equivalent of the church – primary education, imbued with revolutionary and republican principles and content, and conducted by the secular equivalent of the priesthood – or perhaps, given their poverty – the friars – the *instituteurs*.[10] There is no doubt that this was a deliberate construction of the early Third Republic, and, given the proverbial centralization of French government, that the content of the manuals which were to turn not only peasants into Frenchmen but all Frenchmen into good Republicans, was not left to chance. Indeed, the 'institutionalization' of the French Revolution itself in and by the Republic has been studied in some detail.[11]

The second was the invention of public ceremonies.[12] The most important of these, Bastille Day, can be exactly dated in 1880. It combined official and unofficial demonstrations and popular festivities – fireworks, dancing in the streets – in an annual assertion of France as the nation of 1789, in which every French man, woman and child could take part. Yet while it left scope for, and could hardly avoid, more militant, popular manifestations, its general tendency was to transform the heritage of the Revolution into a combined expression of state pomp and power and the citizens' pleasure. A less permanent form of public celebration were the occasional world expositions which gave the Republic the legitimacy of prosperity, technical progress – the Eiffel Tower – and the global colonial conquest they took care to emphasize.[13]

The third was the mass production of public monuments already noted. It may be observed that the Third Republic did not – unlike other countries, favour massive public buildings, of which France already had a large supply – though the great expositions left some of these behind them in Paris – nor gigantic statuary. The major characteristic of French 'statuomania'[14] was its democracy, anticipating that of the war memorials after 1914–18. It spread two kinds of monuments throughout the cities and rural communes of the country: the image of the Republic itself (in the form of Marianne which now became universally familiar), and the bearded civilian figures of whoever local patriotism chose to regard as its notables, past and present. Indeed, while the construction of Republican monuments was evidently encouraged, the initiative, and the costs of, such enterprises were undertaken at a local level. The entrepreneurs catering for this market provided choices suitable for the purses of every Republican commune from the poorest upwards, ranging from modest busts of Marianne, in various sizes, through full-figure statues of varying dimensions, to the plinths and allegorical or heroic accessories with which the more ambitious citizenry could surround her feet.[15] The opulent ensembles on the Place de la République and the Place de la Nation in Paris provided the ultimate version of such statuary. Such monuments traced the grass roots of the Republic – particularly in its rural strongholds – and may be regarded as the visible links between the voters and the nation.

Some other characteristics of the official 'invented' traditions of the Third Republic may be noted in passing. Except in the form of the commemoration of notable figures from the local past, or of local political manifestos, it kept away from history. This was partly, no doubt, because history before 1789 (except perhaps for *'nos ancêtres les Gaulois'*) recalled church and monarchy, partly because history since 1789 was a divisive rather than unifying force: each brand – or rather degree – of Republicanism had its own corresponding heroes and villains in the revolutionary pantheon, as the historiography of the French Revolution demonstrates. Party differences were expressed in statues to Robespierre, Mirabeau or Danton. Unlike the USA and the Latin American states, the French Republic therefore shied away from the cult of the Founding Fathers. It preferred general symbols, abstaining even from the use of themes referring to the national past on its postage stamps until long after 1914, though most European states (other than Britain and Scandinavia) discovered their appeal from the mid-1890s onwards. The symbols were few: the tricolour (democratized and universalized in the sash of the mayor, present at every civil marriage or other ceremony), the Republican monogram (RF) and motto (liberty, equality, fraternity), the 'Marseillaise', and the symbol of the Republic and of freedom itself, which appears to have taken shape in the last years of the Second Empire, Marianne. We may also note that the Third Republic showed no official hankering for the specially invented ceremonies so characteristic of the First – 'trees of liberty', goddesses of reason and ad hoc festivals. There was to be no official national day other than 14 July, no formal mobilizations, processions and marches of the civilian citizenry (unlike the mass regimes of the twentieth century, but also unlike the USA), but rather a simple 'republicanization' of the accepted pomp of state power – uniforms, parades, bands, flags and the like.

## The Production of 'National' Traditions

The Second German Empire provides an interesting contrast, especially since several of the general themes of French Republican invented tradition are recognizable in its own. Its major political problem was twofold: how to provide historical legitimacy for the Bismarckian (Prusso-Little German) version of unification which had none; and how to deal with that large part of the democratic electorate which would have preferred another solution (Great Germans, anti-Prussian particularists, Catholics and, above all, Social Democrats). Bismarck himself does not seem to have bothered much about symbolism, except for personally devising a tricolour flag which combined the Prussian black–white with the nationalist and liberal black–red–gold which he wished to annex (1866). There was no historical precedent whatever for the Empire's black–white–red national banner.[16] His recipe for political stability was simpler: to win the support of the (predominantly liberal) bourgeoisie by carrying out as much of its programme as would not jeopardize the predominance of the Prussian monarchy, army and aristocracy, to utilize the potential divisions among the various kinds of opposition and to exclude political democracy as far as possible from affecting the decisions of government. Apparently irreconcilable groups which could not be divided – notably the Catholics and especially the post-Lassallean Social Democrats – left him somewhat at a loss. In fact, he was defeated in his head-on confrontations with both. One has the impression that this old-fashioned conservative rationalist, however brilliant in the arts of political manoeuvre, never satisfactorily solved the difficulties of political democracy, as distinct from the politics of notables.

The invention of the traditions of the German Empire is therefore primarily associated with the era of William II. Its objects were mainly twofold: to establish the continuity between the Second and First German Empires, or more generally, to establish the new Empire as the realization of the secular national aspirations of the German people; and to stress the specific historical experiences which linked Prussia and the rest of Germany in the construction of the new Empire in 1871. Both, in turn, required the merger of Prussian and German history, to which patriotic imperial historians (notably Treitschke) had for some time devoted themselves. The major difficulty in the way of achieving these objects was firstly the history of the Holy Roman Empire of the German nation was difficult to fit into any nineteenth-century nationalist mould, and secondly that its history did not suggest that the denouement of 1871 was historically inevitable, or even likely. It could be linked to a modern nationalism only by two devices: by the concept of a secular national enemy against whom the German people had defined their identity and struggled to achieve unity as a state; and by the concept of conquest or cultural, political and military supremacy, by means of which the German nation, scattered across large parts of other states, mainly in central and eastern Europe, could claim the right to be united in a single Greater German state. The second concept was not one which the Bismarckian empire, specifically 'Little German', cared to stress, though Prussia itself, as the name implied, had been historically constructed largely by expansion into Slavonic and Baltic areas outside the range of the Holy Roman Empire.

Buildings and monuments were the most visible form of establishing a new interpretation of German history, or rather a fusion between the older romantic 'invented tradition' of pre-1848 German nationalism and the new regime: the most powerful symbols being those where the fusion was achieved. Thus, the mass movement of German gymnasts, liberal and Great German until the 1860s, Bismarckian after 1866 and eventually pan-German and anti-Semitic, took to its heart three monuments whose inspiration was basically not official: the monument to Arminius the Cheruscan in the Teutoburg Forest (much of it constructed as early as 1838–46, and inaugurated in 1875); the Niederwald monument above the Rhine, commemorating the unification of Germany in 1871 (1877–83); and the centenary memorial of the battle of Leipzig, initiated in 1894 by a 'German patriotic League for the Erection of a Monument to the Battle of the Peoples at Leipzig', and inaugurated in 1913. On the other hand, they appear to have shown no enthusiasm for the proposal to turn the monument to William I on the Kyffhäuser mountain, on the spot where folk myth claimed the Emperor Frederick Barbarossa would appear again, into a national symbol (1890–6), and no special reaction to the construction of the monument to William I and Germany at the confluence of the Rhine and the Moselle (the 'Deutsches Eck' or German Corner, directed against French claims to the left bank of the Rhine.[17]

Leaving such variations aside, the mass of masonry and statuary which went up in German in this period was remarkably large, and made the fortunes of sufficiently pliable and competent architects and sculptors.[18] Among those constructed or planned in the 1890s alone, we may mention the new Reichstag building (1884–94) with elaborate historical imagery on its façade, the Kyffhäuser monument already mentioned (1890–6), the national monument to William I – clearly intended as the official father of the country (1890–7), the monument to William I at the Porta Westfalica (1892), the William I monument at the Deutsches Eck (1894–7), the extraordinary Valhalla of Hohenzollern princes in the 'Avenue of Victory' (Siegesallee) in Berlin (1896–1901), a variety of statues to William I in German cities (Dortmund 1894, Wiesbaden 1894, Prenzlau 1898, Hamburg 1903, Halle 1901) and, a little later, a spate of Bismarck monuments, which enjoyed a more genuine support among nationalists.[19] The inauguration of one of these monuments provided the first occasion for the use of historical themes on the postage stamps of the Empire (1899).

This accumulation of masonry and statuary suggests two comments. The first concerns the choice of a national symbol. Two of these were available: a vague but adequately military 'Germania', who played no notable role in sculpture, though she figured extensively on postage stamps from the start, since no single dynastic image could as yet symbolize Germany as a whole; and the figure of the 'Deutsche Michel', who actually appears in a subordinate role on the Bismarck monument. He belongs to the curious representations of the nation, not as country or state, but as 'the people', which came to animate the demotic political language of the nineteenth-century cartoonists, and was intended (as in John Bull and the goateed Yankee – but *not* in Marianne, image of the Republic) to express national character, as seen by the members of the nation itself. Their origins and early history are obscure, though, like the national anthem, they are almost certainly first found in eighteenth-century Britain.[20] The point about the 'Deutsche Michel' is that his image stressed both the innocence and simple-mindedness so readily exploited by cunning foreigners, and the physical strength he could mobilize to frustrate their knavish tricks and conquests when finally roused. 'Michel' seems to have been essentially an anti-foreign image.

The second concerns the crucial significance of the Bismarckian unification of Germany as the *only* national historical experience which the citizens of the new Empire had in common, given that all earlier conceptions of Germany and German unification were in one way or another 'Great German'. And within this experience, the Franco-German War was central. Insofar as Germany had a (brief) 'national' tradition, it was symbolized in three names: Bismarck, William I and Sedan.

This is clearly exemplified by the ceremonials and rituals invented (also mainly under William II). Thus the chronicles of one gymnasium record no less than ten ceremonies between August 1895 and March 1896 recalling the twenty-fifth anniversary of the Franco-Prussian War, including ample commemorations of battles in the war, celebrations of the emperor's birthday, the official handing-over of the portrait of an imperial prince, illuminations and public addresses on the war of 1870–1,

on the development of the imperial idea (*Kaiseridee*) during the war, on the character of the Hohenzollern dynasty, and so on.[21]
[...]

A comparison of the French and German innovations is instructive. Both stress the founding acts of the new regime – the French Revolution in its least precise and controversial episode (the Bastille) and the Franco-Prussian War. Except for this one point of historic reference, the French Republic abstained from historical retrospect as strikingly as the German Empire indulged in it. Since the Revolution had established the fact, the nature and the boundaries of the French nation and its patriotism, the Republic could confine itself to recalling these to its citizens by means of a few obvious symbols – Marianne, the tricolour, the 'Marseillaise', and so on – supplementing them with a little ideological exegesis elaborating on the (to its poorer citizens) obvious if sometimes theoretical benefits of Liberty, Equality and Fraternity. Since the 'German people' before 1871 had no political definition or unity, and its relation to the new Empire (which excluded large parts of it) was vague, symbolic or ideological, identification had to be more complex and – with the exception of the role of the Hohenzollern dynasty, army and state – less precise. Hence the multiplicity of reference, ranging from mythology and folklore (German oaks, the Emperor Frederick Barbarossa) through the shorthand cartoon stereotypes to definition of the nation in terms of its enemies. Like many another liberated 'people', 'Germany' was more easily defined by what it was against than in any other way.

This may explain the most obvious gap in the 'invented traditions' of the German Empire: its failure to conciliate the Social Democrats. It is true that William II initially liked to present himself as a 'social emperor', and made a clear break with Bismarck's own anti-socialist policies. Yet the temptation to present the Socialist movement as anti-national proved too strong to be resisted, and Socialists were more systematically excluded from the state service (including, by a specially passed law, from posts in higher education) than they were, for example, in the Habsburg Empire. No doubt two of the Empire's political headaches were considerably mitigated. Military glory and power as well as the rhetoric of German greatness disarmed the 'Great Germans' or pan-Germans, now increasingly divorced from their liberal or even democratic origins. If they were to achieve their ends at all, it would now be through the new Empire or not at all. The Catholics, as became clear when Bismarck's campaign against them was abandoned, caused no serious problems. Nevertheless, the Social Democrats alone, advancing with apparent inevitability towards majority status in the Empire, constituted a political force which, if other countries during this period are a guide, ought to have moved the German government towards a rather more flexible attitude.

Yet in a nation relying for its self-definition to such a great extent on its *enemies*, external and internal, this was not wholly unexpected;[22] all the more so, since the by definition anti-democratic military elite formed so powerful a device for assimilating the middle class to the status of a ruling class. Yet the choice of Social Democrats and, less formally, of Jews as internal enemies had an additional advantage, though the nationalism of the Empire was unable to exploit it fully. It provided a demagogic appeal against both capitalist liberalism and proletarian socialism which could mobilize the great masses of the lower middle class, handicraftsmen and peasants who felt threatened by both, under the banner of 'the nation'.

Paradoxically, the most democratic and, both territorially and constitutionally, one of the most clearly defined nations faced a problem of national identity in some respects similar to imperial Germany. The basic political problems of the USA, once secession had been eliminated, was how to assimilate a heterogeneous mass – towards the end of our period, an almost unmanageable influx – of people who were Americans not by birth but by immigration. Americans had to be made. The invented traditions of the USA in this period were primarily designed to achieve this object. On the one hand, the immigrants were encouraged to accept rituals commemorating the history of the nation – the Revolution and its founding fathers (the 4th of July) and the Protestant Anglo-Saxon tradition (Thanksgiving Day) – as indeed they did, since these now became holidays and occasions for public and private festivity.[23] (Conversely, the 'nation' absorbed the collective rituals of immigrants – St Patrick's Day, later Columbus Day – into the fabric of American life, mainly through the powerful assimilating mechanism of municipal and state politics.) On the other hand, the educational system was transformed into a machine for political socialization by such devices as the American flag, which, as a daily ritual in the country's schools, spread from the 1880s onwards.[24] The concept of Americanism as an act of *choice* – the decision to learn English, to apply for citizenship – and a choice of specific beliefs, acts and modes of behaviour implied the corresponding concept of 'un-Americanism'. In countries defining nationality existentially there could be unpatriotic Englishmen or Frenchmen, but their status as Englishmen and Frenchmen could not be in doubt, unless they could also be identified as strangers. Yet in the USA, as in Germany, the 'un-American' or '*vaterlandslose*' person threw doubt on his or her actual status as member of the nation.

As might be expected, the working class provided the largest and most visible body of such doubtful members of the national community; all the more doubtful because in the USA they could actually be classified as foreigners. The mass of new immigrants were workers; conversely, since at least the 1860s, the majority of workers in virtually all the large cities of the land appear to have been foreign-born. Whether the concept of 'un-Americanism', which can be traced back to at least the 1870s, was more of a reaction of the native-born against the strangers or of Anglo-Saxon Protestant middle classes against foreign-born workers is unclear. At all events it provided an internal enemy against whom the good American could assert his or her Americanism, not least by the punctilious performance of all the formal and informal rituals, the assertion of all the beliefs conventionally and institutionally established as characteristic of good Americans.

[...]

We may deal more cursorily with the invention of state traditions in other countries of the period. Monarchies, for obvious reasons, tended to link them to the crown, and this period saw the initiation of the now familiar public relations exercises centred on royal or imperial rituals, greatly facilitated by the happy discovery – or perhaps it would be better to say invention – of the jubilee or ceremonial anniversary. Its novelty is actually remarked upon in the *New English Dictionary*.[25] The publicity value of anniversaries is clearly shown by the occasion they so often provided for the first issue of historical or similar images on postage stamps, that most universal form of public imagery other than money.

Almost certainly Queen Victoria's jubilee of 1887, repeated ten years later in view of its notable success, inspired subsequent royal or imperial occasions in this country and elsewhere. Even the most traditionalist dynasties – the Habsburgs in 1908, the Romanovs in 1913 – discovered the merits of this form of publicity. It was new insofar as it was directed at the public, unlike traditional royal ceremonials designed to symbolize the rulers' relation to the divinity and their position at the apex of a hierarchy of grandees. After the French Revolution every monarch had, sooner or later, to learn to change from the national equivalent of 'King of France' to 'King of the French', that is, to establish a direct relation to the collectivity of his or her subjects, however lowly. Though the stylistic option of a 'bourgeois monarch' (pioneered by Louis Philippe) was available, it seems to have been taken only by the kings of modest countries wishing to maintain a low profile – the Netherlands, Scandinavia – though even some of the most divinely ordained rulers – notably the Emperor Francis Joseph – appear to have fancied the role of hard-working functionary living in Spartan comfort.

Technically there was no significant difference between the political use of monarchy for the purpose of strengthening effective rulers (as in the Habsburg, Romanov, but also perhaps in the Indian empires) and building the symbolic function of crowned heads in parliamentary states. Both relied on exploiting the royal person, with or without dynastic ancestors, on elaborate ritual occasions with associated propagandist activities and a wide participation of the people, not least through the captive audiences available for official indoctrination in the educational system. Both made the ruler the focus of his people's or peoples' unity, the symbolic representation of the country's greatness and glory, of its entire past and continuity with a changing present. Yet the innovations were perhaps more deliberate and systematic where, as in Britain, the revival of royal ritualism was seen as a necessary counterweight to the dangers of popular democracy. Bagehot had already recognized the value of political deference and the 'dignified', as distinct from the 'efficient', parts of the constitution in the days of the Second Reform Act. The old Disraeli, unlike the young, learned to use 'reverence for the throne and its occupant' as 'a mighty instrument of power and influence' and by the end of Victoria's reign the nature of the device was well understood.

[ ... ]

Glory and greatness, wealth and power, could be symbolically shared by the poor through royalty and its rituals. The greater the power, the less attractive, one may suggest, was the bourgeois option for monarchy. And we may recall that in Europe monarchy remained the universal state form between 1870 and 1914, except for France and Switzerland.

Sport combined the invention of political and social traditions by providing a medium for national identification and factitious community. This was not new in itself, for mass physical exercises had long been linked with liberal–nationalist movements (the German *Turner*, the Czech *Sokols*) or with national identification (rifle-shooting in Switzerland). Indeed the resistance of the German gymnastic movement, on nationalist grounds in general and anti-British ones in particular, distinctly slowed down the process of mass sport in Germany.[26] The rise of sport provided new expressions of nationalism through the choice or invention of nationally specific sports – Welsh rugby as distinct from English soccer, and Gaelic football in Ireland (1884), which acquired genuine mass support some twenty years later.[27] However, although the specific linking of physical exercises with nationalism as part of nationalist movements remained important – as in Bengal[28] – it was by now certainly less significant than two other phenomena.

The first of these was the concrete demonstration of the links which bound all inhabitants of the national state together, irrespective of local and regional differences, as in the all-English football culture or, more literally, in such sporting institutions as the cyclists' Tour de France (1903), followed by the Giro d'Italia (1909). These phenomena were all the more significant as they evolved spontaneously or by commercial mechanisms. The second consisted of the international sporting contests which very soon supplemented national ones, and reached their typical expression in the revival of the Olympics in 1896. While we are today only too aware of the scope for vicarious national identification which such contests provide, it is important to recall that before 1914 they had barely begun to acquire their modern character. Initially, 'international' contests served to underline the unity of nations or empires much in the way inter-regional contests did. British international matches – as usual the pioneers – pitted the nations of the British Isles against each other (in football: those of Britain in the 1870s, Ireland being included in the 1880s), or various parts of the British Empire (Test Matches began in 1877). The first international football match outside the British Isles confronted Austria and Hungary (1902). International sport, with few exceptions, remained dominated by amateurism – that is by middle-class sport – even in football, where the international association (FIFA) was formed by countries with little mass support for the game in 1904 (France, Belgium, Denmark, the Netherlands, Spain, Sweden, Switzerland). The Olympics remained the main international arena for this sport. To this extent national identification through sport against foreigners in this period seems to have been primarily a middle-class phenomenon.

This may itself be significant. For the middle classes in the broadest sense found subjective group identification unusually difficult, since they were not in fact a sufficiently small minority to establish the sort of virtual membership of a nation-wide club which united, for example, most of those who had passed through Oxford and Cambridge, nor sufficiently united by a common destiny and potential solidarity, like the workers.[29] Negatively the middle classes found it easy to segregate themselves from their inferiors by such devices as rigid insistence on amateurism in sport, as well as by the lifestyle and values of 'respectability', not to mention residential segregation. Positively, it may be suggested, they found it easier to establish a sense of belonging together through external symbols, among which those of nationalism (patriotism, imperialism) were perhaps the most significant. It is, one might suggest, as the quintessential patriotic class that the new or aspiring middle class found it easiest to recognize itself collectively.

This is speculation. Here it is only possible to point out that there is at least some prima facie evidence for it, seen in the appeal of patriotism to the white-collar strata of Britain in the South African War[30] and the role of the right-wing nationalist mass organizations – overwhelmingly of middle-class but not elite composition – in Germany from the 1880s on, the appeal of Schönerer's nationalism to the (German-speaking) university students – a middle-class stratum profoundly marked by nationalism in a number of European countries.[31] The nationalism which gained ground was overwhelmingly identified with the political right. In the 1890s the originally liberal–nationalist

German gymnasts abandoned the old national colours en masse to adopt the new black–white–red banner: in 1898 only one hundred out of 6501 *Turnervereine* still maintained the old black–red–gold.[32]

What is clear is that nationalism became a substitute for social cohesion through a national church, a royal family or other cohesive traditions, or collective group self-presentations, a new secular religion, and that the class which required such a mode of cohesion most was the growing new middle class, or rather that large intermediate mass which so signally lacked other forms of cohesion. At this point, once again, the invention of political traditions coincides with that of social ones.

To establish the clustering of 'invented traditions' in western countries between 1870 and 1914 is relatively easy. Enough examples of such innovations have been given in this chapter, from old school ties and royal jubilees, Bastille Day, May Day, the Internationale and the Olympic Games to the Cup Final and Tour de France as popular rites, and the institution of flag worship in the USA.

[ . . . ]

There remain three aspects of the 'invention of tradition' in this period which call for some brief comment in conclusion.

The first is the distinction between those new practices of the period which proved lasting, and those which did not. In retrospect it would seem that the period which straddles the First World War marks a divide between languages of symbolic discourse. As in military uniforms what might be called the operatic mode gave way to the prosaic mode. The uniforms invented for the interwar mass movements, which could hardly claim the excuse of operational camouflage, eschewed bright colours, preferring duller hues such as the black and brown of Fascists and National Socialists.[33] No doubt fancy dress for ritual occasions was still invented for men in the period 1870–1914, though examples hardly come to mind – except perhaps by way of the extension of older styles to new institutions of the same type and, hopefully, status, such as academic gowns and hoods for new colleges and degrees. The old costumes were certainly still maintained. However, one has the distinct impression that in this respect the period lived on accumulated capital. In another respect, however, it clearly developed an old idiom with particular enthusiasm. The mania for statuary and allegorically decorated or symbolic public buildings has already been mentioned, and there is little doubt that it reached a peak between 1870 and 1914. Yet this idiom of symbolic discourse was destined to decline with dramatic suddenness between the wars. Its extraordinary vogue was to prove almost as short-lived as the contemporary outburst of another kind of symbolism, 'art nouveau'. Neither the massive adaptation of traditional allegory and symbolism for public purposes, nor the improvization of a new and imprecise language of vegetable or female, but in any case curvilinear, symbolism, mainly for private or semi-private purposes, appears to have been suited more than temporarily to whatever social requirements gave rise to them. We can only speculate about the reasons, and this is not the place to do so.

On the other hand, it may be suggested that another idiom of public symbolic discourse, the theatrical, proved more lasting. Public ceremonies, parades and ritualized mass gatherings were far from new. Yet their extension for official purposes and for unofficial secular purposes (mass demonstrations, football matches and the like) in this period is rather striking. Some examples have been mentioned above. Moreover, the construction of formal ritual spaces, already consciously allowed for in German nationalism, appears to have been systematically undertaken even in countries which had hitherto paid little attention to it – one thinks of Edwardian London – and neither should we overlook the invention in this period of substantially new constructions for spectacle and de facto mass ritual such as sports stadia, outdoor and indoor.[34] The royal attendance at the Wembley Cup Final (from 1914), and the use of such buildings as the Sportspalast in

Berlin or the Vélodrome d'Hiver in Paris by the interwar mass movements of their respective countries, anticipate the development of formal spaces for public mass ritual (Red Square from 1918) which was to be systematically fostered by fascist regimes. We may note in passing that, in line with the exhaustion of the old language of public symbolism, the new settings for such public ritual were to stress simplicity and monumentality rather than the allegorical decoration of the nineteenth-century Ringstrasse in Vienna or the Victor Emmanuel monument in Rome;[35] a tendency already anticipated in our period.[36]

On the stage of public life the emphasis therefore shifted from the design of elaborate and varied stage sets, capable of being 'read' in the manner of a strip cartoon or tapestry, to the movement of the actors themselves – either, as in military or royal parades, a ritual minority acting for the benefit of a watching mass public, or, as anticipated in the political mass movements of the period (such as May Day demonstrations) and the great mass sporting occasions, a merger of actors and public. These were the tendencies which were destined for further development after 1914. Without speculating further about this form of public ritualization, it does not seem unreasonable to relate it to the decline of old tradition and the democratization of politics.

The second aspect of invented tradition in this period concerns the practices identified with specific social classes or strata as distinct from members of wider inter-class collectivities such as states or 'nations'. While some such practices were formally designed as badges of class consciousness – the May Day practices among workers, the revival or invention of 'traditional' peasant costume among (de facto the richer) peasants – a larger number were not so identified in theory and many indeed were adaptations, specializations or conquests of practices originally initiated by the higher social strata. Sport is the obvious example. From above, the class line was here drawn in three ways: by maintaining aristocratic or middle-class control of the governing institutions, by social exclusiveness or, more commonly, by the high cost or scarcity of the necessary capital equipment (real tennis courts or grouse moors), but above all by the rigid separation between amateurism, the criterion of sport among the upper strata, and professionalism, its logical corollary among the lower urban and working classes.[37] Class-specific sport among plebeians rarely developed consciously as such. Where it did, it was usually by taking over upper-class exercises, pushing out their former practitioners, and then developing a separate set of practices on a new social basis (the football culture).

Practices thus filtering socially downwards – from aristocracy to bourgeoisie, from bourgeoisie to working class – were probably predominant in this period, not only in sport, but in costume and material culture in general, given the force of snobbery among the middle classes and of the values of bourgeois self-improvement and achievement among the working-class elites.[38] They were transformed, but their historical origins remained visible. The opposite movement was not absent, but in this period less visible. Minorities (aristocrats, intellectuals, deviants) might admire certain urban plebeian sub-cultures and activities – such as music-hall art – but the major assimilation of cultural practices developed among the lower classes or for a mass popular public was to come later. Some signs of it were visible before 1914, mainly mediated through entertainment and above all the social dance, which may be linked to the growing emancipation of women: the vogue for the ragtime or the tango. However, any survey of cultural invention in this period cannot but note the development of autochthonous lower-class sub-cultures and practices which owed nothing to models from higher social classes – almost certainly as a by-product of urbanization and mass migration. The tango culture in Buenos Aires is an example.[39] How far they enter into a discussion of the invention of tradition must remain a matter of debate.

The final aspect is the relation between 'invention' and 'spontaneous generation', planning and growth. This is something which constantly puzzles observers in modern mass societies.

'Invented traditions' have significant social and political functions, and would neither come into existence nor establish themselves if they could not acquire them. Yet how far are they manipulable? The intention to use, indeed often to invent, them for manipulation is evident; both appear in politics, the first mainly (in capitalist societies) in business. To this extent conspiracy theorists opposed to such manipulation have not only plausibility but evidence on their side. Yet it also seems clear that the most successful examples of manipulation are those which exploit practices which clearly meet a felt – not necessarily a clearly understood – need among particular bodies of people. The politics of German nationalism in the Second Empire cannot be understood only from above. It has been suggested that to some extent nationalism escaped from the control of those who found it advantageous to manipulate it – at all events in this period.[40] Tastes and fashions, notably in popular entertainment, can be 'created' only within very narrow limits; they have to be discovered before being exploited and shaped. It is the historian's business to discover them retrospectively – but also to try to understand why, in terms of changing societies in changing historical situations, such needs came to be felt.

# Notes

1   G. L. Mosse, 'Caesarism, Circuses and Movements', *Journal of Contemporary History*, 6:2 (1971), pp. 167–82; G. L. Mosse, *The Nationalisation of the Masses: Political Symbolism and Mass Movements in Germany from the Napoleonic Wars through the 3rd Reich* (New York, 1975); T. Nipperdey, 'Nationalidee und Nationaldenkmal in Deutschland im 19. Jahrhundert', *Historische Zeitschrift* (1968), pp. 529–85, esp. 543n, 579n.
2   Eugen Weber, *Peasants into Frenchmen: The Modernization of Rural France, 1870–1914* (Stanford, 1976).
3   This was conclusively demonstrated in 1914 by the socialist parties of the Second International, which not only claimed to be essentially international in scope, but actually sometimes regarded themselves officially as no more than national sections of a global movement as in 'Section Française de l'Internationale Ouvrière'.
4   Graham Wallas, *Human Nature in Politics* (London, 1908), p. 21.

# The Production of 'National' Traditions

5 Emile Durkheim, *The Elementary Forms of the Religious Life* (London, 1976). First French publication 1912.

6 J. G. Frazer, *The Golden Bough*, 3rd edn (London, 1907–30); F. M. Cornford, *From Religion to Philosophy: A Study of the Origins of Western Speculation* (London, 1912).

7 Jean Touchard, *La Gauche en France depuis 1900* (Paris, 1977), p. 50.

8 M. Agulhon, 'Esquisse pour une Archéologie de la République; l'Allégorie Civique Féminine', *Annales ESC*, 28 (1973), pp. 5–34; M. Agulhon, *Marianne au Combat: l'Imagerie et la Symbolique Républicaines de 1789 à 1880* (Paris, 1979).

9 Sanford H. Elwitt, *The Making of the 3rd Republic: Class and Politics in France, 1868–84* (Baton Rouge, 1975).

10 Georges Duveau, *Les Instituteurs* (Paris, 1957); J. Ozouf (ed.), *Nous le Maîtres d'Ecole: Autobiographies d'Instituteurs de la Belle Epoque* (Paris, 1967).

11 Alice Gérard, *La Révolution Française: Mythes et Interprétations, 1789–1970* (Paris, 1970), ch. 4.

12 Charles Rearick, 'Festivals in Modern France: The Experience of the 3rd Republic', *Journal of Contemporary History*, 12:3 (1977), pp. 435–60; Rosemonde Sanson, *Les 14 Juillet, Fête et Conscience Nationale, 1789–1975* (Paris, 1976), with bibliography.

13 For the political intentions of the 1889 one, cf. Debora L. Silverman, 'The 1889 Exhibition: The Crisis of Bourgeois Individualism', *Oppositions, A Journal for Ideas and Criticism in Architecture* (1977), pp. 71–91.

14 M. Agulhon, 'La Statumanie et l'Histoire', *Ethnologie Française*, nos 3–4 (1978), pp. 3–4.

15 Agulhon, 'Esquisse pour une Archéologie'.

16 Whitney Smith, *Flags through the Ages* (New York, 1975), pp. 116–18. The nationalist black–red–gold appears to have emerged from the student movement of the post-Napoleonic period, but was clearly established as the flag of the national movement in 1848. Resistance to the Weimar Republic reduced its national flag to a party banner – indeed the militia of the Social Democratic Party took it as its title ('Reichsbanner'), though the anti-republican right was divided between the imperial flag and the National Socialist flag, which abandoned the traditional tricolour design, possibly because of its associations with nineteenth-century liberalism, possibly as not sufficiently indicative of a radical break with the past. However, it maintained the basic colour scheme of the Bismarckian empire (black–white–red), while stressing the red, hitherto the symbol only of the socialist and labour movements. The Federal Republic and the Democratic Republic both returned to the colours of 1848, the former without additions, the latter with a suitable emblem adapted from the basic model of the Communist and Soviet hammer and sickle.

17 Hans-Georg John, *Politik und Turnen: die deutsche Turnerschaft als nationale Bewegung im deutschen Kaiserreich von 1871–1914* (Ahrensberg bei Hamburg, 1976), pp. 41ff.

18  'Fate determined that, against his nature, he should become a
    monumental sculptor, who was to celebrate the imperial idea of William
    II in giant monuments of bronze and stone, in a language of imagery
    and over-emphatic pathos.' Ulrich Thieme and Felix Becker, *Allgemeines
    Lexikon der bildenden Künstler von der Antike bis zur Gegenwart* (Leipzig,
    1907–50), iii, p. 185. See also in general entries under Begas, Schilling,
    Schmitz.
19  John, op. cit., Nipperdey, 'Nationalidee', pp. 577ff.
20  J. Surel, 'La Première Image de John Bull, Bourgeois Radical, Anglais
    Loyaliste (1779–1815)', *Le Mouvement Social*, 106 (1979), pp. 65–84;
    Herbert M. Atherton, *Political Prints in the Age of Hogarth* (Oxford, 1974),
    pp. 97–100.
21  Heinz Stallmann, *Das Prinz-Heinrichs-Gymnasium zum Schöneburg, 1890–
    1945. Geschichte einer Schule* (Berlin, n.d. but 1965).
22  H.-U. Wehler, *Das deutsche Kasierreich 1871–1918* (Göttingen, 1973), pp.
    107–10.
23  The history of these festivities remains to be written, but it seems clear
    that they became much more institutionalized on a national scale in the
    last third of the nineteenth century. G. W. Douglas, *American Book of Days*
    (New York, 1937); Elizabeth Hough Sechrist, *Red Letter Days: A Book of
    Holiday Customs* (Philadelphia, 1940).
24  R. Firth, *Symbols, Public and Private* (London, 1973), pp. 358–9; W. E.
    Davies, *Patriotism on Parade: The Story of Veterans and Hereditary Organisations
    in Americas 1783–1900* (Cambridge, Mass., 1955), pp. 218–22; Douglas,
    op. cit., pp. 326–7.
25  The 'jubilee', except in its biblical sense, had previously been simply the
    fifth anniversary. There is no sign before the later nineteenth century
    that centenaries, single or multiple, still less anniversaries of less than
    fifty years, were the occasion for public celebration. The *New English
    Dictionary* (1901) observes under 'jubilee' 'especially frequent in the last
    two decades of the nineteenth century in reference to the two "jubilees"
    of Queen Victoria in 1887 and 1897, the Swiss jubilee of the Postal
    Union in 1900 and other celebrations', v, p. 615.
26  John, op. cit., pp. 107ff.
27  W. F. Mandle, 'Sport as Politics. The Gaelic Athletic Association
    1884–1916', in R. Cashman and M. McKernan (eds), *Sport in History: The
    Making of Modern Sporting History* (St Lucia, 1979), pp. 99–123.
28  John Rosselli, 'The Self-Image of Effeteness: Physical Education and
    Nationalism in 19th Century Bengal', *Past and Present*, 86:1 (1980), pp.
    121–48.
29  It would be interesting, in countries whose language permits this
    distinction, to inquire into the changes in the mutual social use of
    the second person singular, symbol of social brotherhood as well
    as of personal intimacy. Among the higher classes its use between
    fellow-students (and, as with French polytechnicians, ex-students),

brother-officers and the like is familiar. Workers, even when they did not know one another, used it habitually. Leo Uhen, *Gruppenbewusstsein und informelle Gruppenbildung bei deutchen Arbeitern im Jahrhundert der Industrialisierung* (Berlin, 1964), pp. 106–7. Labour movements institutionalized it among their members ('Dear Sir and Brother').

30  Richard Price, *An Imperial War and the British Working-Class: Working-Class Attitudes and Reactions to the Boer War, 1899–1902* (London, 1972), pp. 72–3.

31  It is to be noted that in Germany the elite student Korps resisted the principle of anti-Semitism, unlike the non-elite associations, though de facto applying it (Detlef Grieswelle, 'Die Soziologie der Kösener Korps 1870–1914', in *Student und Hochschule im 19 Jahrhundert: Studien und Materialen* (Göttingen, 1975), p. 353). Similarly, anti-Semitism was imposed on the German gymnastic movement by pressure from below, against some resistance from the old National–Liberal bourgeois leadership of the movement (John, op. cit., p. 65).

32  John, op. cit., p. 37.

33  The brightest such uniforms appear to have been the blue shirts and red ties of socialist youth movements. I know of no case of red, orange or yellow shirts and none of genuinely multicoloured ceremonial clothing.

34  Cf. 'Stadthalle', in *Wasmuth's Lexikon der Baukunst* (Berlin, 1932), iv; W. Scharau-Wils, *Gebäude und Gelände für Gymnastik, Spiel und Sport* (Berlin, 1925); D. R. Knight, *The Exhibitions: Great White City, Shepherds Bush* (London, 1978).

35  Carl Schorske, *Fin de Siècle Vienna: Politics and Culture* (New York, 1980), ch. 2.

36  Cf. Alastair Service, *Edwardian Architecture: A Handbook to Building Design in Britain 1890–1914* (London, 1977).

37  Professionalism implies a degree of occupational specialism and a 'market' barely if at all available among the settled rural population. Professional sportsmen there were either servants or suppliers of the upper classes (jockeys, alpine guides) or appendages to amateur upper-class competitions (cricket professionals). The distinction between the upper- and lower-class killing of game was not economic, though some poachers relied on it for a living, but legal. It was expressed in the Game Laws.

38  A Weberian correlation of sport and Protestantism has been observed in Germany up to 1960. G. Lüschen, 'The Interdependence of Sport and Culture', in M. Hart (ed.), *Sport in the Sociocultural Process* (Dubuque, 1976).

39  Cf. Blas Mantamoro, *Las Ciudad del Tango (Tango Histórico y Sociedad)* (Buenos Aires, 1969).

40  Geoffrey Eley, *Re-shaping the German Right* (London and New Haven, 1980).

# 8

## *Ethnicity, Migration and the Nation-State*

President George H. W. Bush's new world order is a new world disorder, and for the time being, no restoration of stability is visible or even conceivable. It is against this background that we see the present rise of ethnic or nationalist or separatist phenomena in various, but by no means in all, parts of the world. On the other side of the coin is supranationalism or transnationalism, that is, the development of an increasingly integrated world economy or, more generally, a world whose problems cannot effectively be tackled let alone solved within the borders of nation-states.

The paradox of the situation is that some of these agitations are recreating nation-states of the ethnic/linguistic type, often on a much smaller scale than before, at a time when this makes no rational sense and, indeed, is particularly dangerous. This is not a universal tendency. Today, ethnic or similar movements do not necessarily or even typically find a nation-state of their own relevant to their problems. The United States demonstrates this in general and the black population of the United States demonstrates this in particular. In short, we must not equate ethnicity and nationalism or ethnicity and other interests aiming to set up territorial states. However, very often they are confused.

## Ethnicity, Migration and the Nation-State

I want to draw your attention to three aspects of this new instability: first, the specific and explosive situation between the frontiers of Germany, Austria and Italy in the west and those of Japan in the east, including the Middle East and central Asia; second, the phenomenon of ghettoization within states; and third, the actual or potential consequences of living through a period of global mass migration comparable to and potentially much bigger than the European mass migration of 1880 to 1920.

What we are seeing today (1995) is not a proof of the irresistible force of national or ethnic identity, but it is the result of the outcome of the First World War in a situation analogous to that in 1917–20, namely the breakdown of old pluri-ethnic empires. The collapse of the Habsburg and Ottoman empires and the temporary collapse of Tsarist Russia produced two equally impracticable forms of post-war settlement. On the ruins of the European empires, it produced the Wilsonian plan of a Europe of, in theory, homogeneous ethnic linguistic nation-states. In the Middle East, it produced the imposition of British and French formal or informal empire over nominally independent territories with little or no historic political presence, plus a half-hearted Wilsonian formula for the Jews in Palestine.

The European settlement broke down before the Middle Eastern one. It became clear that the distribution of ethnic groups and languages is such that homogeneous national territories could only be achieved by forcible assimilation, by mass population transfer, and/or by genocide. The Turks initiated this in a modest way, by forcible assimilation of the Kurds, mass transfer of the Greeks and genocide of the Armenians. But in the 1940s, the whole matter was taken up again on a much larger scale with the genocide of the Jews and others, and, after the war, the mass expulsion of the Germans from central and eastern Europe.

In short, in spite of this, the basic situation in large parts of Europe remained as before. Homogeneous national territorial states can still only be imposed at the same cost. And meanwhile international migration has created – or recreated – ethnic diversity even in states which previously, through the barbarism of the 1940s, had eliminated it. The former Yugoslavia demonstrates this. Concretely, the explosive issues today in Europe are issues that were created by the First World War and not before. Yugoslavia, the Croats and the Serbs in the same state, the Czechs and the Slovaks in the same state, and so on. This applies also in the explosive Soviet national problems which were of no significance before 1914. Neither the Caucasian nor the Baltic problem was in any important sense an historic problem of nationalism. Conversely, the historic problems of nationalism that were explosive or present before 1914 have been relatively quiescent today. The most obvious example is the Macedonian question in the Balkans, which only became explosive when – for reasons that had nothing to do with Macedonia – Yugoslavia fell apart; and also the Ukrainian question in the former Soviet Union, which similarly came to the fore only as the Soviet Union collapsed. In 1917 there was strong Ukrainian nationalism, though it was not separatist. There was no Baltic nationalism worth mentioning.

A brief note. Replaying 1918 not only creates instability and solves no problem – although actually in a transnational economy it becomes possible to think of an economically viable Slovakia and Serbia, as it was not between the wars – but it is actually dangerous to democracy. It is dangerous to culture. It is dangerous to freedom because the small nations, unlike the big nations, in establishing homogeneity insist on dominating their minorities.

The problem in Quebec is not directed against the English; it is directed against the Italians, the Greeks, the Inuit, the Native Americans who are forced to be culturally assimilated to French culture in Quebec. And the same is true in Slovakia, in Croatia, in Serbia and anywhere else.

A brief word about the second point: ghettoization. The modern pattern of migration produces, at least initially, a diaspora of ghettos, mostly urban. Democracy produces a machine for minority groups to fight effectively for a share of central or national resources, which is why the classic nationalist programme is so totally irrelevant to groups in this situation. Ghettoization is politically effective, which is why it develops so rapidly in countries like the United States. In recent New York elections, redistricting was specifically designed to produce minority representation, not only of ethnic minorities. For instance, in the West Village and Chelsea, it was designed to produce a specific territory of gay representation, and the candidate who won advertised himself as being not only gay, but HIV positive.

Mass migration also produces group friction. In extreme cases, it creates areas barricading themselves against hostile or unacceptable outsiders. This is worse than living side by side, as was possible in the past, within limits. But it is better than mutual massacre or the racist transformation of national politics, which we see in many European countries. In this respect, events in the United States are more acceptable than what is happening elsewhere. Racism in the United States tends to be less dangerous and less pervasive than in other countries because it is much more limited to a grassroots struggle, as opposed to countries like France or even countries with apparently no racist tradition, such as Sweden or Italy. Even when ghettoization turns into civil war at the grassroots, as in Northern Ireland, it has so far proved containable. It is one of the saddest paradoxes that in actual fact, in most sociological terms, Northern Ireland is a more peaceful, more stable and a more sane society than most of the rest of Britain, in spite of the fact that a certain number of people are being killed on the borders of these two ghettos.

The obvious negative side is that no common national ground may remain in the end by the division of the population of a state into self-contained sub-units. And, in fact, the ability which once provided the Democratic Party with its unity, namely the skill to forge a single unit out of ethnic diversity and, if you like, class unity, ceases to be valid. What we find today is the complete absence of the kind of concern with Americanization which one found in the United States in the 1880 to 1922 period. And this is a real problem. Possibly only in Australia, among the countries with mass immigration, does one find a basic concern for integrating and creating a sort of national unity.

We are today in an era of global and not only of European mass migration. It is potentially far bigger than we realize. The percentage of the demographic excess of the European population that migrated between 1880 and 1914 was enormous. Whereas today, even in Latin America, which has the largest mass emigration, it is tiny, relatively speaking, compared to what the Italian or Norwegian or Swedish emigration was in the earlier era. The potential is far greater. The United States, Canada and Australia are quite exceptional so far in permitting, with very little hindrance, free immigration of this kind. Everywhere else, even since the Gulf War, the response has been to close doors and barricade national gates, though this has not prevented the appearance of permanent and growing Third World minorities in most developed countries. The developed world is becoming a steadily tinier percentage of the globe. Between 1750 and 1900, it grew, demographically, absolutely and relatively from about 15 per cent of the world population to about a third of the world population. Since 1900, or more exactly since 1950, it has fallen. It is now back to 15 to 20 per cent, if one takes OECD countries as a percentage of global population. This is the rich world, the land of milk and honey and gold, towards which the poor of the world are naturally drawn, particularly in an international capitalist society theoretically encouraging free movement of the factors of production. What is more, they are being lured by the fact that the developed world, including the ex-socialist countries, do not reproduce themselves and therefore have a problem of labour shortage.

One possible solution to this situation is, of course, to refuse the strangers, to barricade ourselves. I think this is no longer actually possible. The second is an apartheid solution – to admit or accept these new immigrants, but to turn them into a permanent underclass. Whether this is possible any longer now that it has proved impossible even in South Africa is a matter of debate. The third is to allow it and to face a long-term, quite fundamental transformation – such as is happening in the United States, of course, where already in the big cities the majority of the population are of non-European and non-white origins. I do not think that this necessarily means the end of a basic culture, particularly a culture of the kind established in the United States. Essentially, the Roman Empire followed this particular strategy or was forced to follow this political strategy. But in the end, the area of the Roman Empire remains, to this day, culturally marked by the Romans, the Latin culture, whether in the religious or in the civilian form.

Finally, I draw your attention to simply one further possibility. Namely, that modern transportation and the modern globalization of the world make possible simultaneous, bi-national or multinational existence, such as, of course, many members of the upper middle class, especially academics, are already engaged in. There are people who habitually spend part of the year in one country, part of the year in another, without necessarily losing their roots. This may be happening not only at the upper level. There are already many people from Israel who habitually, while either remaining Israelis or permanent Israeli immigrants, spend many months each year in New York making a living and then return to Israel. I have myself come across a case of an Ecuadorian from Guayaquil who comes for six months to New York, earns dollars driving a cab, and then goes back home, where his wife is looking after their business in Guayaquil.

Where does this leave exclusive ethnicity, exclusive nationalism, the exclusive division of the world? I raise these questions not to answer them, because there is no answer. I raise them because they are problems that the left and the right must face today.

# 9

## *Working-Class Internationalism*

This paper distinguishes the problem of how
internationalist working-class parties related to the
policy of nation-states (especially in wars) from two
other aspects of working-class internationalism.
It discusses (1) the differences and similarities
between our internationalism and the bourgeois
and liberal-radical internationalism current in
the nineteenth century, and (2) the varieties of
internationalism existing with labour movements and
their membership. Under (1) it notes the operational
advantage of internationalism in labour struggles,
the specifically international organisation of labour
movements and its lack of interest in 'nation-building'.
Under (2) it warns about applying a rigid nationalist/
internationalist dichotomy, while nevertheless
underlining the significance of the movement's
opposition to chauvinism and racism.

I have the honour of opening the colloquium which has been
organized to mark the fiftieth anniversary of the International
Institute of Social History (founded in 1935), the greatest archive
and institute of its kind in the world. The speaker who opens such
a colloquium has one clear function: to offer congratulations,

on behalf of everyone who has even the slightest contacts with the study of labour and socialist movements anywhere in the world, and to wish the Institute and its collaborators and users another fifty years of equal success. Every one present at this colloquium knows the Institute and is profoundly indebted to its extraordinary and indispensable collections, to the work done by its collaborator or under its auspices and to the remarkable series of its publications. It would be absurd if I were to go into detail about what we already know and appreciate. But I cannot prevent myself from recalling that, but for the foundation of the Institute and the efforts of its pioneers, the extraordinary wealth of historical materials it contains, starting with the manuscripts of Marx and Engels themselves, might not even be in existence. That so many of them survived the tragic era of fascism and war is due to the men and women who decided to found and organize this Institute, to their labours, and to the many people, organizations and institutions in the Netherlands who made its foundation and continued life possible. May the second fifty years of the Institute be as fruitful and distinguished as its first half-century has been.

Beyond congratulating the Institute, the functions of the speaker opening this colloquium are not so clear. I do not wish to anticipate the proceedings of the next three days. However, it may be useful to reflect upon some of the ambiguities of the concept of 'working-class internationalism' as it has come to be understood or misunderstood. These are, I submit, of three kinds. *First*, it is not always clear how 'working-class internationalism', or more precisely the internationalism of the socialist movements speaking on behalf of the working class or claiming to, is related to other forms of internationalism of which there was plenty about in the nineteenth century. In other words, what is specific to the working class and its movements in the internationalist ideology associated with them. *Second*, by identifying the working class and working-class movement, we risk confusing different kinds or levels of internationalism existing within both. And *third*, there is the complex and passionately debated problem of how the internationalism of the working class, or its movements, or the movements claiming to speak on its behalf, relates to the nation, i.e. in practice the nation-states within which these classes and movements have their being; or how they ought to relate.

Practically all political debates about working-class internationalism are concerned with this third set of problems. They have been discussed with particular passion and urgency when states possessing such movements have gone to war with one another, and with even more passion since 1945, when even states claiming to be socialist have undertaken military operations against other socialist states. The Franco-German War of 1870–1 was, I think, the first in which the problem of working-class internationalism in a period of conflict between nations was publicly dramatized. I have placed this problem third, simply because it is unnecessary to underline its significance. I shall return to it later.

Meanwhile let me consider the first set of ambiguities, since it raises problems of theory and history which are too often overlooked. Internationalism is an integral part of the ideology of bourgeois liberalism and progress in the nineteenth century. One might go further and say that it is an integral part of all theories of social evolution. Is there a specific working-class version of it, and if so, in what does it consist?

The reason why this has not been much noticed, and it is not easy to recognize its considerable importance, is that this 'internationalism' exists, as it were, in the penumbra of the concept from which it is obviously derived, namely that of 'the nation' or 'nations'; and as everyone knows, one of the great puzzles of nineteenth-century intellectual history is that while the concepts or terms 'nation', 'nationality' or 'national', are very generally used by most thinkers, their meaning is far from clear. Certainly these terms are undefined in the *Communist Manifesto*. It is as though writers, in the period before the Marxist debates on 'the national question' began in the 1880s, generally felt that the terms were too obvious to require elucidation. As the English liberal Bagehot said of 'the nation': 'We know what it is when you do not ask us, but we cannot very quickly explain or define it.'

I am elsewhere attempting to analyse the nature of 'the nation' in the period of triumphant bourgeois-liberal ideology, and here I only want to sketch its connection with a kind of internationalism. To put the matter briefly, virtually all thinkers deriving from the eighteenth-century Enlightenment took the view that the evolution of human society proceeded from the smaller to the larger scale: from locality to region to state; from kin group to tribe to people – and eventually to a global society, globally organized, with a global culture, a *Weltliteratur*, perhaps even a single global language. Most, without arguing the case too precisely, would take it for granted that the phase of this evolution which coincided with bourgeois and liberal society was that of state and people – i.e. of 'the nation' and the nation-state. Or, more precisely, the nation-state sufficiently large to carry out its historic functions of economic, political and cultural development, which were held to include the exploitation of the undeveloped and backward parts of the globe. The force of historical evolution was on the side of *large* and therefore viable nationalities and their states, against small ones. Beyond them there undoubtedly lay the transnational or internationalist future of world society, to which even nationalists like Friedrich List claimed to look forward, and which generated a great deal of sincere but quite vacuous rhetoric. Internationalism and world society would be the child of a world of nations.

However, at this point a divergence may be noted among bourgeois ideologists. Liberal free traders argued, with Richard Cobden, that the development of capitalism already made the world in some senses a potential unity, so that the instauration of universal free trade would (or ought to) cut the ground from under the conflicts between states and peoples, and make wars impossible. Men should speak directly to men, or rather businessmen to businessmen, bypassing governments. International capitalism meant international peace and understanding *now*. This was not mere political rhetoric. Cobden and Bright opposed the Crimean War almost single-handedly on such grounds, and in 1914 two Liberal ministers (one was Cobden's biographer) actually resigned from the British government rather than support a war they believed to be unnecessary and wrong. On the other hand, ideologists representing less dominant capitalist economies than the British argued that, while the future undoubtedly belonged to a world society, the present belonged, and was likely to belong for a long time to come, to the formation of united states: a state of 30–60 million already offered the advantages which one day would be enjoyed by the whole world.

So much for the classic bourgeois-liberal internationalism. Perhaps one should add a word on two more radical-democratic concepts, also arising out of 'nations' or 'nationality', and peculiarly prominent in 1848, namely the idea of the fraternal reconciliation of nations or *Völkerverbrüderung*, and the idea of the right of nations to self-determination. Both, as is obvious, assume the prior existence of nations which are to fraternise or exercise self-determination. Neither are logically implied in bourgeois liberalism, for which the only 'nation' that exists is the nation-state and its body of citizens. Now fraternization between *individuals* makes sense, but hardly between states. As for self-determination, it is incompatible with the evolutionary theory I have just sketched.

Now it is clear that socialist theory, at least in its Marxist form, is one variant of this form of evolutionary theory. In Marx and Engels this process is specifically linked to the bourgeoisie:

Through its industry, its commerce and its political institutions [ ... ] is already working everywhere to drag the small, self-contained localities which only live for themselves out of their isolation, to bring them into contact with one another, to merge their interests, to expand their local horizons, to destroy their local habits, strivings and ways of thinking, and to build up a great nation [...] out of the many hitherto mutually independent localities and provinces.[1]

And, to cite the *Manifesto*, in turn it 'compels all nations, on pain of extinction, to adopt the bourgeois mode of production' and draws 'from under the feet of industry the national ground on which it stood', because capitalism creates a global economic system, a 'universal interdependence of nations'. And in turn intellectual production itself must become globalised; 'from the numerous national and local literatures there arises a world literature'.[2] What is more, to revert to Engels' reflections à propos of the *Sonderbund* war [the Swiss civil war], this process of development will imply the formation of a single supranational state: 'the democratic proletariat will not only have to centralise every country separately, but will have to centralise all civilised countries together as soon as possible'.[3] In short, the world of nations is an intermediate state on man's progress of localized to global existence, for Marx and Engels as well as for numerous non-socialist thinkers of their time. And other similarities between their view and prevailing contemporary liberal views about nations and global society are easily seen – for instance Engels' scepticism about the future of small or backward nationalities, which is shared by John Stuart Mill and many others.

It is worth noting, however, that in sharing this general view of social development, Marx's and Engels' internationalism is firmly rooted in a world of *nations*, i.e. of nation-states. The reason why the most famous internationalist injunction of all calls upon the workers of all countries to unite, is because they operate in different countries. What is more, 'the struggle of the proletariat with the bourgeoisie is at first a national struggle', at least in form, though not in substance, because 'the proletariat of each country must, of course, first of all settle matters with its own bourgeoisie', and indeed, it 'must first of all acquire political supremacy, must rise to be the leading class of the nation, must constitute itself *the* nation'.[4] In other words internationalism is not the absence of concern with the nation, a-nationalism or cosmopolitanism, but the overcoming of the limits of the nation.

I observe in passing that there are indeed movements, institutions and even social groups which are non-national or cosmopolitan, in that they simply do not recognize 'nations' either in the form of states or of nationalities, except as something which exerts *force majeure*. It would be absurd to speak of Islamic internationalism, since for the pious Muslim the political or ethnic entities to which other Muslims belong are in themselves no more significant than the colour of their eyes. What is alone significant is the faith which binds them together. The belief, which is, as we have seen, not Marx's alone, that a world system will emerge, as it were, through and on the other side of a world of nations, excludes such a-nationalism. And yet, for both bourgeois and proletarian – if in different ways – the world was not *only* 'a world of nations' but also, and directly, a world system, in which individual, class and general social interest could operate independently of, and across state, ethnic or any other lines and in conflict with interests defined in state or national terms. The very fact that there could be bourgeois liberals who fought imperialism and war on the grounds that they made no sense from a capitalist point of view proves the point, even if we do not accept their arguments. The existence of interests and struggles across state and ethnic frontiers therefore had to introduce, at least potentially, an element of cosmopolitanism, inasmuch as, say, class and movement ought to prevail over state and nation if the two were in conflict. And as we shall see, this was particularly clear in an internationally *organized* movement such as the working-class movement.

What, therefore, were the specifically proletarian elements in 'working-class internationalism'? It was not that it looked forward to the end of nations, or even to an era of universal brotherhood and peace. Free traders also expected this to be the result of abolishing restraints on free capitalist development, and Cobden would have agreed with Marx that 'National differences and antagonisms between peoples are daily more and more vanishing, owing to the development of the bourgeoisie, to freedom of commerce, to the word market,' etc.[5] The peculiarity of working-class internationalism, apart from a much more specific analysis of the development of capitalism and its overthrow, was threefold. *First*, it believed in the special role of the proletariat in the overcoming of national and state antagonisms, because as a class it 'had no country'. Or, in Engels' words on the occasion of the Festival of Nations in London, in 1845:

> [...] the proletarians in all countries have one and the same interest, one and the same enemy, and one and the same struggle. The great mass of proletarians are, by their very nature, free from national prejudices and their whole disposition and movement is essentially humanitarian, anti-nationalist. Only the proletarians can destroy nationality, only the awakening proletariat can bring about fraternisation between the different nations.[6]

No doubt the older Engels would not have wished to subscribe to every word of this youthful outburst, but it surely expresses his and Marx's permanent conviction that the collective interest of workers everywhere as workers, their conflict as proletarians with employers outweighed everything else. Internationalism was implied in class struggle.

Now it is easy to see that there is friction between this thesis and the other thesis by which 'the struggle of the proletariat against the bourgeoisie is at first a national struggle', waged in each country under the highly specific economic, political, institutional and other conditions of that state. The struggle of, say, the Italian, Spanish and Portuguese proletariat even today, when all belong to the European Economic Community, may be classified together as against the struggles of farmers, but they are not the *same* struggle, directed against the *same* enemy, in any operational sense; and where national segments of working classes have actually had to struggle against the *same* trans-national employer (e.g. Ford or General Motors), the difficulty of doing so through labour and trade union movements essentially organized for *national* operation, has been only too evident. Moreover, historical experience has shown that the young Engels' generous assumption about national prejudices is not true.

And yet no major or mass labour movement could have been formed with such an ideology unless something in it has represented what workers experienced as realities in their class situation. I think it can be shown that this was so, and I suggest it is a more interesting task of research to investigate the more positive appeal of working-class operational internationalism than to demonstrate, yet again, its obvious limitations. There is no time to pursue the subject, but I would just draw your attention to three things. *First*, the class struggle, in its most elementary but also spontaneous and rooted form of the trade union struggle *was* internationalist, insofar as any division along national, racial, or religious or other lines *inevitably* weakens the collective of workers in dispute with an employer or employers. (Of course workers do not *only* act as trade unionists; at other times and in other roles they may well act – if I may quote a particularly sad case – as Irish nationalists or Ulster Orangemen.) To this extent internationalism made sense, as it still does, especially in factories where workers of different national origins had to strike together in Vienna, Budapest as much as in the Rhondda. *Second*, we actually know that, in certain conditions which should be investigated, national and linguistic differences which might, or subsequently did, prove fatal to unity, were apparently insignificant. A powerful workers' movement in Vienna developed on a mixed German-Czech foundation, the Welsh coalfield was transformed from Welsh- to

English-speaking without any discernible national problems, and, most impressive of all, a single Belgian labour movement was built on the foundation of Flemish and French workers. The linguistic divisions which have since split every Belgian institution down the middle were apparently so insignificant that Emile Vandervelde and Jules Destrée in 1898 did not so much refer to the Flemish problem in their book *Le socialisme en Belgique*.

And *third*, we should not forget the extraordinary mobility of an era which sent thirty to forty million, mainly of future manual workers, into emigration, to make themselves into members of new countries and nations. However, neither should we forget the enormous numbers who came back, or permanently criss-crossed frontiers. All historians know that travelling men, emigrants and returned emigrants were the essence of early labour movements, since they provided so many of their cadres. The mind automatically turns from German journeymen who bring socialist ideas northwards from Germany, to English trade unionists like Tom Mann migrating for some years to Australia to organise workers there, to Norwegians like Martin Tranmæl bringing the experience of the IWW [Industrial Workers of the World] back from the USA to Norway, or Harry Bridges crossing the Pacific from Australia to lead general strikes in San Francisco. Socialist, communist and anarchist movements were full of leaders and militants who transferred readily from one movement to another. More than this: they contained persons who might actually be simultaneously leaders of labour movements in more than one country. Rosa Luxemburg, equally and contemporaneously involved in the politics of the German, Polish, All-Russian and international movements, is the most famous case in point.

The *second* specificity of working-class internationalism was that it was from the start organized as an international movement, because it was conceived as such. Without prejudice to earlier currents of internationalism in bourgeois or liberal revolution (e.g. in the 1820s) this tendency to international organization may be characteristic of proletarian as distinct from bourgeois movements. Bourgeois and democratic-radical *national* revolutions often had a sense that they possessed a mission for *world* liberation, as notably in the case of the French: but this kind of messianism was not confined to *la grande nation*. However, the centre of proletarian internationalism was not a revolutionary country, but, as it were, an international army of which national movements were seen as subordinate units. The international communist movement came to be dominated by the USSR because in 1917–23 revolution failed everywhere except in Russia. Lenin originally envisaged the transfer of the Communist International to Berlin. It is extremely unlikely that any French Jacobin would ever have conceived, even in theory, of another capital of the world revolution than Paris. I would suggest, by the way, that Marx has considerable personal responsibility for this transnational orientation of the movement. Without the memory of the First International there would have been no Second, and without the Second no Third. The regrettable decline of this tradition may tell us something about the historical fortunes of mass proletarian socialist movements. There is no longer any real equivalent to the old Internationals. And while mass proletarian socialist/communist parties appeared and grew in a large number of countries between the 1880s and the 1930s, hardly any new parties of this kind have emerged out of the working classes since then, in countries where they did not previously exist. This is very strikingly the case in the so-called Third World.

This throws light on a *third* peculiarity of working-class internationalism. Actual mass working-class parties and movements, as distinct from their leaders and theorists, were not particularly concerned with that 'nation-building' which Bagehot claimed to be the essential element in nineteenth-century history. In this respect they differed from the liberal bourgeoisie, which always saw itself as a potential ruling class to which the construction of a viable national economy was essential for capitalist development, at least in the nineteenth century. They also differed from petty-bourgeois and other nationalists, for whom the construction of their own nation as a political unit irrespective of size, was the overriding political objective. Both required some control over the state. To put it crudely, a liberal bourgeoisie or a nationalist movement which did not think in terms of government could concentrate its activities on little else except journalism, rhetoric and folklore, whereas a working class had plenty of other concrete tasks to keep it busy: for instance, collective bargaining. The limited scope of spontaneous class consciousness (or 'trade-union' consciousness as Lenin called it) was the reason why Marx insisted from the start that political organization with political power as its objective must be central to the working-class movement.

But the ideal-typical stance of most mass labour movements until the revolution – and how many were to get to this point – was oppositionist, that is to say it left the running of state and economic system to someone else, as the parties of the Second International did before 1914, and the communist parties in the capitalist countries did after 1917. The more a socialist movement was the organized expression of the immediate interests of a working class, the less it had to bother about the frictions between the governments of states, or with other national problems; unless, of course, its own internal affairs were affected by them.

Admittedly this did something to protect movements against state chauvinism, and it certainly made a public commitment to an internationalist ideology easier. But often it led to a tacit acceptance of bourgeois hegemony and working-class subalternity. In politics the major activity of the parties of the Second International was to win or assert full citizenship rights for workers. But what kind of political behaviour was to be expected from the citizen, was defined not by the workers' movement, but by the state: someone else's state. In 1914 when class-conscious workers in belligerent countries rushed to the colours in a spontaneous *levée en masse*, as was certainly the case in Britain, they did not believe themselves to be betraying their parties' convictions. Having won the right to be full members of their nation through their movement, they now behaved as full citizens were supposed to. For socialist leaders the outbreak of war and the collapse of their (Second) International in August 1914 were utterly traumatic. It is very doubtful whether the mass of labour and socialist workers felt the same conflict between the demands of their class consciousness and of their national citizenship. The same Welsh miners, who both followed revolutionary syndicalist leaders and also poured into the army as volunteers in 1914, brought their coalfield out in a solid strike in 1915, deaf to the accusation that they were being unpatriotic in doing so.

These observations on the limitations of working-class internationalism bring me to the need to distinguish the various types and strata of internationalism within working-class movements. At one extreme of these we find a small body of men and women to whom the states and the nation(alities) to which they belonged were genuinely irrelevant, the future revolution being, as it were, their only real 'country'. They are those Brecht refers to in his poem 'To Those Born After' when he wrote '*die Länder öfter wechselnd als die Schuhe*' (we changed countries more often than our shoes), remaining in the same territory wherever he or she found themselves.

In the Second International period we find such people frequently among anarchists, quite often as migrants or re-migrants from one national movement to another, notably among people born in eastern Europe. I am not thinking so much of people permanently assimilated into another national movement, like Kautsky, Hilferding and other Austrian-born German Social Democrats; or even of foreigners essentially associated with a movement not their own, like Dobrogeanu-Gherea with

Romania, Anna Kuliscioff with Italy or Charles Rappoport with France; but of figures like Luxemburg or Rakovsky who were, simultaneously or successively, important in several national movements. Such persons would clearly have put their energies with equal zeal into the struggle in Switzerland or Portugal if this had seemed politically desirable. In the Comintern period these international cadres became institutionalized, a process which has been excellently analysed by Aldo Agosti in the third volume of *Storia del Marxismo* [published by Einaudi]. Under the impact of the collapse of 1914 the Comintern deliberately developed this form of internationalism as a general and overriding obligation of all Communists, and not only Comintern cadres, in the form of loyalty to the international party line and the USSR. How far this duty was actually felt to be compelling outside the cadre of professional revolutionaries and functionaries is a question which still awaits much research. It is impossible to pursue it here. However, we may nevertheless distinguish between a minority of genuinely transnational cadres, whose nationality of origin was of merely biographical interest, and those who remained firmly identified with their nation, while unswervingly doing their duty as the International defined it for them.

I do not particularly wish to defend the elements of Franco-centricity to be found in the French Communist Party, or the Great-German assumptions to be found among harried and illegal cadres of the KPD confronted in the later 1930s by Austrian communists with theories about an Austrian nation. However, these examples undoubtedly prove that nationalist, even chauvinist reflexes in communist movements were not incompatible with absolute loyalty to the international line. It is this combination of effective internationalism with strong national identification which seems to be characteristic of the Comintern period. Once again, one is sadly obliged to note its decline, not only in working-class parties, but even in the states of 'real socialism'.

At the other extreme of labour movements we find those whose horizons were primarily national, and whose internationalism was insignificant in practice: Józef Piłsudski's PPS [*Polska Partia Socjalistyczna* – Polish Socialist Party] and Labour Zionism are familiar examples. Since the topic of this conference is not nationalism in working-class movements but internationalism, I shall only draw your attention to one curious and not insignificant fact. It is striking how often, especially in the period of the Second International, the movements and parties which de facto turned into the major representatives of their nation, or even its nationalist parties, were organizations originally founded not under nationalist but under socialist – i.e. by definition internationalist – auspices. One need mention only the Polish Socialist Party, the Social-Democratic Party in Finland, the Mensheviks in Georgia, the various Armenian nationalist bodies – and even to some extent the Bolsheviks in Latvia. The dialectic of internationalism, national and social liberation deserves more discussion than it has received.

Between these two extremes we find the parties and leaders who tried to cope, as best they could, with 'the national question' as it concerned the states within which they operated and their own parties. They have not always received their due, at least among those of us who were brought up on the official Bolshevik interpretation of the debates in which Lenin and Stalin took so prominent a part. Whatever we may think of Austro-Marxist theory on the matter, and the undoubted German national identification of the leading socialists in Cisleithania, I think the internationalist actions of Victor Adler and Otto Bauer stand up to scrutiny; though probably not those of Karl Renner. But at this point we must, briefly, return to the overlap between bourgeois and working-class internationalism which I noted at the outset of this essay. Some of the least social-patriotic behaviour among socialists in 1914 was to be found in Britain, where the Independent Labour Party, as distinct from Hyndman's Marxist Social Democrats, refused to support the war. But they did so as pacifists, drawing their inspiration chiefly from Liberal protestant non-conformity and Cobdenite rather than socialist internationalism.

Let me finally turn to the ordinary rank-and-file of the organized labour movements. What of their internationalism? I believe this is a senseless question. In the debate of political people, or ideologists, for whom nationalism or internationalism imply major political choices, the two concepts are regarded as mutually exclusive alternatives; just as for nationalists people belong under one national banner or another. Either–or. But as a description of political behaviour this is simply misconceived. In the first place many workers who joined labour movements had as yet no national identification and therefore the question of nationalism or internationalism did not arise. The Italian labour movement in 1914 consisted of people for many of whom being 'Italian' was as artificial a classification as being a member of the European Economic Community is today. They did not read, write or even talk the language, and while they could not escape the laws and officials of the Italian state, practically none of them had had even the right to vote for parliament for more than a year. They were not more internationalist than the French workers because they showed no enthusiasm for the war, and thus made it easy for their Socialist Party to oppose it. Why should an Italian government's war be their war?

In the second place, even if they did see themselves as members of some nation or nationality for certain purposes, they did not necessarily do so for other purposes, let alone for all purposes. It was and is perfectly possible for a man or woman to see themselves simultaneously as – I deliberately choose an extreme case – a proud Irishman, a member of the working class, a Catholic, a Kerryman, a member of the great clan of the O'Connells and a veteran of the Irish Guards of Her Majesty, stressing one identification or another according to the situation.

Thus Irish citizens, who enjoy voting rights in both Ireland and the UK, may be strong supporters of the British Labour Party in Birmingham but vote for Fianna Fáil and not the Irish Labour Party when they return to the Irish Republic. There are times when such a man may himself feel the obligation to choose one such identity and reject another, but it will almost certainly not be when a British or Irish politician thinks he must. We must never forget the multidimensionality of human beings in society. Moreover, even quite strong national identifications may not always have the political implications that governments and political parties read into them. Many a time Welsh nationalists have been disappointed that most of their countrymen, though passionately proud of their Welshness, do not believe that it implies support for a nationalist party.

In the third place, I have already suggested that the development of mass working-class movements paradoxically creates both national consciousness and international ideology *simultaneously*. In many ways what made Italian workers first feel that they were Italians, and not primarily Neapolitans or Pugliesi, was precisely that they identified with a Socialist Party or unions which represented all members of the new nation-state. It was through internationalist movements which operated on a nation-wide or state-wide scale that national consciousness first developed for many a proletarian. Once again, the one-dimensional alternative, 'either internationalist or nationalist', is inadequate for an understanding of the actual historical situation.

However, it *is* relevant in one crucial respect. Workers who joined a class party of the socialist kind certainly did not necessarily share, understand or even know much about the theory, the ideology or even the programme and policy of their leaders. But by identifying with their class through such a party, they undoubtedly accepted all or most of what that party told them, at least in theory, unless it was in head-on conflict with their own experience. In practice they may not have followed the party's injunctions, but in principle they saw them as right and legitimate. The party told them much that some of them would not find particularly congenial, for instance about the equality of women. The party also told them about the brotherhood of man and the equality of races. In practice it may have compromised and prevaricated: more – much more than, say socialist women have expected of the party of Engels and Bebel. It might for instance, as in Austria, make more, much more, concession to the anti-Semitism of supporters by playing down the extent to which its leaders were Jewish, just as the French Communist Party in the Second World War undoubtedly made concessions to French chauvinism in playing down the extent to which the active anti-fascist resistance in France was the work of foreigners.

Yet, when all such fully justified criticism have been made, the fact remains that the working-class movements did teach, by precept, example and practice, the equality of peoples and the brotherhood of man – and woman: Jew and Cossack (as in Babel's wonderful stories), Pole and Frenchman, Indian and English – the Communist MP for Battersea, one of the oldest strongholds of labour politics, was an Indian. In doing so, the movement, a school of civility for workers as well as the expression of their class interests, kept in check old, spontaneous, perhaps atavistic forms of groups, hatred and national friction. If socialism and anti-Semitism diverged, it is for this reason: for there is plenty of evidence in the late nineteenth and early twentieth century that anti-Semitism was not only in Bebel's phrase, the socialism of idiots, but also not by any means instinctively alien to the socialism of proletarians. Where it succeeded, it kept in check the anti-Irish sentiments of the English. It is when the old all-embracing loyalty of class to its party and its ideology dissolves, when the ideological package becomes undone, as it were, then the individual items within it can be taken and left individually, then the effect of the old loyalties can be recognized. In the late 1960s public opinion in Britain was shocked to see demonstrations of London dockers, the most solid of

Labour loyalists, supporting the racist demands of a politician [Enoch Powell] who demanded the repatriation of coloured immigrants. We were shocked not because class-conscious proletarians were revealed to have racist beliefs. That was sad, but not totally unexpected. What was shocking was that on the issue of racism they were prepared publicly and actively to support a *Conservative* politician against their class party. So long as the hold of the class party or class movement on the class remained firm, racism, where it existed among the backward elements of the workers, could only exist in a private, unofficial, shamefaced manner. Loyalty to parties committed to racial equality and internationalism forbade its public emergence. It is the slow, and in the past few years the rapid, erosion of the bond between class and classical working-class parties in many countries, which has allowed such sentiments to emerge, or re-emerge, into the open – especially among young workers. This is tragic. There can be no real internationalism of any kind without a belief not just in the equality of nations and races in the abstract, but in the equality of the West Indian, Pakistani, Bangladeshi working in a factory or an office with the English, Scots, Welsh and Irish.

This is why the flag of internationalism in labour movements must be held high, even today when the storms of history threaten to tear it to tatters. That is why movements like the African National Congress in South Africa deserve our admiration as well as our support: for against racist white rulers and racist or tribalist black rebels, it has won the leadership of the oppressed African people on the basis of a platform of non-racialism: of equality of African and Indian, coloured and white in a free South Africa. In this internationalism there lies the only hope, small and faint though it is, for the future. And that is why the International Institute has done well to celebrate its fiftieth anniversary by inviting us to reflect collectively on this theme.

# Working-Class Internationalism

# Notes

1  Friedrich Engels, 'The Civil War in Switzerland' [1847], in Karl Marx
   and Friedrich Engels, *Collected Works*, vol. 6 (Moscow, 1976), pp. 367–74,
   p. 372.
2  Karl Marx and Friedrich Engels, 'Manifesto of the Communist Party',
   in Marx and Engels, *Collected Works*, pp. 477–519, p. 488.
3  Engels, op. cit., p. 373.
4  Marx and Engels, op. cit., pp. 495, 502, 503.
5  Ibid., p. 503.
6  Friedrich Engels, 'The Festival of Nations in London (To Celebrate the
   Establishment of the French Republic, September 22, 1792)' [1845], in
   Marx and Engels, *Collected Works*, vol. 6, pp. 3–14, p. 6.

# 10

## *Defining Nationalism: The Problems*

### I

Nationalism is probably the most powerful political phenomenon of our century, and one whose importance continues to grow, but analysis has found it remarkably hard to come to grips with it. The literature about it, other than the purely descriptive, is on the whole unsatisfactory and frustrating. Virtually everything that has been written by nationalists (at least about their own nations) is question-begging and therefore negligible. Until recently, most of what has been written by non-nationalists has considered nationalism in some sense intrusive and disturbing. Like that Roman soldier who threatened to blot out Archimedes' diagrams, it was there, real and powerful, and one had to come to terms with it. Also like him, it was fundamentally outside the analytic models of the students concerned. If it had not obtruded itself, they would have been happy to take no notice of it.

Moreover, a considerable proportion of all serious analytical writing on 'the national question' was inevitably concerned with problems of definition, and with the associated activity of demythologizing conventional views about the subject. Criticism was tempting and easy. What nationalists said and say about nations and nationalism, especially their own, is generally so unconvincing to anyone who does not share their emotional commitments, and may be so inconsistent with rational enquiry, as inevitably to provoke extended expressions of scepticism, muffled only by politeness, diplomacy or caution. On the other hand, the difficulty of coming to analytical grips with the problem has meant that most definitions of 'nations' and 'nationalism' have been empirical, and all of them, as can readily be shown, partial or inadequate. The search for objective criteria of nationhood, singly or in combination, quickly breaks down. Is its basis territorial, linguistic, ethnic, historic, or something else – or a combination of these? Exceptions can always be found, if not today then tomorrow. As for the subjective definitions, these are tautological or *a posteriori*. To define a nation by the existence of 'national consciousness' or some analogous sense of solidarity between its members, merely amounts to saying that a nation is what behaves like a nation, or alternatively, that it cannot be predicted but only recognized. Able thinkers have found it difficult to escape from this frustrating predicament.

The most fruitful approach to 'the national question' has undoubtedly been historical. If nations and nationalism are seen as phenomena which develop within a specific historical situation and are determined by it, a good many of our difficulties disappear. We can abandon the search for permanent, let alone eternal, characteristic of either or both, and we shall not be surprised to find that phenomena which converge from different starting points and in different circumstances towards a single objective (let us say, for argument's sake, the 'nation-state'), show substantial variations, if we take a cross-section of them at any given moment. Historically oriented theories of nationalism have therefore been the most useful. Yet even the two most popular varieties of these, Marxism and the group of interpretations covered by the term 'modernization', have their weaknesses.

Marxism has suffered, because, while recognizing nation-alism as a phenomenon arising in the 'bourgeois epoch' it has, largely because of a deep-seated lack of sympathy with it, under-estimated its importance and persistence. It is true that since Lenin, Marxists have recognized and analysed its revolutionary historic significance, and have stressed its political force. Though grossly neglected in the academic literature, the writings of the Leninist tradition of Marxism constitute a major advance in our understanding of the problem, especially as regards the libera-tion movements of colonial and semi-colonial peoples, and the struggle of the European nations against fascism. On the other hand, it is plainly wrong to regard nationalism as a phenomenon *confined* to the bourgeois epoch, or to analyse phenomena power-ful enough to have split the international communist movement in the past decades as mere (petty) bourgeois survivals.

The 'modernization' theories, on the other hand, have suf-fered not merely from the extreme primitivism of their basically single-step model of history, but from their even more striking failure to predict. (I leave aside the question whether such models have any serious predictive value.) Marxism did indeed predict some very important matters, notably the fusion of social and national elements in the liberation struggles of the present century, and the historical importance of such movements in the non-European countries. It failed to analyse 'the national ques-tion' in certain situations, notably those following upon social revolutions. 'Modernization', insofar as it considers 'national consciousness' as 'but one facet' of this process, which is in turn defined in such simple uni-directional terms as 'expanding control over nature through closer interaction among men', must naturally be puzzled by the characteristic current form of western nationalism, which is divisive rather than integrative.[1] 'Modernization' has undoubtedly led political scientists to pay greater attention to the problem of 'nations' than anyone else, or perhaps it would be better to say that the great movements of the 'underdeveloped' countries since the Second World War have led them to take an interest in the complex of problems of which 'nations' are one, unfortunately often with conceptually inadequate tools. Still, the historians are hardly in a position to feel superior, since they have, with few exceptions, neglected the subject shamefully.

The following notes will therefore not discuss the past analytical literature at length. Readers will recognize easily enough where it follows what has already been written and where it diverges from it.

## II

In defining 'the national question' it is more profitable to begin with the concept of 'the nation' (i.e. with 'nationalism') than with the reality it represents. This is not to deny that 'nations', whatever they are, are real, though often they are the products of nationalist movements or nation-states rather than their foundation. The 'nation' as conceived by nationalism, can be defined prospectively; the real 'nation' can only be recognized *a posteriori*. So it is convenient to begin with the first. We know what Mazzini thought a nation was or ought to be, and the objective datum for our investigation is his programmatic idea, which need not, and in fact did not, correspond to the facts he supposed it to represent. We do not know what the 'nations' of his time were, or if they existed in the modern sense, and neither did Mazzini, whose own view of the future structure of a Europe of nations would be rejected by far more nationalist movements than would accept it.[2]

The following propositions about 'the nation' in this programmatic sense may be put forward. They represent not what nationalists actually thought, but the implicit socio-political content of their aspirations.

The 'nation' is a historically novel construct, characteristic of the period since the late eighteenth century, though no doubt anticipations or a few earlier examples may be discovered by those who wish to. Its novelty consists in the combination of two main assumptions.

The first of these is that the bonds of loyalty to (or characteristic of) the 'nation' are not merely superior to all others, but in a sense replace them, so far as political obligation is concerned. A man is no longer definable as the locus of a complex of multiple, possibly overlapping, probably separable, loyalties, but overwhelmingly in terms of a single one, his 'nationality'.

The second of these is the belief that this single collectivity of 'the people' or 'the nation' must find its expression in an independent and sovereign 'nation-state', preferably containing a homogeneous population composed only of members of its 'nation' using a single language.

'The nation' is therefore a combination of elements which have at first sight no necessary or even probable connection: on the one hand those of structural 'modernization', i.e. the territorial state and the transformation (or simplification) of socio-political relations within it; on the other, the appeal to a variety of means of asserting or symbolizing group membership and solidarity in the most emotionally charged personal sense, most of which are deliberately archaic in form, reference or derivation. One might go further and say that before the 'national' era, which, as the very term United Nations demonstrates, has tended to identify the concepts of 'nation' and 'sovereign state', the various 'national' solidarities had only a casual connection, and were not supposed to have any special connection, with obligations to the state centre.[3]

The assumptions discussed above imply, as has often been noted, a strong democratic and egalitarian element, as least within each nation. Political nationalism is revolutionary in its origins. Nationality-citizenship is therefore particularly effective in disrupting traditional hierarchies and ties of dependence. It is, at least potentially, not merely a political device but a movement.

Since nationalisms characteristically define their 'nations' in terms of what they consider natural, permanent, traditional

or even eternal, their revolutionary novelty as a political programme is obscured. 'Nations' are not so much invented as
composed and developed out of pre-existing historical materials, generally with quite different socio-political functions. It is
easy to demonstrate that such concepts as territory, language,
history, culture, even ethnic unity, did not mean the same in the
European fifteenth century as in the twentieth, had quite different functions, if any, and were not necessarily connected with
each other, and even less with a particular state. The novelty of
nationalist procedures can be traced even through their most
traditionalist rhetoric. Thus the most powerful appeal to group
solidarity in modern nationalist movements and states, the met-
aphor of 'kinship', is at once the most ancient and operationally
the least relevant to 'national' social and political systems, in
which actual kinship plays only the most subordinate or marginal role, where it is not actually dysfunctional. Yet it is the
persistent, one might almost say the basic, theme of nationalist
rhetoric. The nation is the motherland or fatherland; its members are brothers. They are linked by ties of 'blood' and 'race'
(i.e. by supposed biological ties) which exclude non-members,
by a common 'home', with common physical and mental furniture whose full meaning cannot be understood by others; they
possess common ancestors, and a common language which is,
almost by definition, inaccessible to those not sharing the family
heritage ('*traduttore-traditore*' is not merely a pun, but a deeply
ambiguous phrase). But it may be observed that the kinship
model adopted, at least in European nationalisms – there has
been little research in this field, so we can only speak with great
caution – seems to be the simple nuclear family, rather than
extended kinship. 'Cousins' ('our American cousins') do not
really belong; a 'family of nations', such as used to form part of
the staple of British imperialist rhetoric, is very different from
a fatherland. In a word, the 'family' of such rhetoric has little
in common with the kind of kinship which actually produced
and implied group loyalty and mutual aid in societies in which

blood really was thicker than water. The conceptual framework of even the most archaizing nationalist argument, tends to be very far from the real past.

## III

Is there a functional connection between the apparently so disparate sets of elements which make up the 'nation-state'? Nineteenth-century observers assumed so, without much thought, and the theorists of 'modernization' have made their most useful contribution in attempting to demonstrate (though not always to explain) it. They have done so by making the nation a function of the development of the modern state (by which we may understand the state in the era of capitalist development, or, more broadly, of the development of all industrial economies). State-building, in modern terms, is 'nation-building'. The analysis rests on the undeniable 'great transformation' of states since the European middle ages.[4] Speaking generally, the 'territorial state' which has developed since then, at first without 'national' implications, later commonly with them, substitutes a unified territorial base for the previous political systems for which this was not essential (any more than it is essential today for units of economic ownership such as a corporation or an estate), a single set of standardized institutions and values for a multiplicity of unstandardized ones, and a single set of direct linkages between a central government (with growing, and eventually total, power) and the individual citizen for a complex of indirect linkages, which run parallel to, or replace, the direct relation between 'centre' and 'periphery'. The early versions of the territorial state may have been unable to realize this programme to the full – even France in 1789 had not quite achieved the sixteenth-century absolutist slogan *Un roi, une loi, une foi* (One King, One Law, One Faith), but that is another question.

Why this model of the state came to be adopted – probably for the first time in history, at least in polities of such size – in the period of developing capitalism, is a question which cannot be discussed here, though we may observe in passing that it has not been irrelevant to capitalist economic development. It may well be argued that something like this kind of territorial state was essential to it. However, granted that such a type of state was to be constructed, models requiring it to be infused with a 'national' content can readily be set up. A familiar ideological version of such a model is Rousseau's argument, taken up by the French Revolution. The 'nation', which is the sovereign people, cannot tolerate intermediate and sectional interests and corporations between itself and its members. But by implication this very elimination of other centres of loyalty makes the relation of loyalty of citizen to 'nation' the only valid, and therefore the strongest, of his emotional-political commitments. It is the content of the other 'civic religion' which the community needs. There is no difference between *'Gemeinschaft'* and *'Gesellschaft'*, because the only valid *Gemeinschaft* (community) is the *Gesellschaft* (society), organized as the polity. Free man equals citizen. It is more irrelevant that Rousseau himself did not think in terms of modern nation-states, for such arguments were applied to them.

They can readily be translated into less ideological terms. A territorial state which functions through a direct linkage between the individual citizens and a strong centre must develop a set of motivations in the citizens which (a) give them a primary and overriding sense of obligation towards it and (b) eliminate or sidetrack the various other obligations which they feel towards other groups and centres within or outside it. The most obvious way to do this is to establish a sense of identity with it, and the most effective way is to transfer the strongest bonds which hold men together from other poles of attraction to the state. It then becomes not merely the emotional equivalent of family, local community, etc., but the family or community itself – and the elimination or demotion of the other centres leaves a void which the symbols of patriotism can fill. (It is probably no accident that the improvised slum communities of immigrants in

187

Chilean cities, drawn from a variety of uprooted countrymen, establish their identity by hoisting the national flag.) The need to provide the citizen with this sense of obligation is obvious, and all the more urgent when the modern territorial state requires mobilizing many of its citizens directly and individually, rather than through the habitual pre-industrial mechanism of relatively autonomous intermediary bodies or superior authorities. Military conscription, for instance, raises the problem in an acute form. Recent research has demonstrated that the percentage of draft evasion in the France of the 1820s was highest in Corsica, in the south and in Brittany, and lowest in the relatively developed north-east of the country, where identification with 'France' was traditionally greater than elsewhere. (It is no historical accident that Joan of Arc came from Lorraine and not, say, the Gironde.)

In European history the process of making such transfers is normally one of adapting and broadening (or changing) existing elements of loyalty, and this obscures the novelty of the phenomenon. There is a formal continuity between the 'France' or even the 'Italy' of nationalism and the political, cultural or other entities bearing this name in the past, so much so that we are struck by surprise at the information that in 1860 the percentage of citizens in the newly united kingdom who actually spoke Italian at home, and not merely (when they knew it at all) used it as a language of literate culture or a lingua franca for communicating with Italians from other regions, probably did not exceed 2.5 per cent. The case is much clearer in a country like the USA, where few of the traditional raw materials for nationalism were available at the time of its revolutionary creation, but where nevertheless the transfer has been made – and in part deliberately engineered (e.g. by the use of the flag as a ritual centre for the daily reaffirmation of national loyalty in schools). Such an example strengthens the argument that some kind of national loyalty is essential to make a modern territorial-centralized state function, and has

Defining Nationalism: The Problems

to be constructed where the materials for adaptation are not available. Where there is no old wine to put into a new bottle, some new liquor must be brewed.

But need this consist of the familiar brew of 'patriotism'? And if so, what are the precise elements of this brew which actually produce the desired effect? The first question cannot at present be answered, except in the general term that any state of the type discussed requires some kind of 'civic religion'. So far none of the alternatives to national patriotism have worked for any length of time, but it ought to be added that, with the single exception of the Soviet Republic in its initial years, no alternative has been seriously tried on any large scale. One might also point out that, so long as the states, set up on whatever principles, have to coexist with other sovereign states, their 'civic religion' cannot but emphasize those things which distinguish their citizens from those of other states. To that extent they provide a natural breeding ground for national patriotism, at least insofar as the common factors stressed are similar to those used to define, or rationalize, national loyalties in more orthodox cases.[5]

This brings us to the second question – a remarkably difficult one, since, with the probable exception of common territory and political organization, the actual content of nationalism *in existing states* may be almost wholly constructed *a posteriori*. None of the commonly accepted criteria are indispensable, or need exist prior to the state: language, common culture, religion, traditions or history, let alone 'race'; even the nation's common economy may follow rather than precede its state. It is by no means established that any combination of them need predate the establishment of the national state. Admittedly cases where some of the more obvious criteria are absent – e.g. multilingual nations such as Switzerland – are rare, and probably confined to certain geographical-historical situations.[6] The contemporary liability of old-established nation-states, in which autonomist and even separatist movements emerge among groups long believed to have been integrated into a single 'nation' (e.g.

189

France) or to have accepted a common economy and polity (e.g. Britain), illustrates the point.

Language is today the commonest de facto criterion of nationhood. At least it is hard to think of a nationalist movement which does not put it forward in some form. Yet there are numerous rival nations sharing the same language (e.g. Latin America), and there are speakers of the same literate idiom who may decide not to 'belong' to their co-linguists, as the Austrians have done since the Second World War, having previously considered themselves German, at least in the opinion of all their political parties with the exception of the Communists in the later 1930s. Conversely, there are more cases than is usually realised, of 'nations' whose common language was the product rather than the precondition of nationalism. The extreme case is Israel, whose national language had virtually to be invented for purposes of modern secular use.[7]

Our question is therefore impossible to answer at present. All that can be said is that, even where the common criteria of belonging to a state are constructed on entirely non-traditional lines (and even when they may actually be deliberately ecumenical in their ideological content), the very fact of their being the possession of one state among several others, is likely to infuse them with a 'national' or 'nationalist' element. 'Americanism', whatever its present political connotation, was originally a universal programme as well as a definition of what the citizen of the USA ought to represent: an invitation to all men to become Americans if they so chose, as well as an ideal description of those who already were. This has not prevented it from turning into a strongly nationalist slogan.[8] It would therefore seem that the best way to avoid states generating their own nationalism is either to merge them all into a global federation, or to have a form of socio-political organization quite different from the modern territorial-centralised one. There is no precedent for the former. As for the latter, there are plenty of precedents, though their circumstances were so different that they can prove nothing except that there are theoretical alternatives to the modern form of state. How likely humanity is to follow either or both these roads, is quite another question.

## IV

It is, as we have seen, not difficult to construct a model of the state which will generate nationalism. This model may well have a certain explanatory power, but it is unfortunately evident that it does not apply to a large part of the phenomena which are patently 'nationalist', namely those who are not functions of an already existing state, notably the movements of national self-assertion and liberation, especially those not linked to an existing or even a historically remembered polity (i.e. what nineteenth-century terminology called the 'unhistoric nations').

Such phenomena are, once again, extremely difficult to analyse, because we know so little about 'national consciousness', and even if we knew more, its social and ideological components would normally be very hard to disentangle. As soon as the phenomenon of 'nationalism' becomes politically so noticeable as to attract the attention of students it emerges – at least since the French Revolution – as a *programme*: in the increasingly common extreme case, as the programme of establishing a sovereign nation-state with certain conventional characteristics.

Now in the first place in the past century such a programme has been adopted almost automatically by all emerging nationalist movements, an example of what the economists call the demonstration effect. We do not know what programmes such movements would have formulated at any stage of their development, had the attraction of this prestigious model from the advanced world not been so great. Its standardised versions conceal many possible divergences between such movements, just as Roman Catholicism and communism have in their time concealed substantial variations between the Catholicism and communism of different regions. In the second place, such a programme is normally formulated and adopted by particular groups within a population, who provide the pioneers, ideologists, leaders, organizers and very often the political spokesmen of their 'nationalism'. The remainder of the population, in becoming 'nationalist', therefore buys a pre-selected package of miscellaneous goods. To acquire one is to acquire all. Support for any form of nationalism therefore normally appears to imply support for one particular kind.

How great these masked divergences may be, is sometimes revealed by time. Thus before 1947 support for the expulsion of the British from India implied, for all except the followers of the Muslim League, support for a unified all-Indian state, which was the programme of the leading cadres of the national movement. It has since become clear (though this was actually anticipated earlier by some Marxist students) that this demand masked a powerful current in favour of linguistic states, which was neither envisaged nor accepted by the Indian National Congress. One need hardly add that even the all-Indian nationalism which emerged when the local and regional activists and bosses were revealed as an effective political force in politics, proved to be quite different from the ideology and programme of the small group of largely westernized évolués who previously provided the programme and charismatic national leadership of the movement. Gandhi, for instance, favoured Hindi as the 'national language' of a free India because a nation needed a common language, and it seemed hardly conceivable that English, the imperial idiom, should be retained for this purpose, even supposing that it had been spoken by more than a tiny minority of the educated. Hindi, though admittedly not ideal – it was spoken by less than half of the population – was the least implausible candidate. Coming from a native Gujarati speaker, who was pretty certainly far more fluent in English than in Hindi, Gandhi's view was presumably unbiased by linguistic loyalties. The briefest glance at the present state of the movement in favour of Hindi reveals a very different situation, carrying a much higher emotional charge, and implying political consequences very different from those envisaged by Gandhi.

Even if we overcome such difficulties, sheer massive ignorance of what actually happens when nationalist movements appear and grow, still bedevils us, thanks to the gross neglect of the subject by historians. (It has proved as disastrous to leave the history of nationalism to nationalists as that of railways to railway enthusiasts.) The social, economic, even the ideological, analysis of the pioneers and early cadres and supporters of such movements has hardly been begun for Europe; and there has been almost no comparative study in this field. Even greater darkness encompasses mass nationalism, especially when this meant the change of meaning of an existing term rather than the formulation of a new one. So long as this is the case, much about nationalism must remain a matter for speculation rather than analysis.[9]

Fortunately one quite first-rate piece of comparative historical analysis has been done recently by a Czech worker on a selection of national movements among small European nationalities – Czechs, Slovaks, Norwegians, Finns, Estonians, Lithuanians and Flemings.[10] This throws much light on our problems, all the more so as [Miroslav] Hroch's results appear to converge with recent work on the apparently very different problem of peasant movements and revolutions.[11] In the following paragraphs I am greatly indebted to this excellent study.

Hroch divides the development of nationalist movements into three phases, of which he considers only phase A (when it is confined to a group of intellectuals without wider influence or even much ambition to mobilize mass support) and phase B (when a group of 'patriots' already attempt systematically to spread 'the national idea' but without as yet penetrating to any extent into the masses). Phase C begins when there is evidence of such mass penetration, as in Bohemia from 1848.

What is interesting about his work is not so much the excellent comparative analysis of the social, age, etc., composition and origins of both the 'patriots' and the circles directly affected by their agitation in phase B, as the geographical analysis, which seeks to define the areas of a 'national' territory within which the agitation is particularly intense or firmly established. National activity was of course rather unevenly distributed at this stage, but normally the zone of maximum nationalism formed (with some qualifications determined by the urban pattern) a fairly coherent and compact area.

Purely geographic, administrative, and linguistic factors and patterns of human settlement appeared to play no predominant role in determining the formation of such areas. (On the other hand, education – especially the density of village schools – was significant, though not all well-schooled areas developed intense national activity.) Economic factors clearly played a highly significant role. However:[12]

1. National zones were not areas in which industry or pre-industrial manufactures were of central importance. They were dominated by small-scale artisan production for the local needs of towns and the peasant hinterland.
2. They were situated in the most fertile part of the national territory (notably in regions of cereal production, sometimes combined with industrial crops).
3. Agrarian production, though no longer part of self-sufficient economies of the medieval type, was distributed through local markets and only through these linked with more distant markets.
4. They consisted of areas whose economic activities and social structure were affected by the influence of the civilization of a rising industrial society, but which were not themselves the main bearers of these processes of industrialization.[13]

In brief, these European national movements emerged first in regions of *intermediate* social change: neither in the traditional peasant regions so remote from the 'new times' that the very concept of 'country' or 'nation' could hardly arise nor in the areas already transformed. The growing suburbs of the Walloon towns, swelled by mass immigration from the Flemish countryside, remained notably uninterested in the Flemish nationalist movement. Similarly, the nationalist activists and supporters of phase B tended to be socially intermediate: weakest among the urban and rural poor and the workers, weak also among entrepreneurs and large merchants, not to mention the higher strata of the old regimes. One might say that such movements tended to take root first in areas (and perhaps strata) for whom 'modernization' was sufficiently present to present problems – not necessarily problems of life or death – but not sufficiently advanced to offer solutions. The well-known phenomenon of an over-production of school and university graduates, whose possibilities of employment and upward social mobility were therefore inhibited, is a special case of such a situation. (With certain exceptions, the 'patriots' of the movements studied were predominantly the sons of parents from the lower ranks, who had risen just about as far as persons of such parentage could.)[14] More generally, as Hroch does not fail to point out, we may observe awareness of 'the difference between the old-style petty producer and modern industrial production, between the petty market and the great market, between the petty-bourgeois idyll and the impersonal, harsh character of the rising civilisation of modernity'.[15]

There is an interesting analogy between these suggestions and Wolf's persuasive argument that the major force of peasant revolutionary movements lies in the 'middle peasants', the rural strata most firmly rooted in traditional agrarian society, fighting to maintain or re-establish the customary way of life – against a growing threat rather than an already accomplished disruption. Those already integrated into the new society (whether as its beneficiaries, like capitalist farmer-peasants, or as its victims, like the rural proletarians), or those who occupy marginal positions within it (like certain sections of the 'village poor'), are less likely to provide a sufficient force of negation.[16] Both early nationalist movements and peasant movements appear subjectively as defensive reactions against a process of (threatened rather than achieved) social transformation. Yet they cannot but be its vehicle. The 'programmes' of both are not merely impracticable but in a sense historically irrelevant, whether they are formulated with great precision, as among the peasants of Emiliano Zapata's Morelos in Mexico, or in terms of vague and barely defined aspirations, as among nationalists. Hence, insofar as such organized movements establish themselves firmly, it is by means of methods, ideas and leadership which belong to the new world, even when their object (like Gandhi's spinning wheels) may be to restore or preserve the old. Insofar as they are historically effective, their effect is at odds with their intentions. But here we are concerned not with results but with motivations.

The situation which stimulated the nationalist defence reactions and is best known to historians, was that of the advancing capitalist market economy and market society. It may be that this provided an unusually favourable breeding ground for 'nations', not only because the medium-sized 'nation-state' provided obvious advantages for 'progress' and the development of the middle class – or alternatively, because the states it replaced were more often than not backward, wrongly structured or both[17] – but also because bourgeois society in the form of liberal capitalism destroyed the older solidarities, communal bonds and structures of society continuously, ruthlessly and as a matter of principle, while deliberately putting nothing in their place except the pursuit of self-interest. During the time it did so, it provoked a defensive, sometimes a militant, nostalgia for older collectivities, notably among the strata which found themselves unable to benefit adequately as individuals from the new society (unlike successful capitalist entrepreneurs and higher professionals) or to evolve their own modern collectivities (as workers did through the labour movement). In Germany and German-Austria we can trace the rise of nationalist, anti-Semitic, potential mass movements among such strata in the last third of the nineteenth century as a double reaction against liberalism and social democracy. After it had done so, it left a void which 'the nation' could fill symbolically.

Yet it does not follow that reactions of this type are confined to this particular historical situation. History does not come to a stop when the state defined by some political scientists as 'modern' has been reached. Social disruption continues, with occasional bouts of particularly drastic change, such as that which has decimated those resistant strata, the peasantry and the traditional small-shopkeeper-type petty bourgeoisie in western Europe since the 1950s. Whenever it threatens the viability of institutions, values and practices within existing social systems, even those formed to come to terms with an earlier bout of change, the pattern of reaction may recur. All the things which can be sheltered under the large conceptual umbrella of 'the community', the set of directly perceived primary social groups and relationships, seem particularly vulnerable. They must be reinforced or replaced, if only symbolically, by something that purports to perform the same function. It need not necessarily take the form of a 'nation', though this has the advantage of an apparently precise delimitation externally ('us' against 'the foreigners') and almost total lack of precision in its internal definition, so that it can simultaneously contain the most changing and contradictory interests and aspirations. However, even if it did not have these advantages, once the stereotype of 'the nation' has been established and reinforced by prestige and a prevalent pattern of international political structure, it probably contains enough force to absorb and assimilate a variety of other expressions of communal nostalgia. Pakistan was clearly not the result of a 'national' movement, but both the original movement, the state, and doubtless the subsequent Pakistani patriotism have evidently been assimilated to the prevalent pattern.[18] Moreover, the very construction of internationally homogeneous nation-states strengthens the 'nationalist' appeal among those groups which are being homogenized, or whose separate communal existence – often institutionally recognized – loses its function. Pluralist polities become monolithic nations with 'minorities', providing twentieth-century governments with headaches from which their pre-industrial ancestors rarely suffered.

The relation of nationalism to the social processes which provoke it, may thus differ widely, though the phenomenon itself appears to remain the same. Thus the characteristic 'nation-building' of the nineteenth century tended to run parallel with the characteristic trend of economic and social development, the creation of larger homogeneous units out of (economically and administratively) smaller heterogeneous ones; so much so that quite a few examples of potential 'nationalism' which diverged from this trend tended to escape wider notice – like the Bretons or the Catalans. In the mid-twentieth century the two trends run at an angle to each other, except insofar as the continuing tendency of economic and political units to grow further in size, power over their subjects or clients, and planned bureau-cratization may have taken them to a size beyond the optimal one for administration and management, or beyond that with which human beings can cope as participants, producing some movement towards decentralization and devolution. Still, by and large the tendency towards gigantism continues (it is, by the way, no longer as closely linked with nation-states as before), while the tendency of nationalism has been increasingly to break up large units into smaller ones.

Where, for instance, are the contemporary equivalents of the unifying national movements of the period from 1815 to 1950 – e.g. the German, Italian, Southern Slav, Indian or Chinese? Conversely we are today familiar with nationalisms which seek to disrupt established 'modern' economies, often of no great size, sometimes with a long history of national integration.

Their success in doing so is evident: as witness the difference between the political problems raised by Flemish nationalism in Belgium before 1914 and since 1945. Subjectively the supporters of such movements may feel similar to those of earlier ones; objectively one cannot but conclude that the case for the small-size sovereign nation-state as a unit of economic or even cultural development is today considerably weaker than it was before 1914, especially in underdeveloped areas.[19]

But if the 'nationalist' reaction today lacks the built-in brake provided by the nineteenth-century aspiration to build viable nation-states – i.e. the assumption that there was something like a minimum size for such units – need they continue to be a 'nationalist' in the established sense? It is true that they can still often borrow the concepts and symbols of historic nationalism. There are still enough 'suppressed nations' to make this easy, though one or two – at present politically insignificant – movements like the Cornish and the Occitan come close to actually having to invent their 'nations'. However, insofar as such movements are primarily reactions against bigness (and they are not entirely this), it is not easy to set lower limits to their ideal units. Logically local patriotism might provide equally possible rallying-points, as was anticipated in 1949 in the British comedy film *Passport to Pimlico*, and in practice in 1970 by the brief 'declaration of independence' of the Isle of Dogs against the rest of London. We need hardly as yet discuss at what point of such development an analysis in terms of 'nationalism' ceases to be realistic.

## V

Nationalism is therefore a dual phenomenon, or rather an interaction of two phenomena, each of which help to give shape to the other. It consists of a 'civic religion' for the modern territorial-centralized state, and of a mode of confronting social changes which appear to threaten and disrupt certain aspects of the complex of social relationships. The former reflects a specific historic situation, characteristic of Europe since the French Revolution, and of most of the non-European world in the twentieth century: the combination of economic development, in the first instance capitalist (whether this is a necessary condition is not yet clear), with the mass participation in politics of a mobilized population. It is possible that we may be approaching the end of this period, at least insofar as the medium-sized sovereign 'nation-state' seems to be losing its role as the necessary or optimal framework for economic development. The latter is in principle not confined to any particular historic period or society, though it only acquired the full features of 'nationalism' as we know it in the specific historical era since 1789, and would probably not have done so in another setting.

Conversely, the state in this period tended to become a 'nation-state' whose civic religion took the form of national patriotism, largely because the elements from which such sentiments could be generated – territorial, linguistic, ethnic, etc. – lay ready to hand, being also those most likely to be used to formulate defensive group reactions. An obvious weakness of most states of technically desirable size was, of course, that they were not 'nationally' homogeneous, a state of affairs likely to lead to acute practical problems once 'national consciousness' ceased to be the property of only a few 'nations', as most nineteenth-century thinkers assumed it was and ought to be.[20] A 'nationalist' civic ideology was convenient, moreover, not only inasmuch as a state required to mobilize its citizens en masse directly, but also insofar as they were already mobilized for their own purposes (not necessarily only under 'national' banners) which conflicted with the interests of their rulers.

The characteristic nationalism of the past 150 years has been a constant interpenetration of these two elements. Hence the difficulty of analysing it. States have aspired to become 'nations', 'nations' to become states. Social movements (in the broadest sense of the term) have tended to become 'national' or to be split among 'national' lines, as the history of the most passionately and systematically internationalist among them demonstrates. 'National' movements have been imbued with a social and ideological content which has no necessary connection with their nationalism. Each tendency has reinforced the other, and given it a more self-conscious expression. The 'nation-state' has created its 'nation' and its 'nationalism' not to mention those of the other potential 'nations' with which it came into conflict. The 'national movement' in turn has forced both states and other political organizations with nationally unspecific aims, to adopt its ambiance and characteristics. The Middle East provides illustrations for both of these developments today.

One error of older students of the subject was to seek for some entity, the 'people' or the 'nation' which, though doubtless subject to the process of growth and evolution, had some sort of permanent objective characteristics. This is not the case, or rather, the search for human groups specifiable in such a manner throws no significant light on 'nations' and 'nationalism'. However, another error, which remains popular, is to assign only one specific historical function to nationalism – whether in the process of 'modernization' or that of the development of bourgeois/ capitalist society. It plainly has had such functions, though these require, as has been suggested, rather more complex analysis than they are often given. But it cannot be confined to such a role, and consequently the 'nationalisms' which fall outside it cannot merely be dismissed as troublesome 'bourgeois' or other survivals, though the establishment of the 'nation' stereotype and of an international system which largely equates states and nations undoubtedly gives them a significant capacity to survive.

However, the capacity of nationalism to fit a wide variety of socio-political situations and to adopt new functions need not lead us to abandon the view that it is not necessarily permanent. Non-nationalist students before 1914 assumed that it would eventually disappear, to be absorbed into or replaced by international forms of government, ideology, or even culture and language, reflecting the increasingly global character of the economy, of science, technology and communications. Such views were oversimplified, and as short-term forecasts were as wrong then as they are today. In spite of increasing evidence of globalization, nationalism is on the increase, and the uneven character of historical change is likely to make it go on increasing, and above all multiplying. As a long-run forecast, on the other hand, the prediction that nationalism will decline may prove to be no more unrealistic than other mid-nineteenth-century predictions (e.g. the disappearance of the peasantry), which looked implausible enough even a century after they were made, but are far from implausible today. Such a prediction does not imply that the differences which nationalism uses to define 'nations' will disappear, that the self-identification of groups in such terms will cease, or that their relations with outsiders will become idyllic. It merely implies that their social, economic and political implications will become transformed to the point where terms like 'nation' and 'nationalism', in our sense, cease to be seriously applicable to them.[21] Still, since this is not a prospect of the politically foreseeable future, and in any case not one to which a timescale can be attached, it is hardly worth pursuing this line of analysis. Nevertheless, it may be worth concluding these reflections by stating the obvious, namely that nationalism is a historic phenomenon, the product of the fairly recent past, itself subject to change, and unlikely to persist indefinitely.

# Notes

1   Dankwart Rustow: 'Nation', in *International Encyclopedia of the Social Sciences*, vol. 2 (New York, 1968).

2   He envisaged: (1) a united Iberian peninsula combining Spain and Portugal; (2) a united Scandinavian peninsula combining Norway, Sweden and Denmark; (3) a United Kingdom of England, Scotland and Ireland; (4) Italy; (5) an 'Alpine Confederation' uniting Switzerland with Savoy, German Tyrol, Carinthia and Slovenia (!!); (6) a confederation of the Balkan peoples under Greek presidency, with its capital in Constantinople, including Greece, Albania, Macedonia,

# Defining Nationalism: The Problems

Rumelia, Bosnia, Serbia and Bulgaria; (7) a Danubian federation of Hungary, the Romanian race – among which he appeared to include the inhabitants of Herzegovina – and Bohemia; (8) Germany, including Holland and Flanders; (9) France, including Walloon Belgium; (10) Russia and (11) Poland dividing between themselves 'the rest' and associated with one another. See Denis Mack Smith, *Il Risorgimento* (Bari, 1968), p. 422.

3   This may be illustrated by an actual example of conflict between them. In 1914 a Baltic baron, from a family settled in Courland since the fifteenth century, found himself, as a German, teaching at a German university. Since he was also a reserve officer in an Imperial Russian cavalry regiment, he returned without a moment's hesitation to St Petersburg to fight and kill his co-nationals, on the ground that 'loyalty to lord comes before loyalty to kin'. The argument, entirely convincing to a feudal noble, seems shocking to a nationalist. What is significant about it is that a man sufficiently 'national' to regard Germany and all Germans as his 'kin', simply did not accept that his nationality had the political implications which nationalism reads into it. By contrast the British government in 1940, in interning German immigrants (including Jews and political refugees) wholesale, acted on the purely 'nationalist' assumption that unless there was strong proof to the contrary, *any* German must be presumed to owe an overriding loyalty to 'his' nation-state.

4   Reinhard Bendix, *Nation-Building and Citizenship* (London, 1964).

5   Federation does not invalidate this. Were western Europe to form a federal union, which is improbable, local nationalisms might be replaced by, or subordinated to, a wider 'Europeanism', as the powerful regional loyalties of Texans have been to 'Americanism'. But this would cease to be really or potentially nationalist only if there were to be a global federation.

6   Stein Rokkan, 'Centre Formation, Nation-Building and Cultural Diversity: Report on a symposium organized by UNESCO', *Social Science Information*, 8:1 (1969), pp. 85–99.

7   It was first used for colloquial domestic intercourse by the socialist Zionist Yisrael Bar Yehuda (born Yisrael Idelson), who invented the Hebrew term for 'nationalism' – characteristically – on his journey of emigration to Palestine.

8   That it lent itself with particular ease to imperialist or expansionist purposes because of its universality, should not mislead us. Even the most restrictionist criteria of nationalism and 'national destiny' have never prevented the generation of expansionist aspirations and slogans.

9   Most of the useful European material comes from two regions: Scandinavia and central-south-eastern Europe, i.e. the now mostly socialist succession states of the nineteenth-century multinational empires of our continent.

10 Miroslav Hroch, *Die Vorkaempfer der nationalen Bewegung bei den kleinen Voelkern Europas* (Prague, 1968); English translation: *Social Preconditions of National Revival in Europe: A Comparative Analysis of the Social Composition of Patriotic Groups among the Smaller European Nations* (Cambridge, 1985).

11 Eric Wolf, *Peasant Wars of the Twentieth Century* (New York, 1969).

12 Hroch, op. cit., p. 160.

13 As Hroch notes, all this implies a higher degree than the current one of 'social communication' in Deutsch's sense (Karl W. Deutsch, *Nationalism and Social Communication* (New York, 1953)), both among 'national' activists and in 'national' regions; but, in my view rightly, he refuses to stop the analysis at this point. (Hroch, op. cit., pp. 167–70.)

14 This appears to apply least in Norway, Finland and perhaps Flanders.

15 Hroch, op. cit.

16 This does not prevent them from acting as channels for the dissemination of new political ideas and methods, which may influence such movements.

17 The three great multinational empires (Tsarist, Austro-Hungarian and Ottoman) against which the bulk of European national movements were directed until 1918, were notorious anachronisms.

18 Generally, 'the nation' replaces older communal structures symbolically. Where it genuinely fills the gap, it tends to do so at disproportionate social cost. As fascism was aware, the most effective examples of a working *Volksgemeinschaft* occur when members of one 'nation' are mobilized in common hostility to foreigners, as in war.

19 Whether such units become de facto dependent on a major capitalist economy ('neo-colonialism') or merge into some larger unit of economic activity, their sovereignty is likely to be infringed. The exceptions which occur, do not invalidate this generalization.

20 Most of them assumed that the rest of the potential 'nations' would either be content to be assimilated to the state-nations, or with something less than sovereign autonomy, or were destined by historical progress to fade away. The serious discussion of 'the national question' began, when it was clear that this did not generally happen.

21 This already is the case with very broad classifications of colour (race), culture and history, such as pan-Africanism, pan-Slavism, pan-Latin-Americanism, which are real enough, but have not the political implications of traditional nationalisms. The attempts to use them as the base of state formation have so far been uniformly unsuccessful.

# 11

# *The State, Ethnicity and Religion*

## I

'Belonging' to some human group, apart from such relations as the biological bond that links mothers to their children, is always a matter of context, and social definition, usually negative – that is to say, specifying the membership of the group by exclusion. Let me be more precise; what I mean by 'identifying' with some collectivity is giving a particular identification priority over all others, for in practice we are all multidimensional beings. There is no limit to the number of ways in which I could describe myself – all simultaneously true, as the constructors of censuses know. I can describe myself in different ways, and for certain purposes I will choose to put forward one identification rather than another, but without for a moment supposing that it excludes the others. I am only expected to choose between identifications if some outside authority or situation forces me to choose one identity because it regards two or more of them as incompatible, or because one is treated as being more important than the others.

The primary identity which has been chosen for most of us in the twentieth century is that of the territorial state, that is to say an institution that claims rights over every inhabitant of a piece of a map. If that person is a 'citizen' the state claims the right to command their loyalty over all other claimants, their love (i.e. 'patriotism') and, in times of war, their life.

These are historically novel arrangements which would have amazed most rulers in the past and most of their subjects, but since the eighteenth century we have got used to them and take them for granted. There is nothing 'natural' about them. Territories clearly demarcated from their neighbours by frontier lines are social innovations. The Franco-Spanish border was not formally fixed until 1869. The assumption that the territorial authority is supreme and has unique power in that territory belongs to modern history. As every medieval historian or orientalist knows, other kinds of state are possible. They may even be preferable, especially as the operations of actual human affairs fit less and less well into the framework of territorial states. At this moment (2006) two transnational corporations in the automobile industry, one officially based in the USA, the other in Germany, are in dispute about a Basque executive who has been lured by the American chief officer of one of these corporations to cross the ocean, with the promise that it will build a plant in the Basque country. In due course political structures will no doubt have to adjust to such realities better than they are able to do today.

I begin with 'state identity', because it is today virtually universal, and because today it provides the model for all other groups which seek a political expression for their existence as a collective. It is, however, a double-sided relationship. In the course of this century all the citizens of such a state belong together as *a community* or 'nation', and *second*, that which binds them together is something like common ancestry, ethnicity, language, culture, race or religion. The words 'state' and 'nation' have become interchangeable, as in the term United Nations. Conversely, any body of people who think of themselves as bound together by ethnicity, language, etc. claim the right to have a territorial state for themselves. This is also a novel concept. Until 1918 there is no evidence that what the Kurds wanted was an independent state, or, since they were partly nomadic, that they even understood what this meant. If they *had* any political demand, it was to have *no* state, not a national territorial one or any other.

The basic confusion is between the state as a territorially defined *political* community and communities in the anthropological, sociological or existential sense. The confusion arose naturally out of the revolutionary origin of the modern political 'nation', which was based on the implicitly democratic concept of sovereignty of the people, which in turn implied a common political will, and common bonds of political action for the common good such as 'patriotism'. So long as full citizenship was withheld from the mass of people, and their active participation in politics was neither necessary nor desired, this was largely academic. However, with the rise of democratic politics and the need to mobilize the population, the 'people' as a whole became an actor, and was – necessarily – addressed as a community across the internal differences that divided it.

Nevertheless, it is essential to note that this communal cohesion of the citizens in the political nation implied no other form of homogeneity, except for pragmatic purposes. The obvious reason why this is so is that, since the world began, no territory of any size has been inhabited by a single culturally or ethnically or in other respects homogeneous population. Moreover, belonging and even being loyal to a national government did not exclude belonging or being loyal to some other community, local, kin-based, religious or whatever. The eighteenth-century founding fathers of the modern 'nation-state' knew this as well as the founders of the post-1945 ex-colonial nation-states, because both operated on the same principle. They defined 'the people' or 'nation' of their state in the only way in which it can be operationally defined, namely as the inhabitants of a pre-existing territory (e.g. the Kingdom of France, the Thirteen American Colonies). In the case of the two founding nations of the modern nation-state, France and the USA, they also included those who would join them by accepting the constitution and laws of the revolutionary state. These inhabitants, as they well knew, constituted a multiplicity of ethnic groups, cultures, languages and cults.

Hence the classic 'nation-states', from the oldest to those founded in the nineteenth century, were with the rarest exceptions (perhaps Portugal?) heterogeneous, and recognized as such. Basques, Castilians, Catalans and Galicians resisted the Napoleonic armies as Spaniards, without abandoning their identity. The idea of ethnic or linguistic homogeneity would have made no sense. Even German nationalism, which is ethnic in character, assumed ethnic multiplicity. Being a 'German' was a function of belonging to one of the various recognized *Stämme* ('tribes' or 'descent groups') – Swabians, Saxons, Bavarians, Franks. After 1934 being a Swabian or Saxon was a secondary characteristic of being a German, not the other way round. As for linguistic uniformity, in societies without primary education this is not even conceivable except for restricted elite.

Nevertheless, for reasons often analysed, the tendency of modern territorial states to develop a socially and functionally necessary standardization of homogenization of the body of their citizens, and to strengthen the bonds linking them to national government, is undeniable. Any means of establishing the continuity and cohesion of the state will be used for this purpose, or invented, notably that great guarantor of continuity, history. Where 'ethnicity', linguistic culture and religion are available, they will be used for this purpose. Historically this has been the easiest where a state was constructed round a *Staatsvolk* which formed the largest body or even the majority of the state's population, such as the English, the Castilians, or the Great Russians. State patriotism and ethnic or religious bonding may therefore overlap.

One last point about state patriotism must be made. In the course of the nineteenth and most of the twentieth century the demands made by states on their citizens have increased enormously, and the ability of the citizens to escape these demands diminished dramatically. So, therefore, has the need to develop incentives for the citizen to identify individually and as part of a collective with the state. The demands of the state become more total. The era of the two world wars and post-war reconstruction probably saw the peak of this tendency. There is considerable evidence of a reaction against it since the 1960s.

## II

Let me turn from the state to ethnicity. There has never been a time in history when groups of human beings have not distinguished themselves from other groups by giving themselves a collective name, assuming that members of the group have more in common with each other than with members of other groups. However, two, perhaps three observations must be made. *First*, that ethnicity in itself is not a political term, or has specific political implications. That is why I prefer the term to 'nationality', which does imply a political programme. *Second*, ethnicity is not a positive characteristic of groups. It describes the way they separate themselves from each other, or demarcate themselves from others. The commonest sense of an intrinsic ethnicity, namely supposed common descent and kinship, is either patently fictitious, as in large modern 'nations', or arbitrary. Almost always the same population could be divided 'ethnically' in different ways. In any case, ethnic membership is often changed and reclassified over time. Without 'the others' there is no need to define ourselves. Let me remind you of the Polish census of 1931 which asked the inhabitants of the Pripet Marshes (whom today we would probably classify as Byelorussians) to state their nationality. They did not understand the question. They answered 'We are from here'. What else needed to be said? In their society, nothing. But there is a *third* point. A large number of ethnic units are not named, i.e. created, by themselves, but from the outside, especially in the nineteenth and twentieth centuries. The history of imperialism is full of colonial administrators who look at the great Rorschach inkblots of their subjects and decide on what shapes to read into them. 'Tribes' are distinguished for administrative purposes which would not have recognized their separate existence before. Conversely, a variety of different peoples are classified together for political or other purposes, e.g. the various tribes of American Indians become members of a new collective, the 'native Americans', which reflects not what the Apache and the Pueblo Indians have in common with the Mohawks, which is very little, but a specific set of legal problems of the federal government of the USA.

The category of 'ethnic Germans' (*Volksdeutsche*) is another such case. Of course, however arbitrary the origin of an ethnic classification, once established it can be as real as any other. A highly heterogeneous ensemble of religions now forms 'the Palestinians', although such a classification could not have had any significance before 1918.

This lack of fixity, or even arbitrariness of the concept of 'ethnicity' creates considerable problems for the definition of ethnic identity. We can observe some of the political consequences in situations like Bosnia. The political 'nation' or 'people' can be defined territorially, at least in the historic era of nation-states. But there is no equally convenient way of defining who belongs to an ethnic unit, however defined. Paradoxically, this identity, which claims to be natural or primordial, can only be defined by a conscious decision as to what constitutes the members of the group as distinct from non-members. Criteria have to be established. Biological racism is one such administrative criterion. Who is a Jew? The Nuremberg laws established one criterion (having one Jewish grandparent), the original Law of Return (1950) of the state of Israel another (being born of a Jewish mother). Both recognize that in real life there are no sharp lines which *objectively* separate Jews from non-Jews. Language is another, though equally arbitrary. How can one deny the status of ethnic Welshmen to my purely Anglophone neighbours on their ancestral farms? In what sense would they be more ethnically if, in an autonomous Wales, they were obliged to use the language that is at present only spoken by 21 per cent of the population? Conscious and arbitrary choice is the third. How else is the child of a mixed Serbo-Croat marriage to decide to which of the two ethnic groups he or she belongs? There were, at the last count, 1.4 million mixed marriages in ex-Yugoslavia. But note that choice can go both ways. Muslim Tamils in Sri Lanka refuse to see themselves as Tamils, and prefer to define themselves as 'Moors'. Most Navarrese prefer their identity as Navarrese to their identity as Basques.

Ethnic national movements therefore face the basic problem of how to separate their constituency from other groups, and, more urgently, how to give all the members who fit their definition convincing reasons to join the movement in its conflicts with the 'others'. The optimal strategy to do so is so to polarize group relations that all members of group 'We' treat all members of group 'They' as potentially dangerous enemies, and therefore total identification with 'our' group as their only protection. Terror designed to produce counter-terror is probably today the most popular strategy for securing this polarization, as we can see in Ulster, in Sri Lanka, in the Punjab and elsewhere – not least in ex-Yugoslavia.

However, a few words must be said about a special aspect of this arbitrary definition of group identity, which is often overlooked. I mean *assimilation*. There are two sides to this coin. Ethnic national movements which encourage the mass assimilation of non-members are not common, though there are some – the Catalan, for instance, or, before 1914, the Magyars. However, as Jews, Gypsies and people with different coloured skins know, even in the best cases the readiness to assimilate outsiders fully is limited. On the other hand, nothing is more

common in the nineteenth and twentieth centuries than individuals who wish to assimilate to some other nationality. In fact,
migration and assimilation were and are probably the chief
agencies for social mobility during this period. Central Europe
is full of people whose family names now show that their ancestors once switched nationalities, and if many of them had not
translated their original names in the language of their chosen
affiliation, this phenomenon would be even more obvious. At
the same time it is a familiar sociological fact about nationalist
movements that many of their pioneers and leaders come from
the fringes rather than from the centre of their ethnic groups,
or even (like some ethnically English leaders of the IRA) from
the outside.

Assimilation illustrates precisely the unreality of ethnic identity, both as a supposedly primordial or natural identity and as
an *exclusive* one. For, you will note, that in accepting a new identity the assimilees do not necessarily deny their old one. My own
father's generation, children of immigrants to England, plunged
themselves passionately into English culture and manners and
even anglicized their names – but without ever denying their
Jewish identity. Americans of Irish origin do not forget their
Irish links. What enrages the zealots of group identity about
assimilation is not that it means a denial of that identity – though
sometimes this does occur – but that it refuses to accept the *specific* criteria of group identity on which they insist, for instance, in
the case of Jews, the practice of the religion, in-group marriage
or – today – a particular attitude to Israel. It is the refusal to
make an either-or choice between group identities.

## III

Let me now turn to *religion*, that is to say the major world
religions which, by definition, cannot serve to define a group
because of their claim to universality. I leave aside religions
which are *ex officio* or in practice identified with one and only one

community. However, as we know, in practice the coexistence of different religions or variants of religion makes it possible for them to function as group markers in many cases. In fact, often there is little sense in distinguishing religion from other markers. Are the conflicts in Northern Ireland or in Bosnia or in Sri Lanka religious or ethnic? It does not matter. (In the first two cases they are clearly not linguistic, since all parties speak and write the same language.) However, the question of religion does enable us to trace certain layers in the phenomenon of national or group identity, and certain changes in it. I shall mention two.

The first is the difference between state patriotism, the nationalism of its leaders and cadres, and the sentiments of the masses.

As we know, from the later seventeenth century to the early twentieth a major tendency of state development has been to separate it from religion. The nation-state was non-religious as it was non-ethnic, i.e. it ruled over a multi-religious and multi-ethnic people. Ethnic-linguistic nationalist movements maintained the principle of a multi-religious nation, though not a multi-ethnic one, especially, of course, in multi-religious states. This was plainly the case of Irish nationalism, Yugoslav nationalism, German nationalism and several others. Yet the constant tension between the American Constitution, which is indifferent to religion, and the popularity of God in the American political discourse shows that in practice some degree of religiosity is one of the popular criteria for 'Americanism'. In Ireland, whatever the official tradition of the Republican movement, it is evident that for the masses Catholicism is the decisive criterion of Irish nationalism. This was, of course, even more marked in Muslim countries even before the recent rise of fundamentalism.

The second is the nature of the recent transformations of religion which are commonly lumped together as 'fundamentalism'. The term is misleading, since it implies a return to some original and authentic version of the faith. However, in practice these groups are not merely often innovatory, but also imply a redefinition of the faith which narrows it and makes it more suitable to separate the in-group from the outsiders. I shall not dwell on the innovations of fundamentalism. Let me merely remind you that the Ayatollah Khomeini's concept of an Islamic state, as preached from the 1970s, was novel, even by the standards of the politically engaged Shiite clergy of Iran. As for the narrowing, this is obvious. The fundamentalism of Jewish zealots like the Chassidim today imposes a degree of ritualism far beyond that traditionally required from pious Jews. 'Hindu fundamentalism' – the phrase is a contradiction in terms – is a movement to make Hinduism more exclusive and turn it into a sort of state religion – another contradiction in terms of Hindus – which will make all non-Hindus into a sort of non-Indian. Similar transformations have turned Sri Lankan Buddhism from a pacific, non-political and indeed household cult into a bloodthirsty collective nationalist religion for the Sinhalese. All these movements are directed against the coexistence of groups on the same territory and within the same state, which has been the basis of the nation-state so far.

However, another point must be borne in mind. The complex of movements called 'fundamentalism' today is, I think, an aspect of the decline of traditional religions, or rather churches. Now such all-embracing churches were always an effective way of expressing group identity, as ethnicity or language were not. They could consist of actual organizations with actual buildings and territorial divisions through which the 'community' could be defined at various levels: for instance, the parish, the diocese, the national or universal church. US presidents address their citizens as 'fellow Americans', but sergeants in the Russian army, both Tsarist and Bolsheviks, addressed their ranks not as 'fellow Russians' but as 'true believers' or Christians. Being a Greek, an Albanian, a Bulgarian or even a Turk in the Balkans was not a defining characteristic of a person. Being an Orthodox Christian or a Catholic or a Muslim was. I am inclined to think that it is the decline of religion as traditionally accepted which has left the way open for forms of religious mobilization which are hard to distinguish from ethnic segregationist movements. I mention this in passing as a field for possible research.

## IV

Let me now consider the historical transformations in these identifications, most of which occur[red] in the twentieth century.

The first of these, as I have argued elsewhere, is the injection of ethnicity and linguistic culture into the French and American revolutionary concept of nation-state, and the historic national monarchies like Russia, Britain and Spain. In short, the doctrine of self-determination to 'nations' defined in the familiar way – shared by John Stuart Mill, Joseph Stalin and President Wilson. To be more precise, the demand, in Mazzini's phrase, that every such 'nation' should have the right to form a sovereign state and the whole nation should be included in one state. This completely unrealistic principle becomes an operational reality with the collapse of the three great multi-ethnic and multi-empires, of Austria-Hungary, Russian and the Ottomans, i.e. in practice at the end of the First World War.

It immediately created problems which had not seriously arisen – which could not – arise in the multi-ethnic non-national empires for these, by definition, stood above all the various groups of their subjects. Bosnia is an excellent illustration of this. Both the Ottoman Empire until 1878 and the Habsburgs from 1878 to 1918 were uncommitted to any of the local communities and thus in a position to mediate between them and to keep their conflicts under control. Communist Yugoslavia was equally uncommitted. The periods when the local Bosnian situation got out of hand were those when the dominant state power was identified with one ethnic group (the Serbs, before and since communism) or when no effective uncommitted state existed. A multinational territorial state identified with one single use of its ethnic-linguistic 'nations' *must* privilege that nation over the others, and thus create problems. This is so even when that state is both democratic and tolerant of its 'minorities', as in inter-war Czechoslovakia, or post-Soviet Kazakhstan. Where the dominant ethnic group had a more aggressive agenda, as in post-1918 Yugoslavia, Romania or Poland, the situation was even more tense.

How nation-states which identified with a particular ethnic group turned into – or came to try to turn themselves into – *mono-ethnic, mono-linguistic* and *mono-cultural* territories is a question that requires more research, but there can be little doubt that this has been a growing tendency, particularly among small ethnic-linguistic movements and states. The logical end-product of this process is and must be one of four policies: mass assimilation or conversion by state force, mass expulsion of populations or 'ethnic cleansing', genocide or the creation, de facto or de jure of an apartheid system which turns non-members of the dominant group into foreigners or a legally inferior underclass of sub-citizens. All of these have been tried. Some are being tried still. This is the second transformation.

Both these are essentially concerned with creating nation-states and a group identification ideally co-extensive with the state and superior to all other group identifications. In the extreme case, a total identification with the state, although in the case of ethnic nationalism expressing themselves through universal religions, divine or secular, this is difficult. However, it is clear that in western states, at any rate from the 1960s, another form of apparently similar group identification has arisen. The rise of these forms of ethnicity was first noted in America by Nathan Glazer and Daniel Moynihan in their edited volume *Ethnicity: Theory and Experience* (1995), but it is also evident that a new terminology has developed since then. Both the term *ethnicity* and the term *identity* as applied to collectivities seem to be neologisms. For that matter we have lately seen all manner of groups which previously claimed no such status, apply such terms as 'community' to themselves, or even the term 'nation' (e.g. 'the queer nation' in the discourse of homosexual activists in the USA). These phenomena may or may not be linked to territorial nationalisms of the old ethnic type, and some of them clearly have been. I am thinking of the radicalization of Basque nationalism and the emergence of Quebec separatism, which both fall into this period. However, I don't think that this is the central characteristic of these new forms of collective identity formation. Certainly it is not in the USA where they have become increasingly prominent; nor in the ethnic movements of Islamic immigrants in European countries, which tend to take the form of fundamentalism. I shall call them *ghetto* movements, since segregation from, and exclusion of, the wider society is their main object, both emotional, intellectual and where possible physical. Ghetto movements among immigrants or the descendants of immigrants are the most typical, but not the only ones. The present phase of such movements differs from the ghettoization of earlier immigrants in one major respect. It has given up the aim of assimilation. The code-word for this in the English-speaking world is 'multi-culturalism'. In practice, of course, the inhabitants of almost all ghettos live and work in a wider society, where they coexist with other groups in a complex economy and under public authorities outside and above the ghetto. Indeed, the major political function of ghetto activists is to compete with other groups for a share in the resources of the wider authority. Their strategy is the opposite of national separatism.

These developments should not, in my opinion, be confused with the changes arising out of very far-reaching changes in the structure of the existing states in most of Europe in the last twenty-five years, and which have enormously accelerated since the collapse of the Soviet bloc. They range from the restructuring of national states, mostly by de-centralization or regionalization to the break-up of old unitary or federal states into their components. Not to mention the move towards a confederal structure of the European Community. What these developments have in common is a weakening of the old model of the nation-state governed from a single centre. This has naturally reinforced national separatist movements both in east and west. Indeed, since the collapse of the Soviet system more new, nominally independent and sovereign states claiming to represent 'nations' have been formed than at any time in the twentieth century, including more than a dozen which had never in their history been independent states of the modern type. I regard the emergence of these new states essentially as a by-product of the weakening or collapse of the previous states, and not as the product of some new wave of powerful nationalist movements or national consciousness. In my view they should be analysed as consequences of breakdown rather than as causes of it. However, once new nation-states have come into existence in whatever manner, their national consciousness becomes as serious force in its own right, and must be regarded as such. The elections of 1917 to the Russian Constituent Assembly – dissolved by the Bolsheviks – show that there was no serious support at that time for Latvian and Estonian ethnic nationalism. But by 1940 there was.

The relations between the changes in the political structure of the late twentieth century states and national consciousness deserve a great deal of research and analysis. However, for reasons of time I must leave them aside, and concentrate on the sociological reasons for the new search for collective identity. It is no accident that we find this happening in the west from the 1960s on, and elsewhere in the course of the 1970s and the 1980s. For during the first half of the twentieth century we have been living – we are living – through the most rapid, profound and universal social transformation in human history. And with it all the old forms of human relationships, all the traditional bonds of community, have lost any but the most residual, or metaphorical, capacity to define us. We are all uprooted people. Is it an accident that Quebec separatism became a serious political force at the end of a decade when the traditional Catholicism that had defined French Canadians collapsed – as the dramatic collapse both of church attendance and of the French-Canadian birth rate shows? In my view it is not an accident. Let me therefore conclude with an example of the way in which such social disorientation can lead directly to the search for a new (and in this case savagely nationalist) identity. I take it from Jonathan Spencer's studies of rural Sri Lanka in the early 1980s.[1]

Sometime in the late 1940s Spencer's Sinhala village – then quite remote from the capital – acquired a road, a temple, a school and a lot more contact than before with the cash economy. As malaria was almost eradicated, it attracted a lot of immigrants and grew from one hundred to one thousand inhabitants. In 1982 nearly half the households had settled in the village in the previous ten years; 85 per cent of the heads of households had been born outside the village. The growth of the cash economy had created wider differences between rich and poor, and differences no longer predictable by a person's family or class/caste. 'Now' – I quote from his book – 'brothers and sisters, parents and children, might find themselves living quite different lives.' This was largely due to, and demonstrated by, school education. This divided those who succeeded in the wider society from those who failed. So it is not surprising – I quote – 'that "unity" and "community" should be the source of some collective anxiety, and this goes some way to explaining the appeal of a higher (ethnic and national) identity'. That higher identity was found through the populism of this national-ethnic Sinhala appeal which 'promised a source of community, solidarity and strength in challenging the local holders of privilege'.

Jonathan Spencer's argument suggests one way in which social change brings about the need for new identities. In my view the collapse of the traditional family structure, followed by the collapse of the traditional structure of (male) manual labour and industrial employment, has produced an analogous form of uprootedness and disorientation in advanced industrial countries; and so has the increasingly sharp break between the generations. The new forms of 'identity politics' may or may not appeal to ethnicity (whatever that means) or create new ethnicities or find expression in religion, or for that matter in what claims to be a state patriotism, as with the neo-fascist English football hooligans who wave the Union Jack. It may do all these things at once. Moreover, it may or may not merge with an older nationalist ideology and movement. However, it is my view that it must be considered and analysed as a novel sociological phenomenon and not as a mere prolongation of older forms of nationalism. In my view it is essentially not political, though it can obviously be exploited by politicians and will be.

It is not my function here to judge them, but I can only conclude that these movements, strong though they are, are essentially negative: they are at best cries of pain and cries for help, at worst blind protests, particularly of those without hope. They offer no political or other solutions because they do not think in terms of solution. My conclusion is a warning against anachronism: do not confuse the neo-Nazis of Germany today even with the original National Socialists. They are different.

## Notes

1 Jonathan Spencer, *A Sinhala Village in a Time of Trouble: Politics and Change in Rural Sri Lanka* (Oxford, 1990).

# 12

# *The Celtic Fringe*

The question of how far the popular classes participated in national movements for independence implies the existence of such movements. However, the historian ought also to be interested in situations where national movements might be expected, but did not occur. The British Isles provide examples of both. Ireland is a classical case of nationalism, whereas Scotland and Wales have developed no serious movements for national independence, in spite of the obvious national sentiments of a large part of their population. Both countries possess Nationalist Parties, though fairly recent ones, but neither enjoys any significant support among the electorate, or has benefited from much participation by the popular masses. Scots and Welsh nationalism exists, but it has so far expressed itself in politics overwhelmingly by the support of all-British parties and movements, though in a manner markedly different from that of the English. Outside politics it has sometimes rested on traditionally separate formal institutions (as in Scotland), or has set out to create separate institutions, notably in the fields of culture and education (as in Wales), but even here it has often operated by a local adaptation of some all-British phenomenon. Ireland has nationalist mass sports – e.g. Gaelic football and hurling. Wales has chosen to adopt as its mass sport a version of football which in England is largely confined to the middle classes, rugby union. Scotland, in spite of several possible sports with a sound basis in Scottish tradition, has not even chosen the limited Welsh form of separatism. It has adopted the characteristic mass sport of England, association football in its standard form, merely organizing it in a special national system of clubs and infusing it with a zeal and passion which has made it a celebrated nursery of eminent players.

What both countries have in common is that – unlike Ireland – no important body of opinion in either has seriously or for any length of time envisaged separation from England. This does not mean that they are English, or have shown any serious tendency to become assimilated to the English, or even lack a certain feeling of hostility to the large country to which they have been attached since 1536 (Wales) and 1707 (Scotland). Nor have they lacked the sort of demands round which nationalist movements can readily crystallize. This common failure to develop typical movements of national independence is all the more striking, because in most respects Wales and Scotland are very different countries. Scotland is, to use nineteenth-century terminology, a 'historic nation', i.e. it entered the Union of 1707 as an independent kingdom with a long history of independence – and in general of hostility to England – and a system of institutions entirely distinct from the English in almost every respect except the linguistic.[1] Except for the superstructure of national politics, this institutional sep-arateness – most marked in law, education, religion and social administration – remained. Scotland possessed an independent social structure, an aristocracy only partly assimilated to the English, a distinct agrarian structure, an energetic bourgeoisie taking its own dynamic part in economic development, espe-cially since the Industrial Revolution, traditional centres of urban life and higher education, and a national church. Until recently it received virtually no English immigration, though a large influx of Irish.

Wales, on the other hand, was – to use nineteenth-century terminology again – a typical 'non-historic nation', a territory inhabited by an agrarian population united by a rather more primitive social and economic structure and by the fact of not speaking English (when the complex of various Celtic dialects may be said to have constituted a single Welsh language is a matter of debate). The Principality as a whole had never been a political unity in any real sense. There is still debate about which of its towns – none of them with any historic claim, hardly any with any record of long urban existence – should be regarded as its capital. Unlike Ireland its landlords were mainly native, but assimilated to the English gentry after the union of 1536. There was no nobility recognized as such in a large country. A Welsh bourgeoisie comparable to the Scottish one hardly existed until the mid-nineteenth century. In a sense the Welsh people consisted entirely of the popular classes – peasants, craftsmen and later industrial workers – though in the nineteenth century a stratum of cadres developed, represented most typically by non-conformist ministers of religion, teachers and small traders. Wales was a nation whose social hierarchy reached no further up than the petty-bourgeoisie, for anything higher was, by function and often definition (e.g. membership of the Church of England) not Welsh but English. Hence Welsh national feeling was invariably strongly radical in sentiment, with the familiar combination of anti-aristocratic agitation (aristocracy being identified with landlordism), a strong penchant for democracy and education, and above all a savage anti-clericalism directed by Protestant dissenters against the established church.

'Welshness' found two main expressions: the Welsh language and vernacular culture, and a variety of Protestant non-conformist sects which, spreading in the eighteenth century, gained majority support after 1800 and had collectively become the national religion by the mid-nineteenth century. Non-conformity, of course, became the national religion largely because it was based on the Welsh language and served to distinguish the Welsh from the (Anglican) English and anglicized upper classes. However, and in spite of the increasingly elaborate apparatus for the protection and propagation of the Welsh language which political pressure constructed, 'Welshness' cannot be identified with either or both. Even in 1851 a large proportion of the population (mainly in the industrial areas) remained outside religion, and industrialization brought an automatic decline of the Welsh language, which owed only very little to the immigration of Englishmen into the rapidly expanding coalmining areas.[2] From the beginning, therefore, there was a potential rift between an *organized* Welsh national sentiment based on non-conformity and the Welsh language (or, in class terms, on the agrarian sector and the petty-bourgeois cadres) and the more general non-linguistic and not so strongly non-conformist Welshness of the industrial working class and the urban masses.

The fortunes of the Scots and Welsh in England have also differed correspondingly, though much research needs to be done on the subject. Except in the areas immediately adjoining Scotland and Wales, selective rather than mass migration to England was the rule. The Lowland Scots migrants to the south were proverbially successful. At virtually all levels there was an emigration of cadres, and they frequently dominated the English activities with which they associated themselves. Certain activities were captured by the Scots almost from the start of the industrial revolution (e.g. industrial and agricultural technology), others only at the end of the century (e.g. politics – there were no Scottish prime ministers before 1894, but seven Scots out of the sixteen prime ministers since then), but England at all times provided ample outlets for Scottish talent, attracted by the higher wages and better prospects of the south. Meanwhile the separateness of Scottish institutions preserved a virtual monopoly of professional posts in Scotland for the natives. For instance, Scots law may, as nationalists claim, be eroded by the influence of English law, but nevertheless it is a field into which no English lawyer is qualified to venture.

The fortunes of the Welsh in England were considerably more modest until parliamentary democracy provided an outlet for Welsh politicians (after 1868 and 1884), the rise of the socialist and labour movement scope for Welsh labour leaders (after 1898), and above all, until the construction of a national system of education and the modern bureaucratic and professionalised society after 1870, provided employment opportunities for the education of office workers, teachers, and other intellectual and non-manual professions which formed the main export of skilled manpower from Wales. Except as non-conformist ministers, few Welshmen before 1900 played a prominent role in English affairs, certainly far fewer – even allowing for the difference in size – than the Scotsmen. Even after 1900, and until the reluctant mass migration of Welshmen from their economically ruined country between the wars, the Welsh success in England was more modest than the Scots', and the concern of the emigrants for Wales itself correspondingly more intense. The Welsh national movement was largely a movement of unemployed intellectuals and middle strata seeking to establish a large and growing reserve of posts for Welshmen in Wales by the expansion of the local educational cultural and administrative system, and its monopolization by those capable of speaking Welsh. Since no such system existed or was recognized, one of the main concerns of Welsh nationalists was to form it and to exclude the non-Welsh occupying such posts already.

Given the general recognition that Scotland was a separate country with separate institutions and problems, and given also the existence of an influential and not wholly anglicized Scottish aristocracy and commercial or industrial bourgeoisie, there was no great opposition in London to the granting of administrative devolution and even something like a modest autonomy; at least when Liberal governments were in power. (Conservative ones had no taste for strengthening the separateness of a country permanently dominated by the Liberals.) In Scotland as in Wales the revival of Irish nationalist agitation from the 1860s, the domination of English politics by the Home Rule question, and the economic depression of the 1880s, produced some national discontent and even some demand for Home Rule, faintly echoing the Irish. There was little force in this. But for the existence of the Irish question, little would have been heard about Home Rule for Scotland and Wales, and even so there was always a major distinction, quite apart from the lack of support for nationalism in the two British countries. For the Irish 'Home Rule' was a euphemism for independence from England, for the Scots and Welsh merely a synonym for administrative devolution and adequate financial support from London. The Scots demands were largely – and quietly – conceded with the setting up of the Scottish Office in 1885, the 'Goschen Formula' which guaranteed financial allocations and posts corresponding to the Scottish share of the total population, and the tacit convention that the English MPs should not intervene in the discussion of Scottish affairs in the House of Commons, for which a Scottish Grand Committee was set up in 1894, and after a period of Conservative opposition, revived and made permanent. 'Home Rule', though forced on the Scottish Liberal Party by a middle-class pressure group, was not seriously pressed. If governments even talked about it, it was largely to make the granting of Home Rule to Ireland palatable to the Scots who were by no means enthusiastic about it. It was of course natural that Scottish political organizations should organize on a Scottish basis, but it is equally significant that they did so not in opposition to the English – or rather the all-British – organizations (such as the National Liberal Federation or the Trades Union Congress), but in addition to them. For this reason their political functions and effectiveness have often been diminished, for they tended to lack both the power of pressure groups concentrating on influencing the all-British organizations, and the power which comes from frank secession. The emerging labour movement naturally also tended – though to a lesser extent – to organize Scottish organizations. Except for the Scottish Trades Union Congress (1897) those formed between 1885 and 1914 have disappeared.

No comprehensive form of local autonomy for Wales, however unofficial, was achieved in the last decades of the nineteenth century, though the nationalist agitation in Wales was undoubtedly far more militant and serious than that in Scotland. The separate treatment of Wales for legislative purposes was achieved, in principle, with the passing of the Welsh Sunday Closing Act of 1881, and some sort of national recognition with the setting up of a federal University of Wales. The two crucial demands of Welsh nationalism, bilingual teaching in Welsh schools (1888) and the disestablishment of the Church of England in Wales (1914), were achieved before the First World War, while the local government reform of 1888 handed over the administration of the Welsh counties to the Welsh. Nevertheless, the demands for some more formal recognition of Wales as a separate country – whether by a 'general council' for Wales or by a Secretary of State for Wales – made no headway. (Only since the early 1960s has a somewhat shadowy Minister for Wales formed part of British governments.) At one point – between 1886 and 1896 – it looked as though the Liberal Party in Wales might be absorbed into, or fused with, a typical nationalist movement (Cymru Fydd or Young Wales), inspired by intellectuals and emigrants, and propagated by militant young politicians of whom Lloyd George is the most famous, but this product of the era of agrarian depression and Irish nationalist agitation had no real mass basis, and there was much unreality about it even after 1891. It was killed by the refusal of the South Wales Liberals from the industrial areas which now represented the great bulk of Welsh population and wealth to allow themselves to be led into utopia by the unrepresentative rural regions of the north. In effect this failure killed the nascent Welsh nationalism.

We must now consider the reasons for this failure of mass nationalism to develop in Scotland and Wales.

The first reason is clearly economic. Both Wales and Scotland have (with the exception of unrepresentative and thinly populated regions of small peasant agriculture) developed since the Industrial Revolution as integrated parts of an all-British economy, more particularly as specialized centres of mining, metallurgy and heavy industry, though not as the only ones. They therefore differ from Ireland which remained overwhelmingly an agrarian country whose economic problems were quite different from those of most parts of Britain,[3] or from Catalonia and the Basque country in Spain, which were relatively industrialized regions in a non-industrial country whose central government was dominated by the non-industrial Castile. Economically, there was no obvious advantage in separation. Both countries were notably poorer and more backward than England – indeed their low production costs helped to concentrate industry there – and might well feel neglected, but neither can be regarded in any realistic sense as subject to 'exploitation'. Though Scots and Welsh industrialism was unstable in the first half of the nineteenth century, with the era of the railway and the steamship both entered a period of abnormally dynamic expansion. They may be called the last great boom regions of classical British industrial capitalism before 1914; the centres of coal export, shipbuilding etc. So far as the workers were concerned, they remained worse off, on the whole, than in England but, on average, better employed. In 1913–14 national unemployment averaged 3.8 per cent, Welsh and Scots unemployment 2.3 and 2.1 per cent respectively. The workers had plenty of causes of discontent as workers, but no very obvious ones – so long as this industrial dynamism lasted – as Scotsmen or Welshmen.

Industrial expansion in Scotland merely reinforced the position, and the vested interest in attachment to Britain, of the powerful Scottish bourgeoisie – especially of Glasgow and the West of Scotland. In Wales the expansion actually did much to create a native bourgeoisie, no longer automatically tending to assimilate to the English or anglicized gentry and the English immigrant entrepreneurs of the early industrial age: P. A. Thomas, David Davies, Edward and David Davies, etc. It also reinforced the national cadres. Yet at the same time it left the Welsh bourgeoisie, insofar as its fortunes rested on industry and trade, without economic discontent. Welsh hill-farmers might agitate during agrarian depressions, unemployed Welsh graduates might be discontented, but Welsh coal-owners had no reason for dissatisfaction.

The collapse of Britain's basic industries affected Scotland and Wales with corresponding severity between the wars. Both became abnormally depressed areas, and unemployment rose dramatically: in Aberdare from 0.2 per cent in 1914 to 25.7 at the peak of the revival of the 1903s (1937), in Merthyr Tydfil from 1.4 per cent to 41.6 per cent, in Greenock from 1.6 per cent to 21.4 per cent and so on. Between the wars therefore Welsh and Scots nationalism, which began to organize their own nationalist parties in 1925 and 1928 respectively, had a more plausible case for protesting against the economic inferiority of the two countries, and their neglect by London, though the catastrophe which hit the Celtic fringe was only a more acute form of the crisis which hit all the old industrial areas of Britain, and no worse than that which hit some entirely English zones. However, by that time the Welsh and Scottish working class put its faith in the labour movement, and the local industrialists were too realistic to expect any solution from the utopian slogans of separatism or autonomy.

The second reason lies in the character and function of the Liberal Party which became the major expression of Scottish and Welsh political interests. In Scotland the attachment to the Whigs can be traced far back into history, in Wales Liberalism hardly emerges as the national party until after the middle of the nineteenth century, but in both it reflected the relative poverty and backwardness of their countries, the relatively slight economic differences between peasantry, workers and a modest middle class, and the penchant for radicalism, democracy and a puritan Protestantism which went with it. The local industrial bourgeoisie was of course also Liberal, if only for economic reasons. In both cases the democratization of the electorate in 1867 and 1884 made the Liberals the permanent majority party. In Wales its hold was quite overwhelming – at its peak (1892) thirty-one Members of Parliament against three Conservatives. In Scotland it sufficed to control most – on four occasions all – urban seats and to establish strong support, mainly in the northern counties. With the rise of the Irish question, which split the Liberal Party (1886), normally by the secession of its richer and more aristocratic supporters, the influence of the Celtic fringe within it increased dramatically. Since England became predominantly Conservative, the Liberal fortunes depended largely on the combination of its Scots and Welsh supporters and the alliance with the Irish nationalists. It was during the period when Home Rule for Ireland dominated British politics – 1886–95, to a lesser extent 1895–1914, and still to some degree 1914–22 – that Welsh and Scottish nationalism tended to infuse Welsh and Scottish Liberalism, sometimes, as in Wales, to the point where the nationalists of Young Wales actually threatened to take over the Welsh Liberal Party from within. This temporary nationalist euphoria, specially marked among the Welsh, which reached its peak under the weak Liberal government of 1892–5, was based on illusion. Its strength was never overwhelming, for the main centres of industry (South Wales, the industrial West of Scotland with Glasgow) were always lukewarm and the working class not deeply involved. The concessions which the Liberal Party was willing to make to Wales and Scotland, though real, were always strictly limited, so long as neither country used the threat of actual secession like the Irish – and neither country was willing to. The restoration of Liberal fortunes in Britain depended not on the support of the Welsh and Scots, which even at its virtual maximum as in 1892[4] could produce only the weakest of Liberal governments, but on England. Once the limits of the Celtic influence were recognized – as they were, with some emotional disillusion – in the 1890s, the Scots and Welsh could settle down as effective regional pressure groups, so long as they were not in conflict with the English senior partners, aided by the rise of Scottish and Welsh politicians to national influence in the early twentieth century. This rise – the appearance of men like Henry Campbell-Bannerman and David Lloyd George as important national figures – appeared to weaken the case for separatism, or at least made the failure of the more ambitious nationalist aspirations a little more tolerable.

With the breakdown of the Liberal Party between 1916 and 1922 Welsh and Scottish nationalism lost its main political expression. The working class seceded to the Labour Party, and the Welsh and Scottish nationalist parties which arose in the 1920s on the ruins of Liberalism never got very far. In Wales they have never elected a single MP, in Scotland only they had one brief and freakish victory for some months in 1945, during the wartime electoral truce, when the rivalry was temporarily suspended. The strength of these nationalist parties of the main parties has lain among intellectuals, and the professional strata in stagnant provincial areas without much industry (as in Perth), or in the untypical regions of declining peasant traditionalism, linguistic Welshness etc.

This breakdown of a united bloc of Scots or Welsh nationalism within the regional Liberal Party brings us to the third reason for the failure of the nationalism of the Celtic fringe: the rise of the labour movement. Both economic development and class interest divided the nationalists from labour. Both Scots Liberalism and the cadres of Welsh nationalism – native capitalists, small traders, non-conformist sects – were normally hostile to militant labour organization and socialism, or at best indifferent to trade unions. Thus, while the electoral breakthrough of the Labour Party in 1906 was due to an electoral pact with the Liberals, which gave a number of seats to Labour candidates,

Scottish Liberalism remained solidly hostile to Labour through-out. With two exceptions all independent labour and socialist candidates in Scotland were opposed by Liberals between 1892 and 1914. The existence in both Scotland and Wales of a pow-erful group of native industrialists without economic reasons for nationalism, allowed class conflict to prevail over national soli-darity. Again, in both Wales and Scotland the nationalist sector of Liberalism became increasingly irrelevant to the industrial areas, however strong its appeal in the backward peasant high-lands or to non-industrial strata. Welsh and Scottish Liberalism still subsist – and the latter has recently revived – in remote and thinly populated traditional regions, but not in the heart of their countries' populations and economies.

The Welsh and Scottish labour movements were of course national, but not nationalist in the orthodox sense. Until the end of the nineteenth century they tended to be weaker, and sometimes more moderate, than the corresponding English movement. Their emergence in both countries was part of a sharp turn to the left – to trade union militancy and social-ism – which was to turn both Wales and Scotland into areas of unusually strong, but also unusually extremist labour organ-ization. The inspiration in both cases came from the socialist and trade union revival of the 1880s and 1890s, whose interests were not specifically national. Indeed, the new movement often found itself with an anti-nationalist orientation, because it was opposed by older and more moderate leaders with a strong taste for Liberalism, and the traditional non-conformist preaching, hymn-singing and Welsh-language oratory, such as William Abraham (widely known as 'Mabon'). The ideology of the South Wales miners, diffused by a nucleus of young militants, was to be a combination of Marxism and revolutionary syndicalism, and the best-known Welsh labour leaders of the twentieth century – the best-known in England as well as in their own country – were men identified with the coal mines and with the extreme left of the Labour Party or the Communist Party (A. J. Cook, Arthur

Horner, Aneurin Bevan) and not with Welsh language or culture. Scotland also functioned as a sort of vanguard or extreme wing of the all-British labour movement, and probably more effectively than Wales, for it provided national leaders for the Independent Labour Party, Labour Party and Communist Party, for some important unions, and at one point at least (in 1922) the chief impetus which shifted the Parliamentary Labour Party in London to the left.

Both movements, moreover, had their strength in the areas of their countries least affected by the traditional symbols of nationalism. In Scotland a large part of the working class, consisting as it did of immigrant (Catholic) Irishmen, who still form 15 per cent of the population, was unlikely to be touched by appeals to Robert Bruce, John Knox or the Battle of Flodden. The South Wales miners, even in the least anglicized parts of the coalfield such as the Rhondda, conducted their business in English, though as late as 1914 they still added a Welsh summary to their minutes. And in Wales certainly ideology prevailed over mere ethnic Welshness. The coalfield was the first industrial area to provide a seat in parliament for the (Scottish) socialist leader Keir Hardie in 1900, it later provided a seat for the (Scottish) leader of the Labour Party, Ramsay MacDonald, and was for long regarded as the best electoral hope for the (English) leader of the Communist Party, Harry Pollitt.

The national colouring was somewhat more obvious in Scotland, where, as we have seen, most political organizations formed on a Scottish basis, including those of the new labour movement. Labour organizations also seem to have been more inclined in the 1880s to adopt nationalist slogans such as Home Rule. Nevertheless, such gestures were not decisive. The Scottish Labour Party of 1888, in spite of its Home Rule platform, merged with the all-British Independent Labour Party, of which it is best regarded as the ancestor. Beyond a tendency to maintain more support in the Glasgow area than anywhere else, there was to be nothing specifically Scottish about this party. Other organizations, also largely confined to Scotland like the Socialist Labour Party (followers of the American socialist Daniel De Leon) were even less nationalist in orientation. During the years of inter-war depression Home Rule resolutions appeared in the Labour Party in Scotland, and the movement was more deeply involved in the nationalist agitation for a Scottish parliament, the 'Scottish Covenant' which reached its peak in 1949–50, but disintegrated rapidly with the economic recovery of the 1950s. Fundamentally, in spite of an attachment to Scottish patriotism, the Scottish working class put its faith in the all-British or international programmes of various socialist parties. Independence was never a serious issue.

Whether with the erosion of the traditional labour movement, nationalist slogans may in future have a greater appeal to the Scottish or Welsh working class, is a question to which only the future can give an answer.[5]

If we are able to sum up the problem of Celtic fringe nationalism, we shall conclude that it provides one of the comparatively rare illustrations of what classical nineteenth-century socialist theory hoped for: proletarian nations whose working classes resisted the attractions of nationalist agitations, preferring to organize under the banner of an international ideology based essentially on class interest. Both Wales and Scotland became essentially Labour nations as they had previously been Liberal nations,[6] which left nationalism confined to rural areas, small towns, and the non-proletarian strata. Welsh nationalism in its classic form of a Welsh-oriented local Liberalism, is therefore an historic interlude between the emergence of a self-conscious Welsh lower middle class and bourgeoisie, and the rise of a class-conscious proletarian movement, i.e. between the 1860s and the early 1920s. Scots nationalism, though more pervasive, has also been less militant or widespread than Welsh, if only because the actual existence of a 'historic' Scottish nation was universally accepted, whereas in Wales the existence of a Welsh nation had to be established and institutionalized by nineteenth-century agitation, references to Mazzini, etc.; and perhaps also because England provided greater opportunities for the potential cadres of a Scottish national movement who, on winning positions of importance in the south, tended to lose interest in the regional problems of their native country.[7] It may be added that Scotland was also a less homogeneous country and society than Wales, a fact reflected in greater political heterogeneity. For the past hundred years, a Welsh Conservative of any prominence has been very rare, whereas there have been and are plenty of Scottish Conservative politicians, intellectuals, not to mention administrators, soldiers and noblemen. But the crucial fact, as in Wales, is that Scottish nationalism has not been able to survive the secession of the bulk of the Scottish industrial working class from the radical-democratic Scottish Liberalism which was, as in Wales, the nearest thing to a national movement and ideology.

If either Wales or Scotland had suffered from anything that could be described as 'exploitation' *as a country*, or even if the problems of Wales and Scotland had been – like those of Ireland – so different from those of England as to make it virtually impossible to reduce them to a common denominator, there might nevertheless have been a basis for Celtic fringe nationalism, for the different classes and regions of the two countries might have had strong reasons to cooperate against the English. But in fact, neither of them did. Both were somewhat poorer than most parts of England. Both had some cause to feel neglected, or (especially in times of depression) to suffer from an all-British policy which did not concentrate specially on their difficulties. Both could rightly complain of a certain degree of discrimination, and of a tendency of both Englishmen and foreigners to forget that Britain included not only one country, but three rather different ones. Yet the mere fact that both formed part of a single all-British industrial economy, which grew up simultaneously in all three countries, meant that their economic problems were not fundamentally different from those of any other region of Britain, including several purely English ones. Much of the discrimination they felt was no different from that felt for long periods by sections of the English population – e.g. the Non-conformists. There remained a number of internal problems of both countries, which required Scottish or Welsh solutions – but these solutions hardly affected England, and were therefore not in serious conflict with English interests. The typical pattern of Celtic fringe politics reflects this situation: they might develop national organizations like the Scottish Liberal Party or the Scottish Trades Union Congress, but without abandoning their membership of the corresponding all-British organizations such as the National Liberal Federation and the Trades Union Congress. The basis for separatist nationalism was therefore reduced to the few (and untypical) areas whose problems really were quite different from any English ones (e.g. the respective highlands with their specific agrarian, linguistic and other problems), to that section of the educated strata which could not, or was not content to, seek an outlet in the larger labour market of England or the British Empire, and to a core of ideologues.

One final weakness of Celtic fringe nationalism remained, though it was probably not decisive. Both countries were small, and might well be regarded as unviable as independent entities (though this argument never affected the Irish). Nevertheless, had they had the prospects of attaching themselves to some large outside nation, their nationalism might have been somewhat strengthened. There was no such outside nation to claim them as irredentas or kinsmen. The only possibility might have been a collective Celtic nationalism uniting the Welsh, Scots – and perhaps other Celtic fragments with the Irish, but though there have always been ideologues to advocate Celtic solidarity, it foundered, and was bound to founder, on the impracticability of uniting either the Welsh or the Scots with the Irish. Ireland had no more in common with the British Celts than what interested archaeologists, anthropologists, linguists and historians. The Irish (separated from the militantly Protestant Scots and Welsh by religion) were not present in any large quantity in Wales, but existed as a large minority in Scotland, and in far from perfect relations with their neighbours. Wales had no strong views on the subject as is shown by the solid support of the Welsh Liberals for Gladstone after the Home Rule crisis of 1886. Scotland had; as is shown by the profound split this crisis produced in the ranks of the Scottish Liberals. In neither case was an all-Celtic independence, or any other combination with outside nations more than the dream of a few fanatics.

# Notes

1   Except among the increasingly small minority of Gaelic-speaking Highlanders, the language of culture and administration has long been English, the colloquial language, also used to some extent in belles-lettres, but for no other literary purpose, a dialect of English no more sharply distinct from the official language than most German dialects from cultured German.

2   Thus in the Rhondda valleys under 10 per cent of the population were non-Welsh by birth even in 1911; but as early as 1901 35 per cent of the population were monoglot English-speakers (a figure not dissimilar for the less comprehensive statistics available for 1891), while between 1901 and 1911 the percentage of monoglot Welsh-speakers fell from 11 to just over 4 per cent.

3   It may be no accident that the only industrialized part of Ireland, the north-east, failed to join the rest of the country in its demand for independence, and remains part of the United Kingdom.

4   Out of 34 seats in Wales and Monmouthshire, 31 went Liberal, and out of 72 Scottish seats, 51.

5   This question can now (1968) be answered. Since 1966 disillusion with a Labour government has turned both Scottish and Welsh nationalism into major electoral forces for the first time in history.

6   By 1918 Labour held 10 Welsh seats, by 1922 18, by 1929 25 out of 35. In Scotland the major swing – a combined product of the transfer of Irish votes after independence, depression and the memory of wartime militancy – occurred in 1922. By 1929 the party held 37 out of 70 seats, and its domination of the industrial Lowlands was far greater. Both nations remain predominantly Labour even in periods of Conservative triumph in England.

7   J. Ramsay MacDonald was, at a very early stage of his career, secretary of a Scottish Home Rule association in London, but this was before he made a name in all-British politics.

# II

# THE PERILS
# OF NATIONALISM

# 13

# *The Limits of Nationalism*

Nationalism is probably the strongest political force of the twentieth century, and in practice we are all obliged to come to terms with it in a manner ranging from quasi-religious enthusiasm to diplomatic politeness. Few people publicly maintain the general scorn of all nationalisms which was once common among the educated: even within the international communist movement 'cosmopolitanism' became a term of abuse. It is much harder to come to terms with it theoretically, and for no body of people more so than historians. For the theories and beliefs of nationalism are peculiarly difficult to reconcile with a rational understanding of human affairs, and as for the past, Ernest Renan's observation is more than ever true: 'To forget and – I will venture to say – to get one's history wrong, are essential factors in the making of a nation.'

There are two main reasons for this. In the first place, nationalist beliefs represent an almost total historical innovation of the past two centuries, whereas it is an essential article of such theories that 'the nation' is in some sense a natural and permanent part of the human landscape. This is demonstrably not so. Of course the Welsh have always been aware of their Welshness as against the Saxons, the Jews of their Jewishness as against gentiles, and probably all other communities, large or small, have always distinguished 'us' favourably from 'them' in various ways, though not necessarily those recognized by the modern nations to which they are attached today.

However, modern nationalism has not merely changed such sentiments very substantially (for example, by introducing the novel concept of a single standardized national language), but added certain quite unprecedented concepts to them. The most significant of these are the belief that the 'nation' is the primary, even the only, focus of an individual's political and social loyalties and obligations, and the belief that nations aspire to form independent sovereign, nationally homogeneous territorial states. Neither of these ideas can be traced back, for other than pedantic purposes, beyond the era of the French Revolution. Both are now so automatically accepted that the very term 'independent state' is virtually identified with 'nation' (cf: 'United Nations'), and that even states which still claim to be based on an entirely different principle of cohesion, such as Islam, tend to define themselves – perhaps rightly – as 'nations'.

This may or may not be realistic in the twentieth century, but it is quite certainly a fantasy when applied to the past. The relation between, say, the modern Italian nation and the peoples living on its territory in the past is not much closer than that of a modern office building erected on the site of a house where Charles Dickens once lived, to its predecessor, whose GLC plaque it has transferred to its walls. There is a link, but it is less obvious than the differences. Some particularly untraditional nationalisms are not unaware of this fact. Zionism and Israeli nationalism defined themselves in deliberate opposition to the actual past of the Jewish people, and therefore prefer to stress their continuity with the last fighting Jewish inhabitants of Palestine, skating lightly over the intervening eighteen hundred years which, though Jewish enough, are not in any modern sense 'national'. Other nationalisms unselfconsciously produce books with titles like *Five Thousand Years of Pakistan*, in which the pre-historic civilizations of the Indus valley are annexed to a nation or state whose very idea was not invented until the 1930s, and whose criterion of definition (Islam) did not come into existence until seventeen hundred years or so after its alleged beginnings.

The second reason is that nationalism, for sociological reasons which are still largely unexplored, today carries an exceptionally heavy burden of emotional needs. Nationalism is not a programme but a passion which has political consequences. It is therefore quite impervious to reason, though its more intellectual supporters may try to find rationalizations for it according to the prevailing fashions of the day (liberal in the nineteenth century, socialist today). It is easy for those not seized by the passion to see how unconvincing nationalist claims or arguments may be, but this has no effect whatever on those who are. These, in the last analysis, can always fall back on the argument of all who think with their blood – namely that those who do not share that blood cannot by definition understand, and furthermore are not entitled to try.

Paradoxically this denial of possible communication is in practice a plea for understanding, at any rate if the nationalism concerned is weak enough to need sympathy. For a negro to answer criticisms of American Black Power arguments by the statement 'You are not black, you can't know' is another way of saying 'Impracticable though our programme may be, you must understand that its function is to give self-confidence and pride to a people which has been deprived of both, and this is the necessary basis of its regeneration, whatever that may turn out to be. If you were black, you would understand this without argument.'

I, who belong to a people of refugees whose experience has been such as to make me still vaguely uneasy if I don't possess a valid passport and enough cash to transport me to the nearest suitable country at short notice, can understand the situation of the Kenya Asians and feel horrified by British immigration officials in a more profound and visceral way than those for whom the question is primarily one of equal rights and civil liberty in general. But the feeling is neither esoteric nor incomprehensible, and if, like nationalism, I were to deduce from it that the interests of refugees and migrants have absolute priority over everything else, I should be wrong.

Nevertheless, this tendency of nationalism to live intellectually in a closed and self-sealing circle is a fact, and so are its consequences for political and intellectual argument.

It throws the burden of criticizing its irrationalities and excesses on those within. Lenin, who like all Marxists rejected 'the present division of mankind into small states, and all-national isolation', was right to believe that the Russian Bolsheviks must totally accept the non-Russian nationalities' claim to secession, not only because a refusal to do so would mask and encourage 'Great-Russian chauvinism', but also because the task of fighting against secession could not be conducted politically, except by the revolutionaries belonging to the non-Russian nationalities. From outside they could be coerced, but not convinced.

It is for Irishmen to criticize the absurdities of Irish nationalism, Welshmen those of Welsh nationalism, Englishmen those of their own brand – which are harder to detect than the others, at any rate for themselves. Nobody else can do it for them. This may be difficult, unpopular, and at times even hopeless, but the nation which lacks internal critics is lost, like Germany in Hitler's days.

It is not easy for outsiders to conceive how difficult the situation of the internal critic may be, especially at times when, as during wars or movements of passionate national mobilization, the emotional – and practical – pressure on them may be overpowering. It is harder today for a Jew to be anti-Zionist, critical of the policy of Israel, or even non-Zionist, than ever before, because dissent from the majority position, whether right or wrong, carries the stigma of some sort of treason.

When the dissenters form a mass movement, this is not so

serious. The French communists have been unaffected by the accusation of being 'separatists' or foreign agents, because the bulk of their supporters have never had the slightest sense of conflict between their Frenchness, and indeed their instinctive Jacobin nationalism, and their political beliefs. The problem is acute when, say, the Union Jack is not just something waved by politicians at suitable moments but painted by poor men on slum walls, as in Belfast.

For then even ideas become emotionally charged. The discovery of an interesting archaeological site becomes the foundation of a national ritual, as at Masada, and the ownership of fragments of ancient manuscript (the Dead Sea scrolls) a question of furnishing a national shrine. This may be a joke for outsiders, like those debates about the precise ethnic or linguistic status of the inhabitants of Macedonia, about which Yugoslav, Bulgarian and Greek scholars still come to blows. It is no joke for those whose business it is to pursue the truth, or indeed for those within reach of the same armies which still stand behind the embattled scholars.

Nothing may be harder than to reject such emotions. But it must be done and done from within. Some day some Jewish investigator must brave outside pressure and publish a critical study of even the most highly charged of all historical statistics, the six million dead of his people, facing the possibility that, however terrible the actual figure, the accepted one should turn out to be exaggerated. There must be men who demonstrate that belonging to a people is not identical with the acceptance of the prevailing view of what such membership implies.

# 14

## *Tower of Babel*

Some students are ready to go to prison for the right to print road signs in Welsh. Le Corbusier's Chandigarh, built as the capital of one Indian state, is disputed between the Hindi-speaking and the Punjabi-speaking states into which its original country has now split. Belgium is paralysed by the impossibility of finding any political formula to reconcile the demands of Flemings and Walloons. French diplomacy is devoting a considerable, if largely unadvertised, effort to making French the official international language of the Common Market. Anyone glancing at the world news at any time can find evidence of the explosive character of language, though native speakers of English, secure in their linguistic world domination, are probably wondering what the trouble is all about. And well they might, for the problem is by no means clear.

The myth of the Tower of Babel is ancient, but there is no sign that its results caused humanity any real difficulties until the last hundred years or so. There are several reasons for this. In the first place, situations in which people speaking mutually incomprehensible languages meet, or have to communicate, are today vastly more common than in the past. In the second,

language has undergone a major and unnoticed political transformation. It has ceased to be simply what people speak, or more
emotionally loaded, their 'mother tongue', and has become an
attribute of 'the nation'. In consequence knowledge of languages
has become mixed up with questions of prestige, political and
economic rights and a number of other formerly secondary, or
at least self-regulating, matters.

We are in fact living a paradox. At the moment when the
technical unification of the globe makes multilingualism more
essential than ever before, the speakers of all languages except
the ones which happen to have become international lingua
francas resent the need to learn any idiom other than their
own with increasing bitterness. Curiously enough, in the pre-
industrial past, when most people – i.e. the peasants – could
almost certainly manage for practically all purposes with nothing but their local patois, there was no such prejudice against
multilingualism.

This was due partly to social immobility (the fact that lords
talked a different language among themselves hardly affected
peasants), partly to the prevailing illiteracy (documents in Latin
were no harder to understand than documents in the vernacular), partly to the social neutrality of the prevailing international
idioms. Dead classical languages, improvised commercial
pidgins or barrack languages like Urdu were utilitarian and
(apart from scholarly snobbery) little else. Their analogy is with
the 'computer languages' of today, which have so far raised no
political jealousies.

But chiefly it was due to a linguistic division of functions,
such as that which most children still know in places where the
formal (school or home) language and the informal (home or
peer-group) language are different. What Swiss-German children learn is German, what they talk is Schweizerdeutsch, and
there is no problem about which is used when, and virtually
no occasion which does not call clearly for one or the other.
In extreme cases mass bilingualism was (and still is) the rule:

80 per cent of Alsatians practise it today. There is no technical reason why it should not be more general. In less extreme cases, groups whose business brought them into contact with people of different idioms were bilingual or multilingual. But basically languages were non-competitive.

This is plainly no longer so. The present climate of linguistic intolerance is obviously due in part to literacy, which raises the problem of the language of schools, bureaucratic forms and other politically sensitive matters; and even more to democracy and egalitarianism, which naturally make men refuse to accept the low status which goes with being a monoglot speaker of, say, a peasant language. But not entirely. The explosive linguistic issues are sometimes entirely divorced from practical considerations.

What excites Flemings and Welshmen is not that they are at an educational disadvantage because bilingually educated – as a matter of fact, the opposite is true – but that they have to learn English or French in addition to Welsh and Flemish. What nags French governments is that their language is no longer the international code. The explosive factor in language is nationalism.

But the nationalist attitude to language mixes the rational and irrational in a characteristic way. If we suppose (as was historically reasonable until recently) that the basic unit of 'modernization' in societies was a territory of a particular order of magnitude, it almost certainly required, among other things, the supplementation of numerous and often mutually non-intelligible languages or dialects by a single standardized language for an increasing number of purposes.

On the other hand, there is no rational basis to the belief that this standardized 'national language' is in some indefinable sense the basic criterion of nationality and state (so that new nation-states are almost by definition linguistic states); that it should be sufficient for all purposes; still less that it should exclude other languages. It is rarely the basis, and much more often the consequence of nationalism. In extreme cases it is an artefact, like modern Hebrew, which nobody used as a domestic language before 1881 when the eccentric Eliezer Ben Yehuda (who had recently invented the Hebrew word 'nationalism') decided to use nothing else; or a conscious corollary to nationalism, like Hindi, which has no claim to be the national language of India except that a nation ought to have one. This claim in turn threatens to lead to the counterclaim that a historically pluralist and multilingual society 'ought' to fragment into monoglot 'linguistic states', and this in turn approaches the black *reductio ad absurdum*, widely applied in Europe and elsewhere in the past twenty-five years, that 'nations' cannot live with their minorities but must massacre or expel them.

A single language is not enough for all purposes, as the international standardization of traffic signs and the irresistible advance of international and interregional languages demonstrates. Today it is not only people of secondary or higher education who find the disadvantages of being monoglot overwhelming, unless they speak English. The trouble is that languages are no longer seen as functionally distinct and non-competitive.

They are seen as interchangeable and not functionally distinct – except by immigrants who retain (insofar as their new countries let them) some of the pluralism of the past, and airport controllers, who can't afford monolinguistic nationalism. They are seen as equal, which they plainly are not, for several practical purposes. No force on earth will at present make Finnish as useful an international medium as English or give a Georgian the advantage which every Costa Rican has, of naturally speaking a widely understood language.

To produce a 'Journal of Biochemistry' in Basque would be a purely symbolic luxury, which does not mean that national pride might not – or has not – felt such exercises to be essential. It would of course be more convenient if the neutral and dead 'classical' second languages had been replaced by Esperanto or some other politically unexceptional medium, but up to the present history has decided otherwise. Some languages are more equal than others, and natural resentment will not change this.

It is of course almost impossible for an English speaker, even a moderately polyglot one, to say these things, since he will be accused of linguistic chauvinism: more often than we suspect, with justice. Our only acceptable and courteous attitude is to give, say, the Welsh all the support they want if they think they require bilingual road signs in Wales, or for that matter – since we are a multilingual country – in England. Nevertheless, some things must be said. They are unlikely to be said by linguistic zealots, and in the absence of Scandinavians or Dutch, who do not regard the need to supplement the limited currency of their language as a national affront, they may have to come even from the English.

They are first, that the identification of nation and language is not a fact but an ideological invention; secondly, that the coexistence of different languages in one country, or in the same person, is historically quite normal; and thirdly that the modern world requires some multilingualism in every nation, including, of course, those which happen to speak regional or world languages. It goes without saying that all living languages should have equal rights to be taught, printed and officially used where they are spoken, though this implies not only that Bretons should be allowed to learn Breton but also that Irishmen should be at a disadvantage because they do not know Irish.

But if one thing is 100 per cent certain it is that these observations will not have the slightest effect on the Flemings or Walloons, on those who wish to impose Hindi in Madras, or on the gentleman who has lately been arguing that Hebrew is essentially a western language. Linguistic politics are the politics of unreason. Rationalists can merely, like the late Bertrand Russell, keep on trying.

# 15

# *The Unconvincing 'Sociobiology' of Nationalism*

Nationalism as a political phenomenon is enormously influential, totally unpersuasive except to those who don't need persuading in the first place, and, perhaps for this reason, extremely puzzling to the analyst. Its own arguments carry no general conviction, which is why so many nationalists deny that anyone not belonging to their people can 'really' understand them.

At most, we can all agree on a sort of polite convention which in theory accepts the right of any group to call itself a 'nation' and to put forward the same claims as any other nation, however absurd they seem to the outsider. In practice, even this convention breaks down when, as is almost always the case, there is dispute about what group constitutes the nation, and the claims of two or more nationalisms conflict with each other. One would like to hear the reactions of the Scottish National Party if Mar, Buchan, Angus and Moray claimed to be nations (following their classification of such at the ancient University of Aberdeen). Almost all the concepts associated with nationalism are very fuzzy.

This explains the air of desperation which surrounds all

attempts to make some sort of objective sense of nationalism, and to explain its enormous political appeal today; but also the ease with which incautious analysts can fall flat on their faces. The latest, Professor Richard Lynn ('The sociobiology of nationalism', in *New Society*, 1 July 1976), is an unfortunate illustration of both. While rightly convinced that neither sociology nor his own discipline of psychology have satisfactorily interpreted nationalism, his own attempt to do so is a great deal less successful than he appears to think.

Lynn's argument seems to run as follows. Nationalism is simply another form of something which occurs throughout human history – namely the tendency of human beings to separate themselves into largely endogamous in-groups versus the rest. Such groups generate their own culture and 'are variously known as tribes, societies, ethnic groups, cultures or nations'. Since their separatist behaviour often runs counter to reason, we assume it to be instinctive. Since it is otherwise inexplicable, we must, following the usual Darwinian argument, assume that it 'has evolved because it has some survival value'. Various possible survival values are suggested, from the value of in-group loyalty in conquering other groups to the supposed genetic advantages of a population divided into inbreeding sub-populations. Nationalism is therefore part of human nature, explained by 'sociobiology'.

It is not my purpose here to discuss the validity of such sociobiological speculations, and in any case I am no better qualified to do so than Professor Lynn, who is no geneticist either. There is a curious and perhaps rather more naive teleological air about them ('Mum, what are flies *for*?'), but the real objection to Lynn's arguments has nothing to do with the sociobiological hypotheses he is popularizing.

It is that sociobiology has no bearing on nationalism, which is, historically speaking, a very recent phenomenon indeed. It simply cannot be equated with the general tendency of humans to form in groups, whether in-born or not. No doubt nationalism expresses this too, among many other age-old social attitudes, as it annexes anything else it finds convenient in the heritage of the past, adding the wormholes of antiquity to a lot of newly constructed furniture such as a largely fictional national history or even, in many cases, a newly constructed standard national language. But to identify human nature and all history with a specific phenomenon of the past two centuries – and during most of this period mainly European – is to fall into the same absurdity as that which entitled the book on the archaeology of the Indus valley *Five Thousand Years of Pakistan*.

It is possible to speculate about the genetic results of an adaptation to hunting existence in the Americas, but not about the genetic effects of a horseman's life, since there were no horses in the Americas until the Spaniards brought them there. Professor Lynn wastes his time and ours by failing to recognize the distinction between the two kinds of speculation.

Of course, even a psychologist is likely to recognize the difference between societies which ride horses and those that don't by the presence or absence of the horse. Abstractions such as 'nationality', 'independence' or 'separatism' are less easily subdivided. Like cloaks and blankets, and unlike gloves and shoes, their function is to cover a great many parts of a body in an approximate manner and not a specific part exclusively. This semantic vagueness is precisely what allows nationalists to substitute one historically specific reading of such terms as, say, 'England' for any of the others covered by this particular blanket. For the analyst, failure to make conceptual distinctions is dangerous, and, when combined with historical ignorance, fatal.

What Richard Lynn does is, *first*, to adopt the currently prevalent self-definition of nationalism, without being quite aware that he does so; and *second*, quite wrongly, to read it backwards and sideways into history and geography as a universal phenomenon. The 'model' of current nationalism is a politically independent sovereign state, separate from all others, embracing a preferably coherent and continuous territory whose citizens all belong to a single homogeneous 'people', different from all others, preferably using a single specific language, which is – where possible – the preferred criterion for belonging to the 'people'.

Both elementary historical knowledge and a moment's thought will show that this simply could not have been the norm of human history. For one thing, it covers neither the great historical empires such as the Chinese, the Roman or the Ottoman, nor most of the non-imperial parts of the world, including those which could be made to look like 'nations' when seen through nineteenth-century spectacles, such as the ancient Greeks or the Italians and Germans before the French Revolution. In short, for most of history the basic political unit was not – and indeed could not have been – anything like the modern territorial state, and the 'instinct' of separatism was either quite compatible with the membership of vast empires or sought expression on a much smaller scale than that of tribe, ethnic group or culture, which in any case had little in common with the modern nation.

Once we accept that nationalism is a fairly recent historical phenomenon, sociobiology becomes irrelevant to its explanation. It nor more tells us why, say, many Scots want independence from England than it tells us why the Americans prefer base-ball to soccer. Neither question can be answered by generalities about the universality of in-group loyalty, xenophobia and playing team games in human societies, since both questions are essentially specific, whether we think of them primarily as concerned with certain *kinds* of in-group behaviour or team games (spectator sports, modern nationalism) or particular cases (Scotland, baseball).

The danger of such combinations of historical ignorance and intellectual confusion is that, so far from explaining, it merely reinforces myths. Naturally nothing, one assumes, could be further from Lynn's intention. Nevertheless, it is a safe bet that he will be read by interested parties as having demonstrated sci-entifically that Paki-bashing is what makes humanity advance, or that nature has designed the Isle of Man to join the United

Nations. And he will be so read, not simply because interested parties will look for or invent confirmation of their views anyway – if magical prophecy had nationalist sales potential the Quebec separatists would no doubt cite oracles – but because the deficiencies of his argument encourage misrepresentation.

This is a great pity. The least one can expect of scientists who tackle a difficult, complicated and still rather confused problem is conceptual clarity and a modicum of historical and political homework. For want of both, Professor Lynn's attempt is, I am afraid, a total write-off.

# 16

## *State of the Nations*

Review of *Nations and States* by Hugh Seton-Watson.

In our century all politics, whatever else it does, has to come to terms with nationalism. No politicians or political thinkers are happy about the fact, except nationalist ones; and even these are happy only about their own nationalism and about movements sufficiently remote to provide arguments and moral backing for their own. They take a less dispassionate view about those with which they are themselves involved. As the book under review reminds us, the Polish National Democrats were as completely convinced of the injustice of denying Poland its freedom – i.e. against the German and Russian oppressor nations – as they were hostile to Ukrainians, Byelorussians, Lithuanians, Romanians and Jews, who merely lived within or adjoining the boundaries of Poland. Moreover, though most of us agree that politics must come to terms with nationalism, nobody quite knows how to. Today few would care to put forward a programme for doing so with any confidence.

Hugh Seton-Watson's lengthy and fairly encyclopaedic

'inquiry into the origins of nations and the politics of national-ism' illustrates this lack of enthusiasm and confidence in various ways. It is essentially a historical survey, and a very comprehensive one. Hardly any nationalist movement anywhere is not at least mentioned, though the author is clearly most at home in his own field of central-eastern Europe and Euro-Asian Russia, and he drifts into potted textbook history more than once. Perhaps because, unable to find a satisfactory way of defining a nation except *ex post facto*, he does not seriously try to analyse the phenomenon theoretically. This is a pity, for while an analytical model of nations and nationalism is implicit in his wide-ranging and excellently informed survey, it is incomplete, even historically. On the other hand, he is very good at recognizing the historical moment when particular groups or states can be described as nations and when (in spite of nationalist rhetoric) the time to do so has not yet come. He sees that the term is more applicable to, say, Brazil than to Mexico, and hardly at all applicable as yet to much of the African continent.

Perhaps he also tends to avoid generalization, because it might imply a greater commitment to the idea of nationhood than he feels happy about. For him, as for many of us, the most obvious aspects of nationalism are negative: 'Extreme nationalism has been a crude substitute religion, replacing withered faiths by fanatical hatreds. Too often its leaders have been frustrated social misfits and self-important semi-intellectuals. At its worst [it] has led to massacres and forcible expulsions of mainly inno-cent people.'

And once again: 'Nationalists, fanatically determined to set up their own independent state, determined to impose their nationality on peoples within their jurisdiction who do not own it, or to seize territories under another government's rule which they claim should be theirs; are capable of terrible civil wars, and of interstate wars which, in the age of nuclear warfare, may threaten the whole human race with extinction.' Quite rightly, he dismisses the belief which every nationalist movement holds:

namely, that these characteristics apply only to other nations and not, of course, to its own.

Such disenchantment is not to be taken seriously, not only because it is based on wide knowledge, but also because, as every historian of the Habsburg Empire and Czechoslovakia knows, the name Seton-Watson occupies a place of honour in the struggle for the independence of the nations of central-eastern Europe. Yet the author also knows, again quite correctly, that the emergence of nations is an aspect of the emergence of the common people into history, whether we call this the rise of mass society or of democracy. Once nations exist, they are virtually indestructible. We have to live with and mostly in them.

They have not always existed. Some, like the French, the English, the Scots, the Castilians, the Portuguese, Danes, Swedes, Hungarians, Russians and Poles, were already in existence at the time of the French Revolution – the French and English perhaps since the fourteenth century. Some, he argues, were already then on the way to nationhood: the Germans, the Italians, perhaps the Irish, Catalans and Norwegians. Others emerged in the nineteenth and twentieth centuries. Yet others may still emerge. But once on the scene, they are here to stay. It is easy to sympathize with them while they are struggling for identity and liberation, especially when they do so against tyrannical or otherwise undesirable regimes. Enthusiasm diminishes when we observe them after their triumph.

But what to do about nationalism? Leaving aside specific proposals such as federalism for Spain and Britain, Seton-Watson seems to hanker after the solution of 'cultural autonomy', championed before 1914 by the Austro-Marxists and the Jewish *Bund* in Russia – i.e. by a definition of the 'nation' as essentially a community of a specific 'culture' in the widest sense. In theory this is attractive for two reasons. It separates nationalism from state sovereignty, which provides it with its most dangerous weapons. It also separates nationality from territory, thereby recognising that most 'national problems', especially today, are not soluble by independence, separation or partition. As in Belfast, they occur between communities which cannot be effectively unscrambled from one another, except by mass expulsion or massacre. As in the lands of the Bible, the claims of both Jews and Arabs to exclusive possession and control of the city of Jerusalem, which is historically sacred to both (not to mention to Christians), merely leads to permanent war. There is no way of settling such disputes by territorial-nationalist criteria.

In practice the author sees that 'cultural autonomy' is likely to fail, as it did in Austro-Hungary and among the Jews, when applied to nation-states or to groups with national consciousness: though he suggests that it may still be tried with some success in the de facto multi-communal states of Africa and Asia. Yet even this does not quite face the crucial difficulty. Nation and territorial state, as Seton-Watson recognizes, are historically intertwined. This has not always been so, and may not last for ever. However, so long as the territorial state ('nation-state') remains the standard international political unit, there is not much chance of disentangling the 'nation' from the territory which it regards, rightly or often wrongly, as its exclusive preserve. States will create 'nations' to fill their structures. Nations will correspondingly feel incomplete without state sovereignty. If the nation could really be defined simply as a cultural community, as the Austro-Marxists held, the problems of national coexistence in the Middle East might indeed be manageable, as they were under the Ottoman Empire. But alas, the Leninists were right to include territory in their definition. That is why there is no formula for peace which is acceptable to both Israelis and Palestinians today.

We may speculate about the future of the 'nation-state', but it remains alive and strong, though with its external sovereign powers undermined and attenuated. Nobody therefore has a solution to the problem of nationalism except, in such states as are prepared to use it, coercive force. Even in Yugoslavia, whose achievement in progressing 'towards a solution of national conflicts within a multinational state' Seton-Watson rightly admires, national tensions have led to a reassertion of a policy of force. His optimistic assessment of Yugoslav federalism may be justified, but, alas, not all of us can share it.

As the author does not know what to do about nationalism any more than his readers and reviewers, his book is best read for comparative information about it. Since comprehensive surveys are rare, and most people interested in the subject, starting with most nationalists, are extremely ignorant about all but a tiny handful of national movements and situations, *Nations and States* is a very useful book. Its thirteen chapters cover old and new European nations, national and multinational states, European colonial nations overseas, the Muslim world, East Asia, Africa, race and nation, diaspora nations, class and ideology.

The author's bias – notably about the Soviet Union – has to be discounted from time to time, and his treatment of some significant national movements, such as the Vietnamese, is plainly more cursory than of others. The index, essential in a book such as this, could have been better. The bibliography is sometimes curious, and not many of us will benefit by the titles in Romanian, Magyar, Slovak and Serbo-Croat. Still, every reader will learn a great deal from this book that he or she did not know before. It may lend itself to reference rather than to breathless reading. But who among us would not wish to have written a work which will be constantly referred to and, probably, plagiarized without acknowledgement? And who among us will predict that Seton-Watson's subject is likely to lose its interest and urgency?

# 17

## *Are All Tongues Equal?*

'Language, culture and national identity' is the title of this paper, but its central subject is the situation of languages in cultures, written or spoken languages still being the main medium of these. More specifically, my subject is 'multiculturalism' insofar as this depends on language. 'Nations' come into it, since in the states in which we all live political decisions about how and where languages are used for public purposes (for example, in schools) are crucial. And these states are today commonly identified with 'nations' as in the term United Nations. This is a dangerous confusion. So let me begin with a few words about it.

Since there are hardly any colonies left, practically all of us today live in independent and sovereign states. With the rarest exceptions, even exiles and refugees live in states, though not their own. It is fairly easy to get agreement about what constitutes such a state, at any rate the modern model of it, which has become the template for all new independent political entities since the late eighteenth century. It is a territory, preferably coherent and demarcated by frontier lines from its neighbours, within which all citizens without exception come under the exclusive rule of the territorial government and the rules under which it operates. Against this there is no appeal, except by authorization of that government; for even the superiority of European Community law over national law was established only by the decision of the constituent governments of the Community. Within the state's territory all are citizens who are born and live there except those specifically excluded as 'foreigners' by the state, which also has the power to admit people to citizenship – but not, in democratic states, to deprive them of it. Foreigners are taken to belong to some other territorial state, though the growth of inhumanity since the First World War has produced a growing, and now very large, body of officially invisible denizens for whom special terms had to be devised in our tragic century: 'stateless', 'apatride', 'illegal immigrant', or whatever.

At some time, mainly since the end of the nineteenth century, the inhabitants of this state have been identified with an 'imagined community' bonded together, as it were laterally, by such things as language, culture, ethnicity and the like. The ideal of such a state is represented by an ethnically, culturally and linguistically homogeneous population. We now know that this standing invitation to 'ethnic cleansing' is dangerous and completely unrealistic, for out of the almost two hundred states today only about a dozen correspond to this programme. Moreover, it would have surprised the founders of the original nation-states. For them, the unity of the nation was political and not socio-anthropological. It consisted in the decision of a sovereign people to live under common laws and a common constitution, irrespective of culture, language and ethnic composition. 'A nation,' said the Abbé Sieyès, with habitual French lucidity, 'is the totality of individuals united by living under a common law and represented by the same legislative assembly' (*Qu'est-ce que le Tiers-État?*, January 1789). The assumption that communities of ethnic descent, language, culture, religion and so on ought to find expression in territorial states, let alone in a single territorial state, was, of course, equally new. It could actually be a reversal of historic values, as in Zionism. 'Strangers have arisen,' wrote in 1900 an orthodox rabbi from Dzików (Poland), who undoubtedly represented the tradition of Judaism,

> who say that the people of Israel should be clothed in secular nationalism, a nation like all other nations, that Judaism rests on three things, national feeling, the land and the language, and that national feeling is the most praiseworthy element in the brew and the most effective in preserving Judaism, while the observance of the Torah and the commandments is a private matter depending on the inclination of each individual. May the Lord rebuke these evil men and may He who chooseth Jerusalem seal their mouths.[1]

A third observation brings me closer to the main theme of this lecture. The concept of a single, exclusive, and unchanging ethnic or cultural or other identity is a dangerous piece of brainwashing. Human mental identities are not like shoes, of which we can only wear one pair at a time. We are all multi-dimensional beings. Whether a Mr Patel in London will think of himself primarily as an Indian, a British citizen, a Hindu, a Gujarati-speaker, an ex-colonist from Kenya, a member of a specific caste or kin group, or in some other capacity depends on whether he faces an immigration officer, a Pakistani, a Sikh or Muslim, a Bengali-speaker, and so on. There is no single platonic essence of Patel. He is all these and more at the same time. David Selbourne, a London ideologue, calls on 'the Jew in England' to 'cease to pretend to be English' and to recognize that his 'real' identity is as a Jew. The only people who face us with such either-or choices are those whose policies have led or could lead to genocide.

Moreover, historically multiple identity lies behind even national homogeneity. Every German in the past, and vestigially even today, had simultaneously two or three identities: as members of a 'tribe' – the Saxons, the Swabians, the Franks – a

German principality or state, and a linguistic culture combining a single standard written language for all Germans with a variety of spoken dialects, some of which also had begun to develop a written literature. (The Reformation brought not only one, but several Bible translations into German languages.) Indeed, until Hitler, people were regarded as Germans by virtue of being Bavarians, Saxons, or Swabians who could often understand one another only when they spoke the written standard culture-language.

This brings me naturally to my central theme of multilingualism and multiculturalism. Both are historically novel as concepts. They could not arise until the combination of three circumstances: the aspiration to universal literacy, the political mobilization of the common people, and a particular form of linguistic nationalism.

Historically, the coexistence of peoples of different languages and cultures is normal; or, rather, nothing is less common than countries inhabited exclusively by people of a single uniform language and culture. Even in Iceland, with its three hundred thousand inhabitants, such uniformity is only maintained by a ruthless policy of Icelandization, including forcing every immigrant to take an ancient Icelandic name. At the time of the French Revolution, only half the inhabitants of France could speak French, and only 12–13 per cent spoke it 'correctly'; and the extreme case is Italy, where at the moment it became a state only two or three Italians out of a hundred actually used the Italian language at home. So long as most people lived in an oral universe, there was no necessary link between the spoken and the written language of the literate minority. So long as reading and writing were strictly affairs for specialized minorities, it did not even have to be a living language. The administration of India in the 1830s switched from written classical Persian, which nobody in India spoke, to written English, which was equally incomprehensible. If illiterates needed to communicate with those who spoke other languages, they relied on intermediaries who could speak or else learned enough of the older language to get by, or developed pidgins or creoles which became unwritten but effective means of communication and have become a fashionable topic for study among linguists.

A single national language only became important when ordinary citizens became an important component of the state; and the written language had to have a relation to the spoken language only when these citizens were supposed to read and write it. But remember that universal primary education, outside of a few exceptional countries, is not much more than a century old.

The original case for a standard language was entirely democratic, not cultural. How could citizens understand, let alone take part in, the government of their country if it was conducted in an incomprehensible language – for example, in Latin, as in the Hungarian parliament before 1840? Would this not guarantee government by an elite minority? This was the argument of the Abbé Grégoire in 1794 (see his *Rapport sur la nécessité et les moyens d'anéantir les patois et d'universaliser l'usage de la langue française*; 'Report on the need and the means to wipe out dialects and make the use of French universal'). Education in French was, therefore, essential for French citizens, whatever the language they spoke at home. This remained essentially the position in the United States, another product of the same age of democratic revolution. To be a citizen, an immigrant had to pass a test in English, and readers of Leo Rosten's *The Education of Hyman Kaplan* (1937) will be familiar with this process of linguistic homogenization. I need not add that Mr Kaplan's struggles with the English language were not intended to stop him from talking Yiddish with his wife at home, which he certainly did; nor did they affect his children, who obviously went to English-speaking public schools. What people spoke or wrote among themselves was nobody's business but their own, like their religion. You will remember that even in 1970 – that is to say before the onset of the present wave of mass immigration – thirty-three million

Americans, plus an unknown percentage of another nine million who did not answer the relevant question, said that English was not their mother tongue. Over three-quarters of them were second generation or older American-born.[2]

In practice, education in languages other than the standard national language was traditionally left to private effort, to special voluntary provision by minority communities, as in the case of the Czech Comenius schools which were set up in Vienna after 1918 with help from the Czech government for the large Czech minority in the city, or by local option, as often happened in America. Thus, bilingual education in English and German was introduced in Cincinnati in 1840. Most such arrangements – and there were several in the second half of the century – had quietly faded away by the time the demand for official federal bilingual education surfaced in the 1960s and 1970s. Let me say that this was a political rather than an educational demand. It was part of the rise of a new kind of ethnic and identity politics during this period.

The situation was different, of course, where there was no single predominant national language, spoken or even written, or where a linguistic community resented the superior status of another language. In the multinational Habsburg Empire, 'the language of (public) office and school' became a political issue from 1848, as it did somewhat later in Belgium and Finland. The usual minimum formula here was – and I quote the Hungarian Nationality Law of 1868 – that people should be educated in their own language at primary school level and under certain circumstances at secondary school level, and that they should be allowed to use it directly or through interpreters in dealings with public authorities. (But note that what was a language was politically defined. It did not include Yiddish nor the creole spoken in Istria, where experts in the 1850s counted thirteen different national varieties.[3] To have a language, as distinct from a dialect or 'jargon', you needed to be classified as a nation or nationality. The minimum formula could work in areas of solid settlement by one language group, and local or even regional government could be substantially conducted in what was called the 'language of common use' (*Umgangsprache*), but it raised big problems in areas of mixed settlement and in most cities. The real educational issue, of course, was not primary, but secondary and tertiary education. This is where the major battles were fought. Here, the issue was not mass literacy, but the linguistic status of unofficial elites. For we must remember that until the Second World War not more than 2 per cent of the age group fifteen to nineteen went to high school, even in countries with a reputation for democracy like Denmark and the Netherlands. Under the circumstances, any Fleming or Finn who had gotten to university level was certainly capable of pursuing it in French or Swedish.

In short, once again the issue was not educational, but political.

Basically, this system of one official language per country became part of everyone's aspiration to become a nation-state, though special arrangements had to be made for minorities which insisted on them. Multilingual nations like Switzerland were regarded as freaks; and de facto, given the great cantonal autonomy of that country, even Switzerland is hardly multilingual because every canton except one (Grisons) is in fact monoglot. Colonies winning their independence after the Second World War automatically thought in terms of some home-grown national language as the base of national education and culture – Urdu in Pakistan, Hindi in India, Sinhala in Sri Lanka, Arabic in Algeria. As we shall see in a moment, this was a dangerous delusion. Small peoples which define themselves ethnic-linguistically still hanker after this ideal of homogeneity: Latvia only for Lettish-speakers, Moldavia only for Romanians. As it so happened in 1940, when this area once again passed to Russia, almost half its population consisted not of Romanians, but of Ukrainians, Russians, Bulgarians, Turks, Jews and a number of other groups. Let us be clear:

in the absence of a willingness to change languages, national linguistic homogeneity in multi-ethnic and multi-lingual areas can be achieved only by mass compulsion, expulsion, or genocide. Poland, which had a third non-Polish population in 1939, is today overwhelmingly Polish, but only because its Germans were expelled to the west; its Lithuanians, Byelorussians and Ukrainians were detached to form part of the USSR in the east; and its Jews were murdered. Let me add that neither Poland nor any other 'homogeneous' country can stay homogeneous in the present world of mass labour migration, mass flight, mass travel and mass urbanization except, once again, by ruthless exclusion or the creation de jure or de facto of apartheid societies.

The case for the privileged use of any language as the only language of education and culture in a country is, thus, political and ideological or, at best, pragmatic. Except in one respect, it is not educational. Universal literacy is extremely difficult to achieve in a written language that has no relation to the spoken vernacular – and it may be impossible unless the parents and the community are particularly anxious for their children to become literate in that language, as is the case with most immigrants into anglophone countries today. Whether this requires formal bilingual education is another matter. Basically, the demand for official education in a language other than the already established one, when this does not bring obvious advantages to the learners, is a demand for recognition or for power or for status, not for easier learning. However, it may also be a demand for ensuring the survival and development of a non-competitive language otherwise likely to fade away. Whether official institutionalization is necessary to achieve this today is an interesting question, but, according to the best expert in the field, bilingual education alone will not do the trick.[4]

Let me just add one important point. Any language that moves from the purely oral to the realm of reading and writing, that is, a fortiori any language that becomes a medium for school teaching or official use, changes its character. It has to be standardized in grammar, spelling, vocabulary and perhaps pronunciation. And its lexical range has to be extended to cover new needs. At least a third of the vocabulary of modern Hebrew has been formed in the twentieth century, since biblical Hebrew, rather like the Welsh of the Mabinogion, belonged to a people of ancient herdsmen and peasants. The established culture-languages of modern states – Italian, Spanish, French, English, German, Russian and one or two others – went through this phase of social engineering before the nineteenth century. Most of the world's written languages did so in the past hundred years, insofar as they were 'modernized', and some, like Basque, are still in the process of doing so. The very process of turning language into a medium of writing destroys it as a vernacular. Suppose we say, as champions of African-Americans sometimes say: our kids should not be taught in standard English, which is a language they do not speak, but in their own black English, which is not a 'wrong' version of standard English, but an independent idiom of its own. So it may be. But if you turned it into a school language, it would cease to be the language that the kids speak. A distinguished French historian, whose native language was Flemish, once said: 'The Flemish they now learn in school in Flanders is not the language the mothers and grandmothers of Flanders taught their children.' It is no longer a 'mother tongue' in the literal sense. A lady who looked after my apartment in New York, bilingual in Spanish and Galician like all from her region in Spain, has difficulty in understanding the purified and standardized Gallego which is now an official language in Galicia. It is not the language of common use in the region, but a new social construct.

What I have said so far may be true or not, but it is now largely out of date. For three things have happened which were not thought of in the heyday of nationalism and are still not thought of by the dangerous latecomers to nationalism. First, we no longer live entirely in a culture of reading and writing. Second, we no longer live in a world where the idea of a single all-purpose national language is generally feasible; that is, we live in a necessarily plurilingual world. And third, we live in an era when at least for the time being there is a single language for universal global communication, namely, a version of English.

The first development is basically the effect of film and television and, above all, the small portable radio. It means that spoken vernacular languages are no longer only face-to-face, domestic, or restricted idioms. Illiterates are, therefore, directly within the reach of the wider world and wider culture. This may also mean that small languages and dialects can survive more easily, insofar as even a modest population is enough to justify a local radio programme. Minority languages, thus, can be cheaply provided for. However, exposure to some bigger language through the media may speed up linguistic assimilation. On balance, radio favours small languages, television has been hostile to them, but this may no longer be true when cable and satellite television are as accessible as FM radio. In New York, in 1994, television programmes were available in Italian, French, Chinese, Japanese, Spanish, Polish, Greek, and even occasionally in Albanian. In short, it is no longer necessary to make a language official if it is to be moved out of the home and off the street into the wider world. Of course, none of this means that illiterates are not at a severe and growing disadvantage compared to literates, whether in written languages or in computer languages.

In Europe, national standard languages were usually based on a combination of dialects spoken by the main state people which was transformed into a literary idiom. In the postcolonial states, this is rarely possible, and when it is, as in Sri Lanka, the results of giving Sinhalese exclusive official status have been disastrous. In fact, the most convenient 'national languages' are either lingua francas or pidgins developed purely for intercommunication between peoples who do not talk each other's languages, like Swahili, Pilipino or Bahasa Indonesia, or former imperial languages like English in India and Pakistan. Their advantages are that they are neutral between the languages actually spoken and put no one group at a particular advantage or disadvantage. Except, of course, the elite. The price India pays for conducting its affairs in English as an insurance against language-based civil wars such as that in Sri Lanka is that people who have not had the several years full-time education which make a person fluent in a foreign written language will never make it above a relatively modest level in public affairs or – today – in business. That price is worth paying, I think. Nevertheless, imagine the effect on Europe if Hindi were the only language of general communication in the European Parliament, and *The Times*, *Le Monde* and the *Frankfurter Allgemeine Zeitung* could be read only by those literate in Hindi.

All this is changing, or will profoundly change, the relation of languages to each other in multinational societies. The ambition of all languages in the past which aspired to the status of national languages and to be the basis of national education and culture was to be all-purpose languages at all levels, that is, interchangeable with the major culture-languages. Especially, of course, with the dominant language against which they tried to establish themselves. Thus, in Finland, Finnish was to be capable of replacing Swedish for all purposes, in Belgium Flemish of replacing French. Hence the real triumph of linguistic emancipation was to set up a vernacular university: in the history of Finland, Wales and the Flemish movement, the date when such a university was established is a major date in nationalist history. A lot of smaller languages have tried to do this over the past centuries, starting, I suppose, with Dutch in the seventeenth century and ending, so far, with Catalan. Some are still trying to do it, like Basque.

Now in practice this is ceasing to be the case operationally, although small-nation nationalism does what it can to resist the trend. Languages once again have niches and are used in different situations and for different purposes. Therefore, they do not need to cover the same ground. This is partly because for international purposes only a few languages are actually used. Though the administration of the European Union spends one-third of its income on translation from and into all the eleven languages in it which have official status, it is a safe bet that the overwhelming bulk of its actual work is conducted in not more than three languages. Again, while it is perfectly possible to devise a vocabulary for writing papers in molecular biology in Estonian, and for all I know this has been done, nobody who wishes to be read – except by the other Estonian molecular biologists – will write such papers. They will need to write them in internationally current languages, as even the French and the Germans have to do in such fields as economics. Only if the number of students coming into higher education is so large and if they are recruited from monoglot families is there a sound educational reason for a full vernacular scientific vocabulary – and then only for introductory textbooks; for all more advanced purposes, students will have to learn enough of an international language to read the literature, and probably they also will have to learn enough of the kind of English which is today for intellectuals what Latin was in the Middle Ages. It would be realistic to give all university education in certain subjects in English today, as is partly done in countries like the Netherlands and Finland which once were the pioneers of turning local vernaculars into all-purpose languages. There is no other way. Officially, nineteenth-century Hungary succeeded in making Magyar into such an all-purpose language for everything from poetry to nuclear physics. In practice, since only ten million speak it, every educated Hungarian has to be, and is, plurilingual.

What we have today are not interchangeable but complementary languages, whatever the official position. In Switzerland, there is no pressure to turn the spoken idiom of Schweizerdeutsch into a written language because there is no political objection to using High German English, and French for this purpose. In Catalonia, the cost of turning Catalan into an all-purpose language is to deprive poor and uneducated inhabitants of this bilingual region of the native advantage of speaking and writing one of the few major international languages, namely Spanish. In Paraguay everybody speaks Guarani (well, strictly speaking 45 per cent of the population are bilingual), the Indian language which has, ever since the country was established as a Spanish colony, served as a regional lingua franca. However, though it has long had equal rights, so far as I can see it is written chiefly for purposes of belles-lettres; for all other purposes, Spanish is used. It is extremely unlikely that in Peru, where Quechua (rightly) acquired official standing in the 1970s, there will be much demand either for daily newspapers or university education in that language. Why should there be? Even in Barcelona, where Catalan is universally spoken by the locals, the great majority of daily papers read, including the local Catalan edition of national papers, are in Spanish. As for the typical Third-World state, as I have pointed out, they cannot possibly have just one all-purpose language.

This is the situation which has encouraged the rise of lingua francas in countries and regions and of English as a worldwide medium of communication. Such pidgins or creoles may be culture and literary languages, but that is not their main purpose. Medieval clerk's Latin had very little to do with Virgil and Cicero. They may or may not become official languages – for countries do need languages of general public communication – but when they do, they should avoid becoming monopoly culture-languages. And the less we let the poets get their hands on such communication languages the better, for poetry encourages both incommunicability and linguistic nationalism. However, such languages are tempted to let themselves be dominated by bureaucratic or technical jargon since this is their primary use. This also should be fought in the interests of clarity. Since American English is already one of the most jargon-ridden idioms ever invented, the danger is real.

Let me conclude with some remarks about what one might call purely political languages – that is, languages which are created specifically as symbols of nationalist or regionalist aspiration, generally for separatist or secessionist purposes. The case for these is non-existent. The extreme example is the attempted reconstitution of the Cornish language, last spoken in the mid-eighteenth century, which has no other purpose except to demarcate Cornwall from England. Such constructed languages may succeed, like Hebrew in Israel – that is, they may turn into real spoken and living languages – or they may fail, like the attempt by nationalist poets between the wars to turn the Scots dialect into a literary language ('Lallans'), but neither communication nor culture is the object of such exercises. These are extreme cases, but all languages have elements of such political self-assertion, for in an era of national or regional secessionism there is a natural tendency to complement political independence by linguistic separatism. We can see this happening in Croatia at the moment. It has the additional advantage of providing a privileged zone of employment for a body of nationalist or regionalist militants, as in Wales. Let me repeat: politics and not culture is at the core of this language manipulation, as the experts in the study of language purism have established. Czech language purism was directed mainly at the elimination of German elements but did not resist the mass influx of French borrowings or the old Latin loan-words.[5] This is natural enough. The Ruthenes do not define themselves as a 'nation' with a 'language' in general, but specifically against the Ukrainians.[6] Catalan nationalism is directed exclusively against Spain, just as linguistic Welsh nationalism is directed exclusively against English.

However, there is today a new element encouraging the political creation of languages, namely, the systematic regionalization of states, which assimilated regions without special linguistic, ethnic or other characteristics, to the potentially separatist areas – for example, Murcia to Catalonia. If Spain is a guide, this will lead to the creation of localized 'official' languages, no doubt eventually – as in Catalonia – demanding monopoly status. What is true of Valencia today may be true of Picardy tomorrow.

# Are All Tongues Equal?

This raises the spectre of general Balkanization. Given the European Union's policy of favouring regions against existing nation-states, which is de facto a policy favouring separatism, as the Scots and Catalan nationalists have quickly recognized, this is a real problem. Balkanization will not solve any problems of linguistic and cultural identity. We shall continue as before. Brussels may spend one-third of its income on translation and interpretation, and if Europe can afford it, why not? But the affairs of the community will not be primarily or at all conducted in Portuguese or Greek or even Danish and Dutch. What linguistic Balkanization will do is to multiply the occasions for conflict. If the Croats can create a separate language for themselves out of the unified Serbo-Croat which their forefathers constructed to unify the southern Slavs – not with much success – then anybody can. So long as language is not as firmly separated from the state as religion was in the United States under the American Constitution, it will be a constant and generally artificial source of civil strife.

Let us remember the Tower of Babel. It remained forever uncompleted because God condemned the human race to everlasting linguistic conflict.

# Notes

1　Cited in Elie Kedourie, *Nationalism* (London, 1960), p. 76.
2　S. Thernstrom et al. (eds), *Harvard Encyclopedia of American Ethnic Groups* (Cambridge, Mass., 1980), p. 632.
3　Rolf Wörsdörfer, '"Ethnizitaet" und Entnationalisierung', *Oester reichische Zeitschrift fur Geschichtswissenschaften*, 5 (Jg 2/1994), p. 206.
4　Joshua Fishman, 'Language Maintenance', in S. Thernstrom et al. (eds), op. cit., p. 636.
5　Bjorn Jernudd and Michael Shapiro, eds, *The Politics of Language Purism* (Berlin, 1989), p. 218.
6　Paul Robert Magocsi, 'The Birth of a New Nation or the Return of an Old Problem? The Rusyns of East Central Europe', *Canadian Slavonic Papers/Revue canadienne des slavistes*, 34:3 (1992), pp. 199–223.

# 18

## *Falklands Fallout*

> Patriotism in the hands of the labour movement is a
> powerful weapon. Patriotism in the hands of the right
> is fraught with danger. The Falklands War sounded
> some alarm bells which the left ignores at its peril.

More has been talked about the Falklands than about any
other recent issue in British and international politics and more
people lost their marbles about this than about almost anything
else. I don't mean the great bulk of the people, whose reactions
were probably considerably less passionate or hysterical than
those whose business it is to write, and formulate opinions. I
want to say very little indeed about the origins of the Falklands
War because that war actually had very little to do with the
Falklands. Hardly anybody knew about the Falklands. I suppose
the number of people in this country who had any personal
relations with the Falklands or even knew anybody who had
been there, is minimal. The 1680 natives of these islands were
very nearly the only people who took an urgent interest in the
Falklands, apart of course from the Falkland Island Company,
which owns a good deal of it, ornithologists and the Scott Polar
Research Institute, since the islands are the basis of all the
research activities in the Antarctic. They were never very important, or at least they haven't been since the First World War or

perhaps just the beginning of the Second World War. They were
so insignificant and so much out of the centre of interest that
parliament let the running be made by about a dozen MPs, the
Falklands lobby, which was politically a very, very mixed lot.
They were allowed to stymie all the not very urgent efforts of
the Foreign Office to settle the problem of the islands' fixture.
Since the government and everybody else found the Falklands
totally without interest, the fact that they were of urgent interest
in Argentina, and to some extent in Latin America as a whole,
was overlooked. They were indeed far from insignificant to the
Argentinians. They were a symbol of Argentinian nationalism,
especially since Perón. We could put the Falklands problem off
for ever, or we thought we could, but not the Argentinians.

## A question of neglect

Now, I'm not judging the validity of the Argentinian claim.
Like so many nationalist claims it can't bear much investigation.
Essentially it's based on what you might call 'secondary-school
geography' – anything that belongs to the continental shelf
ought to belong to the nearest country – in spite of the fact that
no Argentinians had ever actually lived there. Nevertheless,
we're bound to say that the Argentinian claim is almost certainly
rather stronger than the British claim and has internationally
been regarded as rather stronger. The Americans for instance
never accepted the British claim, whose official justification
changed from time to time. But the point isn't to decide which
claim is stronger. The point is that, for the British government,
the Falklands were about as low as they could be on its list of
priorities. And it was totally ignorant of Argentinian and Latin
American views, which are not merely those of the junta but of
all Latin America. As a result it managed, by withdrawing the
one armed ship, the *Endurance*, which had always been there
symbolically indicating that you couldn't take the Falklands
over, to suggest to the Argentinian junta that the UK wouldn't

resist. The Argentinian generals, who were patently crazy and inefficient as well as nasty, decided to go ahead with the invasion. But for mismanagement by the UK government, the Argentinian government would pretty certainly not have decided to invade. They miscalculated and they should never have invaded but it's perfectly clear that the British government actually precipitated the situation, even though it did not mean to. And so, on 3 April the British people discovered that the Falklands had been invaded and occupied. The government should have known that an invasion was imminent, but claimed it didn't, or at any rate if it did know it took no action.

## An upsurge of popular feeling

But what was the situation in Britain when war broke out and during the war itself? Let me try to summarize it fairly briefly. The first thing that happened was an almost universal sense of outrage among a lot of people, the idea that you couldn't simply accept this, something had to be done. This was a sentiment which was felt at all levels right down to the grass roots and it was unpolitical in the sense that it went through all parties and was not confined to the right or to the left. I know of lots of people on the left within the movement, even on the extreme left, who had the same reaction as people on the right. It was this general sense of outrage and humiliation which was expressed on that first day in parliament when the pressure for action actually came not from Thatcher and the government, but from all sides, the ultra-right in the Conservatives, the Liberals and Labour, with only the rarest of exceptions. This I think was a public sentiment which could actually be felt. Anybody who had any kind of sensitivity to the vibes knew that this was going on, and anyone on the left who was not aware of this grass-roots feeling, and that it was not a creation of the media, at least, not at this stage, but genuinely a sense of outrage and humiliation, ought seriously to reconsider their capacity to assess politics. It may not be a particularly desirable sentiment, but to claim that it didn't exist is quite unrealistic.

## Irresistible decline

Now, this upsurge of feeling had nothing to do with the Falklands as such. We have seen that the Falklands were simply a far-away territory swathed in mists off Cape Horn, about which we knew nothing and cared less. It has everything to do with the history of this country since 1945 and the visible acceleration of the crisis of British capitalism since the late 1960s and in particular the slump of the late 70s and early 80s. So long as the great international boom of western capitalism persisted in the 50s and 60s even the relatively weak Britain was to some extent gently borne upwards by the current which pushed other capitalist economies forward even more rapidly. Things were clearly getting better and we didn't have to worry too much although there was obviously a certain amount of nostalgia around the place. And yet at a certain stage it became evident that the decline and crisis of the British economy were getting much more dramatic. The slump in the 70s intensified this feeling and of course since 1979 the real depression, the deindustrialization of the Thatcher period and mass unemployment, have underlined the critical condition of Britain. So the gut reaction that a lot of people felt at the news that Argentina had simply invaded and occupied a bit of British territory could have been put into the following words: 'Ours is a country which has been going downhill for decades, the foreigners have been getting richer and more advanced than we are, everybody's looking down on us and pitying us, we can't even beat the Argentinians or anybody else at football any more, everything's going wrong in Britain, nobody really quite knows what to do about it and how to put it right. But now it's got to the point where some bunch of foreigners think they can simply march some troops onto British territory, occupy it and take it over, and they think the British are so far gone that nobody's going to do anything about it, nothing's going to be done. Well, this is the straw that breaks the camel's back, something's got to be done. By God we'll have to show them that we're not really just there to be walked over.' Once again, I'm not judging the validity of this point of view but I think this is roughly what a lot of the people who didn't try to formulate it in words felt at that moment.

## Decline of the empire

Now, in fact, we on the left had always predicted that Britain's loss of empire, and general decline, would lead to some dramatic reaction sooner or later in British politics. We hadn't envisaged this particular reaction but there's no question that this was a reaction to the decline of the British Empire such as we had predicted for so long. And that is why it had such very wide backing. In itself it wasn't simply jingoism. But, though this feeling of national humiliation went far beyond the range of simple jingoism, it was easily seized by the right and it was taken over in what I think was politically a very brilliant operation by Mrs Thatcher and the Thatcherites. Let me quote her in the classic statement of what she thought the Falklands War proved: 'When we started out there were the waverers and the faint-hearts, the people who thought we could no longer do the great things we once did, those who believed our decline was irreversible, that we could never again be what we were, that Britain was no longer the nation that had built an empire and ruled a quarter of the world. Well they were wrong.'

In fact, the war was purely symbolic; it didn't prove anything of the kind. But here you see the combination of somebody catching certain popular vibes and turning them in a right-wing (I hesitate, but only just, to say a semi-fascist) direction. That is why from the right-wing point of view it was essential not simply to get the Argentinians out of the Falklands, which would have been perfectly practicable by a show of force plus negotiation, but to wage a dramatic victorious war. That is why the war was provoked by the British side whatever the Argentinian attitude. There's little doubt that the Argentinians, as soon as they discovered that this was the British attitude, were looking for a way out of an intolerable situation. Thatcher wasn't prepared to let them because the whole object of the exercise was not to settle the matter now but to prove that Britain was still great, if only in a symbolic fashion. At virtually every stage the policy of the British government in and out of the United Nations was one of total intransigence. I'm not saying that the junta made it easy to come to a settlement but I think historians will conclude that a negotiated withdrawal of the Argentinians was certainly not out of the question. It wasn't seriously tried.

## A new alliance

This provocative policy had a double advantage. Internationally, it gave Britain a chance to demonstrate her hardware, her determination and her military power. Domestically, it allowed the Thatcherites to seize the initiative from other political forces within and outside the Conservative Party. It enabled a sort of takeover by the Thatcherites not only of Conservative camp but of a great area of British politics. In a curious way the nearest parallel to the Thatcherite policy during the Falklands War is the Peronist policy which, on the other side, had first launched the Falklands into the centre of Argentinian politics. Perón, like Mrs Thatcher and her little group, tried to speak directly to the masses using the mass media, over the heads of the establishment. In our case that included the Conservative establishment as well as the Opposition. She insisted on running her own war. It wasn't a war run by parliament. It wasn't even run by the cabinet; it was a war conducted by Mrs Thatcher and a small war cabinet. At the same time she established direct lateral relations, which I hope will not have long-term political effects, with the military. And it is this combination of a direct demagogic approach to the masses, by-passing the political processes and the establishment, and the forging of direct lateral contact with the military and the defence bureaucracy, that is characteristic of the war. Neither costs nor objectives counted, least of all of course the Falklands, except as symbolic proof of British virility, something which could be put into headlines. This was the kind of war which existed in order to produce victory parades. That is why all the symbolically powerful resources of war and empire were mobilized on a miniature scale. The role of the navy was paramount anyway, but traditionally public opinion has invested a lot of emotional capital in it. The forces sent to the Falklands were a mini museum of everything which could give the Union Jack particular resonance – the Guards, the new technological strong men, the SAS, the Paras; all were represented, down to those little old Gurkhas. They weren't necessarily needed but you had to have them just because this was, as it were, a recreation of something like the old imperial durbars, or the processions at the death or the coronation of British sovereigns.

### *Clochemerle* rides again

We cannot in this instance quote Karl Marx's famous phrase about history repeating itself, the first time as tragedy, the second time as farce, because no war is a farce. Even a little war in which 250 Britons and two thousand Argentinians get killed is not a matter for jokes. But for foreigners who didn't realize the crucial role of the Falklands War in British domestic politics, the war certainly seemed and absolutely incomprehensible exercise. *Le Monde* in France called it a *Clochemerle* of the South Atlantic. You may remember that famous 1934 novel by Gabriel Chevallier, in which the right and the left in a small French town come to enormous blows over the question of where to situate a public lavatory. Most Europeans simply could not understand what all the fuss was about. What they did not appreciate was that the whole thing was not about the Falklands at all and not about the right of self-determination. It was an operation concerned basically with British politics and with the British political mood. Having said that, let me just say very firmly that the alternative was not between doing nothing and Thatcher's war. I think it was politically absolutely impossible at this stage for any British government not to do anything. The alternatives were not simply to accept the Argentinian occupation by passing the buck to the United Nations, which would have adopted empty resolutions, or on the other hand, Mrs Thatcher's intended replay of Kitchener's victory over the Sudanese at Omdurman in 1898.

The pacifist line was that of a small and isolated minority, if indeed a minority with a respectable tradition in the labour movement. That line was simply politically not on. The very feebleness of the demonstrations which were being organized at the time showed this. The people who said the war was pointless, and should never have been started, have been proved right in the abstract, but they themselves have not benefited politically and aren't likely to benefit from having been proved right.

## A split in public opinion

The next point to note is more positive. Thatcher's capture of the war with the aid of the *Sun* produced a profound split in public opinion, but not a political split along party lines. Broadly it divided the 80 per cent who were swept by a sort of instinctive patriotic reaction and who therefore identified with the war effort, though probably not in as strident a manner as the *Sun* headlines, from the minority which recognized that, in terms of the actual global politics concerned, what Thatcher was doing made no sense at all. That minority included people of all parties and none, and many who were not against sending a task force as such. I hesitate to say that it was a split of the educated against the uneducated; although it is a fact that the major holdouts against Thatcherism were to be found in the quality press, plus of course the *Morning Star*. The *Financial Times*, the *Guardian* and the *Observer* maintained a steady note of scepticism about the whole business. I think it is safe to say that almost every single political correspondent in the country, and that goes from the Tory ones right down to the left, thought the whole thing was loony. Those were the 'faint-hearts' against whom Mrs Thatcher railed. The fact that there was a certain polarization but that the opposition, though it remained quite a small minority, was not weakened, even in the course of a brief and, in technical terms, brilliantly successful war, is significant. Nevertheless, the war was won, fortunately for Mrs Thatcher very quickly and at a modest cost in British lives, and with it came an immediate and vast pay-off in popularity. The grip of Thatcher and the Thatcherites, of the ultra-right, on the Tory Party unquestionably increased enormously as a consequence. Mrs Thatcher in the meantime was on cloud nine and imagined herself as a reincarnation of the Duke of Wellington, but without that Irish realism which the Iron Duke never lost, and of Winston Churchill but without the cigars and, at least one hopes, without the brandy.

### Short-term effects

Now let me deal with the effects of the war. I shall here only mention briefly the short-term effects; that is, between now and the general election. The first of these is likely to concern the debate on whose fault it is.

The second issue is the cost of the operation and the subsequent and continuing expense of maintaining the British presence in the Falklands. The official statement is that it is going to be about £700 million so far, but my own guess is that it almost certainly will run into thousands of millions. Accountancy is, as is well known, a form of creative writing, so exactly how you calculate the cost of a particular operation of this kind is optional, but whatever it is, it will turn out to be very, very expensive. Certainly the left will press this issue and they ought to. However, unfortunately, the sums are so large as to be meaningless to most people. So while the figures will go on being much quoted in political debate, I suspect this issue won't be very prominent or politically very effective.

The third issue is the bearing of the Falklands on British war policy, or defence policy as everybody now likes to call it. The Falklands War will certainly intensify the savage internal warfare among admirals, air marshals, generals and the Ministry of Defence which has already led to one post-Falklands casualty, the Minister of Defence himself, John Nott. There is very little doubt that the admirals used the Falklands affair to prove that a large navy, capable of operating right across the globe, was absolutely essential to Great Britain – whereas everybody else knows that we can't afford it and what's more it just isn't worth keeping a navy of that size in order to be able to supply Port Stanley. These discussions will certainly raise the question of whether Britain can afford both a global navy and Trident missiles, and what exactly the role and importance of independent British nuclear weapons is. So to this extent they can play a part in the development of the campaign for nuclear disarmament which should not be underestimated. Next, the future of the Falkland Islands themselves. This, once again, is likely to be of little general interest since the islands will cease to be of any serious interest to most Britons again. But it will be an enormous headache for civil servants, for the Foreign Office and for anybody else involved because we have no policy for the future. It wasn't the object of the war to solve the problems of the Falkland Islands. We are simply back to square one, or rather back to square minus one, and something will sooner or later have to be done to find a permanent solution for this problem unless British governments are simply content to keep an enormously expensive commitment going for ever, for no good purpose whatever, way down there by the South Pole.

## Patriotism and the left

Finally, let me deal with the more serious question of the long-term effects. The war demonstrated the strength and the political potential of patriotism, in this case in its jingo form. This should not perhaps surprise us, but Marxists haven't found it easy to come to terms with working-class patriotism in general and English or British patriotism in particular. British here means where the patriotism of the non-English peoples happens to coincide with that of the English; where it doesn't coincide, as is sometimes the case in Scotland and Wales, Marxists have been more aware of the importance of nationalist or patriotic sentiment. Incidentally I suspect that while the Scots felt rather British over the Falklands, the Welsh didn't. The only parliamentary party which, as a party, opposed the war from the start was Plaid Cymru and of course, as far as the Welsh are concerned, 'our lads' and 'our kith and kin' are not in the Falklands, but in Argentina. They are the Patagonian Welsh who send a delegation every year to the National Eisteddfod in order to demonstrate that you can still live at the other end of the globe and be Welsh. So as far as the Welsh are concerned the reaction, the Thatcherite appeal on the Falklands, the 'kith and kin' argument, probably fell by the wayside. Now, there are various reasons why the left and particularly the Marxist left has not really liked to come to terms with the question of patriotism in this country. There's a particular historical conception of internationalism which tends to exclude national patriotism. We should also bear in mind the strength of the liberal/radical, anti-war and pacifist tradition which is very strong, and which certainly has passed to some extent into the labour movement. Hence there's a feeling that patriotism somehow conflicts with class consciousness, as indeed it frequently does, and that the ruling and hegemonic classes have an enormous advantage in mobilizing it for their purposes, which is also true. Perhaps there is also the fact that some of the most dramatic and decisive advances of the Left in this century were achieved in the fight against the First World War, and they were achieved by a working class shaking off the hold of patriotism and jingoism and deciding to opt for class struggle; to follow Lenin by turning their hostility against their own oppressors rather than against foreign countries. After all, what had wrecked the Socialist International in 1914 was precisely the workers failing to do this. What, in a sense, restored the soul of the international labour movement was that after 1917, all over the belligerent countries the workers united to fight against the war, for peace and for the Russian Revolution.

## The British tradition

These are some of the reasons why Marxists perhaps failed to pay adequate attention to the problem of patriotism. So let me just remind you as an historian that patriotism cannot be neglected. The British working class has a long tradition of patriotism which was not always considered incompatible with a strong and militant class consciousness. In the history of Chartism and the great radical movements in the early nineteenth century we tend to stress the class consciousness. But when in the 1860s one of the few British workers actually to write about the working class, Thomas Wright the 'journeyman engineer', wrote a guide to the British working class for middle-class readers, because some of these workers were about to be given the vote, he gave an interesting thumbnail sketch of the various generations of workers he'd known as a skilled engineer. When he came to the Chartist generation, the people who had been born in the early nineteenth century, he noted that they hated anything to do with the upper classes, and would not trust them an inch. They refused to have anything to do with what we would call the class enemy. At the same time he observed that they were strongly patriotic, strongly anti-foreign and particularly anti-French. They were people who had been brought up in their childhood in the anti-Napoleonic Wars. Historians tend to stress the Jacobin element in British labour during these wars and not the anti-French element which also had popular roots. I'm simply saying you cannot write patriotism out of the scenario even in the most radical period of the English working class. Throughout the nineteenth century there was a very general admiration for the navy as a popular institution, much more so than the army. You can still see it in all the public houses named after Lord Nelson, a genuinely popular figure. The navy and our sailors were things that Britons, and certainly English people, took pride in. Incidentally, a good deal of nineteenth-century radicalism was built on an appeal not just to workers and other civilians but to soldiers. *Reynold's News* and the old radical papers of those days were much read by the troops because they systematically took up the discontents of the professional soldiers. I don't know when this particular thing stopped, although in the Second World War the *Daily Mirror* succeeded in getting a vast circulation in the army for precisely the same reason. Both the Jacobin tradition and the majority anti-French tradition are thus part of English working-class history though labour historians have stressed the one and played down the other. Again, at the beginning of the First World War the mass patriotism of the working class was absolute genuine. It was not something that was simply being manufactured by the media. It didn't exclude respect for the minority within the labour movement who failed to share it. The anti-war elements and the pacifists within the labour movement were not ostracized by the organized workers. In this respect there was a great difference between the attitude of workers and of the petty-bourgeois jingoists. Nevertheless, the fact remains that the largest single volunteer mass recruitment into any army ever was that of British workers who joined up in 1914–15. The mines would have been empty but for the fact that the government eventually recognized that if it didn't have some miners in the mines it wouldn't have any coal. After a couple of years many workers changed their mind about the war, but the initial surge of patriotism is something we have to remember. I'm not justifying these things, simply pointing to their existence and indicating that in looking at the history of the British working class and the present reality, we must come to terms with these facts, whether we like them or not. The dangers of this patriotism always were and still are obvious, not least because it was and is enormously vulnerable to ruling-class jingoism, to anti-foreign nationalism and of course in our days to racism. These dangers are particularly great where patriotism can be separated from the other sentiments and aspirations of the working class, or even where it can be counterposed to them: where nationalism can be counterpoised to social liberation. The reason why nobody pays much attention to the, let's call it, jingoism of the Chartists, is that it was combined with and masked by an enormous militant class consciousness. It's when the two are separated, and they can be easily separated, that the dangers are particularly obvious. Conversely, when the two go together in harness they multiply not only the force of the working class but its capacity to place itself at the head of a broad coalition for social change and they even give it the possibility of wresting hegemony from the class enemy.

## Extraordinary 1945

That was why in the anti-fascist period of the 30s, the Communist International launched the call to wrest away national traditions from the bourgeoisie, to capture the national flag so long waved by the right. So the French left tried to conquer, capture or recapture both the tricolour and Joan of Arc, and to some extent it succeeded. In this country, we didn't pursue quite the same object, but we succeeded in doing something more important. As the anti-fascist war showed quite dramatically, the combination of patriotism in a genuine people's war proved to be politically radicalizing to an unprecedented degree. At the moment of his greatest triumph,

Mrs Thatcher's ancestor, Winston Churchill, the unquestioned leader of a victorious war, and a much greater victorious war than the Falklands, found himself, to his enormous surprise, pushed aside because the people who had fought that war, and fought it patriotically, found themselves radicalized by it. And the combination of a radicalized working-class movement and a people's movement behind it proved enormously effective and powerful. Michael Foot may be blamed for thinking too much in terms of 'Churchillian' memories – 1940, Britain standing alone, anti-fascist war and all the rest of it, and obviously these echoes were there in Labour's reaction to the Falklands. But let us not forget that our 'Churchillian' memories are not just of patriotic glory – but of victory against reaction both abroad and at home: of Labour triumph and the defeat of Churchill. It's difficult to conceive this in 1982 but as an historian I must remind you of it. It is dangerous to leave patriotism exclusively to the right.

## Rule Britannia

At present it is very difficult for the left to recapture patriotism. One of the most sinister lessons of the Falklands is the ease with which the Thatcherites captured the patriotic upsurge which initially was in no sense confined to political Conservatives, let alone to Thatcherite ones. We recall the ease with which non-jingos could be tagged, if not actually as anti-patriotic, then at least as 'soft on the Argies'; the ease with which the Union Jack could be mobilized against domestic enemies as well as foreign enemies. Remember the photograph of the troops coming back on the troopships, with a banner saying 'Call off the rail strike or we'll call an air strike'. Here lies the long-term significance of the Falklands in British political affairs. It is a sign of very great danger. Jingoism today is particularly strong because it acts as a sort of compensation for the feelings of decline, demoralization and inferiority which most people in this country feel, including a lot of workers. This feeling is intensified by economic crisis. Symbolically jingoism helps people feel that Britain isn't just foundering, that it can still do and achieve something, can be taken seriously, can, as they say, be 'Great' Britain. It is symbolic because in fact Thatcherite jingoism hasn't achieved anything practical, and can't achieve anything practical. 'Rule Britannia' has once again, and I think for the first time since 1914, become something like a national anthem. It would be worth studying one day why, until the Falklands period, 'Rule Britannia' had become a piece of musical archaeology and why it has ceased to be so. At the very moment when Britain patently no longer rules either the waves or an empire, that song has resurfaced and has undoubtedly hit a certain nerve among people who sing it. It is not just because we have won a little war, involving few casualties, fought far away against foreigners whom we can no longer even beat at football, and this has cheered people up, as if we had won a World Cup with guns. But has it done anything else in the long run? It is difficult to see that it has, or could have, achieved anything else.

## Saviour on a white horse

Yet there is a danger. As a boy I lived some formative and very young years in the Weimar Republic, among another people who felt themselves defeated, losing their old certainties and their old moorings, relegated in the international league, pitied by foreigners. Add depression and mass unemployment to that and what you got then was Hitler. Now we shall not get fascism of the old kind. But the danger of a populist, radical right moving even further to the right is patent. That danger is particularly great because the left is today divided and demoralized, and above all because vast masses of the British, or anyway the English, have lost hope and confidence in the political processes and in the politicians: any politicians. Mrs Thatcher's main trump card is that people say she isn't like a politician. Today

with 3.5 million unemployed, 45 per cent of the electors at
Northfield, 65 per cent of the electors at Peckham, don't bother
to vote. In Peckham 41 per cent of the electorate voted for
Labour in 1974, 34 per cent in 1979, and 19.1 per cent today.
I'm not talking of votes cast but of the total number of people
in the constituency. In Northfield, which is in the middle of the
devastation zone of the British motor industry, 41 per cent voted
for Labour in 1974, 32 per cent in 1979 and 20 per cent today.
The main danger lies in this de-politicization, which reflects dis-
illusionment with politics born of a sense of impotence. What we
see today is not a substantial rise in the support for Thatcher and
the Thatcherites. The Falklands episode may have temporarily
made a lot of Britons feel better, though the 'Falklands factor'
is almost certainly a diminishing asset for the Tories; but it has
not made much difference to the basic hopelessness, apathy and
defeatism of so many in this country, the feeling that we can't do
much about our fate. If the government seems to hold its support
better than might be expected, it is because people (quite mis-
takenly) don't put the blame for the present miserable condition
of the country on Thatcher, but, more or less vaguely, on factors
beyond her or any government's control. If Labour hasn't so far
regained enough support – though it may still just do so – it isn't
only because of its internal divisions, but also, largely, because
many workers don't really have much belief in any politicians'
promises to overcome the slump and the long-term crisis of the
British economy. So why vote for one lot rather than another?
Too many people are losing faith in politics, including their
own power to do much about it. But just suppose a saviour were
to appear on a white horse? None is likely to, but just suppose
someone were to appeal to the emotions, to get that adrenalin
flowing by mobilizing against some foreigners outside or inside
the country, perhaps by another little war, which might, under
present circumstances, find itself turning into a big war, which,
as we all know, would be the last of the wars? It is possible. I don't
think that saviour is going to be Thatcher, and to that extent I

can end on a slightly upbeat note. Free enterprise, to which she is committed, is not a winner, as fascist propaganda recognized in the 1930s. You can't win by saying: 'Let the rich get richer and to hell with the poor.' Thatcher's prospects are less good than Hitler's were, for three years after he had come to power there was not much unemployment left in Germany, whereas three years after Thatcher came to power unemployment is higher than ever before and likely to go on climbing. She is whistling in the dark. She can still be defeated. But patriotism and jingoism has been used once to change the political situation in her favour and can be used again. We must be on the lookout. Desperate governments of the right will try anything.

# 19

## *Benefits of Diaspora Jews*

Originally a lecture given on 10 May 2005 on the
fiftieth anniversary of the Leo Baeck Institute, with
the title 'Enlightenment and Achievement: the
Emancipation of Jewish Talent since 1800'.

Most work in the field of Jewish history deals with the almost
invariably vast impact of the outside world on the Jews, who
are almost invariably a small minority of the population. My
concern is with the impact of the Jews on the rest of humanity.
And, in particular, with the explosive transformation of this
impact in the nineteenth and twentieth centuries: that is to say,
since the emancipation and self-emancipation of the Jews began
in the late eighteenth century.

Between their expulsion from Palestine in the first century
AD and the nineteenth century, the Jews lived within the wider
society of gentiles, whose languages they adopted as their own
and whose cuisine they adapted to their ritual requirements;
but only rarely and intermittently were they able and, what is
equally to the point, willing to participate in the cultural and

intellectual life of these wider societies. Consequently their original contribution to this life was marginal, even in fields in which, since emancipation, their contribution has been enormous. Only as intermediaries between intellectual cultures, notably between the Islamic and western Christian worlds in the (European) Middle Ages, did they have a significant part to play.

Consider a field of outstanding Jewish achievement: mathematics. So far as I am aware no significant developments in modern mathematics are specifically associated with Jewish names until the nineteenth century. Nor do we find that Jewish mathematicians made major advances which were only discovered by the wider mathematical world much later, as was the case of the Indian mathematicians whose work between the fourteenth and the sixteenth centuries, written in the Malayalam language, remained unknown until the second half of the twentieth. Or take chess, the excessive practice of which was actively discouraged by religious authority in general and Maimonides in particular as a distraction from the study of the Law. No wonder the first Jewish chess player to gain a wider reputation was the Frenchman Aron Alexandre (1766–1850), whose life coincided with the emancipation.

This segregation or ghettoization, both imposed and self-imposed, was at its most stringent between the fourteenth and the eighteenth centuries, and reinforced after 1492 by the expulsion of non-converting Jews from the Spanish dominions, including those in Italy. This reduced the occasions for social and intellectual contact with non-Jews, other than those that arose out of the professional activities that linked Jews to the gentile world. Indeed, it is difficult to think of Jews during that period who were in a position to have informal intellectual contact with educated gentiles outside the only major urban Jewish population remaining in the west, the largely Sephardi community of Amsterdam. Most Jews, after all, were either confined to ghettos or prohibited from settling in large cities until well into the nineteenth century.

As Jacob Katz observed in *Out of the Ghetto* (1973), in those days 'the outside world did not overly occupy the Jewish mind'. The elaborate codification of the practices of Orthodoxy that constituted the Jewish religion in the compendia of the time, notably the *Shulchan Aruch*, reinforced segregation; and the traditional form of Jewish intellectual activity, the homiletic exposition of Bible and Talmud and its application to the contingencies of Jewish life, left little scope for anything else. Rabbinical authority banned philosophy, science and other branches of knowledge of non-Jewish origin – even, in parts of Ukraine, foreign languages. The gap between intellectual worlds is best indicated by the fact that the rare advocates of emancipation among eastern Jewry felt they needed to translate into Hebrew work evidently available to any educated person in the gentile print culture – Euclid, for example, or works on trigonometry, as well as on geography and ethnography.

The contrast between the situation before and after the era of emancipation is startling. After many centuries during which the intellectual and cultural history of the world, let alone its political history, could be written with little reference to the contribution of any Jews acceptable as such to the Orthodox, other than perhaps Maimonides, we almost immediately enter the modern era when Jewish names are disproportionately represented. It is as though the lid had been removed from a pressure cooker. Yet the prominence of certain names – Heine, Mendelssohn-Bartholdy, Ricardo, Marx, Disraeli – and the flourishing milieu of wealthy educated Jews in a few favoured cities, notably Berlin, should not mislead us. At the end of the Napoleonic Wars the great bulk of Ashkenazi Jews remained unintegrated in gentile society, in Germany as much as in Holland or the Habsburg Empire, except – a very recent development – administratively, as subjects with civil surnames. Even top families had some way to go: Marx's mother never felt entirely at home in High German, and the first two generations of Rothschilds corresponded with one another in *Judendeutsch* in the Hebrew script. The Jews of the central European hinterlands of the Habsburg Empire remained unaffected by emancipation until the 1840s at the earliest, when immigration into cities became possible, and very much later, in the case of those of Galicia and the Russian shtetls. Even in America, as Stephen Thernstrom reports in the *Harvard Encyclopedia of American Ethnic Groups*, 'until well into the 20th century the majority of the immigrants could recall, or had come directly from, a traditional Jewish society'. The bulk of the Sephardim too remained in segregated enclaves. In fact, I doubt whether we can find any places before the French Revolution, except for small refugee communities in France and the Netherlands and the ancient communities in northern Italy and the South of France, where the totality of Jews, and not merely the elite, were integrated into the surrounding society, where, for example, they habitually spoke the local gentile vernacular among themselves.

The process of Jewish emancipation therefore resembles not so much a suddenly gushing fountain as a tiny stream rapidly turning into a massive river. I have grouped together the mathematicians, physicists and chemists listed in the respective articles of the *Encyclopaedia Judaica* by birth dates. Only one in all these three groups was born before 1800, thirty-one were born in the first half of the nineteenth century, and 162 in the second half. (The analogous curve for medicine, the intellectual field in which pre-emancipation Jews were already established in the wider world, is less dramatic.) I need hardly add that at this stage we are concerned overwhelmingly with the Ashkenazi wing of Jewry, which formed a large and growing majority of the world's Jewish population, and in particular with its increasing urbanization. The number of Jews in Vienna jumped from fewer than four thousand in 1848 to 175,000 on the eve of the First World War.

It's important not to underestimate the impact of small elites of the wealthy and educated – of the 405 Jewish families in early nineteenth-century Berlin, say. Pre-democratic liberal societies were constructed for the benefit of such groups. Thus the Italian Jews, though they represented 0.1 per cent of the population, might, under the restrictions of Italian electoral law, amount to 10 per cent of the electorate; the election of Cavour in the kingdom of Savoy in 1851 was helped by the votes of the Turin Jewish community. This may help to explain the rapid emergence of Jews on the western and central European public scene. So far as I am aware, they hardly appear in the French Revolution or among its European sympathizers, except, as one might expect, in the bourgeois milieu of the Netherlands. But by the time of the 1830 revolutions, the Jewish presence in French politics, especially in the Midi, was already impossible to overlook. The same was true for Germany and northern Italy: Mazzini's secretary as well as several of his activists and financiers were Jews. By 1848, the prominence of Jews was quite startling. Adolphe Crémieux, for example, immediately became a minister in the new French revolutionary government, while Daniel Manin became the leader of revolutionary Venice. Three Jews sat prominently in the Prussian constituent assembly, four in the Frankfurt parliament (it was a Jew who, after its dissolution, saved its Great Seal, which was returned to the Federal Republic a few years ago by his British descendant). In Vienna, it was Jewish university students who launched the call for the March revolution, and Jews provided eight of the twenty-nine signatures on the Manifesto of Viennese Writers. Metternich's list of subversives in Austrian Poland contained no obvious Jewish names, but only a few years later Jews in Poland were expressing their enthusiasm for Polish freedom and a rabbi, elected to the Imperial Reichstag, sat with the Polish faction. In pre-democratic Europe, politics, even revolutionary politics, belonged to a small squadron of the educated.

There was no doubt in the minds of emancipators that two changes were essential: a degree of secularization and education in, as well as the habitual use of, the national language, preferably, but not necessarily, an accepted language of written culture (think of the enthusiastically Magyarised Jews of Hungary). By 'secularization' I don't mean that the Jewish faith had to be abandoned, though among the emancipated there was a rush to conversion, sincere or pragmatic, but that religion was no longer the unremitting, omnipresent and all-embracing framework of life. Instead, however important, it filled only part of life. This kind of secularization ideally allowed the intermarriage or partnership of educated Jewish women with gentiles, which was to play a major role both culturally and later in (left-wing) politics. The relationship of women's emancipation to Jewish emancipation is a very significant subject.

Primary education, necessarily in the vernacular, did not become universal until the last third of the nineteenth century, although near universal literacy could be assumed in large parts of Germany by mid-century. After 1811 it would have been technically difficult for a Jewish boy in Germany to avoid the public education system, and it was no longer virtually compulsory to learn the Hebrew letters in a religious establishment as it still was in the east. West of the borders of Russian and Austrian Poland, the *cheder* was no longer a competitor to the secular school. Secondary education, however, remained highly restricted throughout, ranging from a mid-century minimum of less than 0.1 per cent in Italy to a maximum in Prussia of less than 2 per cent of the relevant age group; university education was even more restricted. As it happens, this maximized the chances of the children of disproportionately prosperous small communities such as the Jews, especially given the high status that learning enjoyed among them. That is why the Jewish share in Prussian higher education was at its maximum in the 1870s. It declined thereafter, as higher education began its general expansion.

To speak, read and write the same language as educated non-Jews was the precondition of joining modern civilization, and the most immediate means of desegregation. However, the passion of emancipated Jews for the national language and culture of the gentile countries in which they lived was all the more intense, because in so many cases they were not joining, as it were, long-established clubs but clubs of which they could see themselves almost as founder members. They were emancipated at the time when a classic literature was coming into being for German, Hungarian and Polish, alongside the various national schools of music. What could be closer to the cutting edge of German literature than the milieu of Rahel Varnhagen in early nineteenth-century Berlin? As Theodor Fontane said of one impassioned Jewish emancipator, 'only in the region he inhabits do we find a genuine interest in German literature'. In much the same way, two or three generations later, emancipated Russian Jewish intellectuals fell, in Ze'ev Jabotinsky's words, 'madly, shamefully in love with Russian culture'. Only in the multilingual Levant did the absence of national linguistic cultures make language change less crucial. There, thanks to the *Alliance Israélite Universelle* of 1860, modernising Jews received their education in French, while continuing to speak, but no longer to write, in Judeo-Spanish, Arabic or Turkish.

Of all the emancipatory languages, German was by far the most crucial, for two reasons. Throughout half of Europe – from Berlin deep into Great Russia, from Scandinavia to the Adriatic, and into the far Balkans – the road from backwardness to progress, from provincialism to the wider world, was paved with German letters. We tend to forget that this was once so. German was the gateway to modernity. Karl-Emil Franzos's story 'Schiller in Barnow', written on the occasion of the centenary of the birth of Schiller, the classical voice of moral and political freedom for common readers of German in the nineteenth century, illustrates this wonderfully well. In the story a small, badly printed volume of Schiller's poems becomes the medium through which a Dominican monk, a young Ruthenian village schoolmaster and a poor Jewish boy from a shtetl in what the author bitterly calls 'Demi-Asia' ('Halb-Asien') find the liberation that the nineteenth-century version of education and modern culture had to offer. The story culminates in a reading of the 'Ode to Joy'. In the darkest east, Schiller was even translated into Hebrew. The emancipatory role of German explains why the city fathers of the most Jewish centre in Galicia, the town of Brody (76 per cent of its population was Jewish), insisted on German as the language of instruction in their schools. In 1880 they even fought – and won – their case in the imperial court in Vienna on the grounds, patently implausible, that this was a language of common use in Galicia.

It was not. Almost all eastern Jews spoke Yiddish, a German dialect, relic of a past bond with the wider society, now – like Sephardic Spanish after 1492 – a badge of linguistic separation. A priori one might have expected Yiddish to coexist as an oral medium with the written national language, as other German dialects did and as Schweizerdeutsch still does but, unlike these, it was a barrier to joining the modern world that had to be removed linguistically and ideologically, as the language of the most obscurantist communities.

Speaking Polish or German, and wearing a 'German jacket', were ways used by the pioneers of emancipation in Warsaw to distinguish themselves. In any case, the children of Yiddish-speaking immigrants in German schools found themselves handicapped by their grammatical usages, correct enough in Yiddish but not in written German. Wealthier Jews, parvenus in an established society, were even more likely to abandon visible and audible marks of their origins. Characteristically, in Arthur Schnitzler's novel *Der Weg ins Freie* [1908, translated as *The Road to the Open*, 1913], that wonderfully perceptive account of the nuances of Jewish assimilation in *fin-de-siècle* Vienna, Ehrenberg, the rich businessman, renounces the old German liberal hope of Viennese Jews in his wife's salon with a deliberate relapse, in the presence of gentile 'society', into semi-Yiddish: 'vor die Jours im Haus Ehrenberg is mir mieß'.

The division between non-assimilated Yiddish-speaking Ostjuden and assimilated Westjuden thus became and remained fundamental until both perished in the same Holocaust. Though no doubt familiar in educated conversation, it seems first to have been formally made in the Bukowina in the 1870s, where a proud and extraordinarily distinguished educated middle class encountered the first attempts (by the doubters of Germanization) to give Jews a national status through their own national language – i.e. Yiddish. For emancipated Jews in Mitteleuropa, 'Ostjuden' defined what they were not, and did not want to be: people so visibly different as almost to constitute a different species. After listening to the adults' conversation as a young boy in Vienna I remember asking an older relative, 'What sort of names do these Ostjuden have?' – to her obvious embarrassment, since she knew that our family, the Grüns and Koritschoners, had come straight to Vienna from Austrian Poland, as such distinguished figures in German Jewry as Rudolf Mosse, Heinrich Graetz, Emmanuel Lasker and Arthur Ruppin had come directly from Prussian Poland.

And yet it was the mass movement of the Ostjuden from the late nineteenth century which played the greatest part in transforming the impact of the Jews in the modern world. While there is obvious continuity, the Jewish influence or effect on the gentile world in the twentieth century is of a different order from its effect in the nineteenth. The liberal-bourgeois century turned into what Yuri Slezkine in his book of that title calls 'the Jewish Century'. The American Jewish community became the largest by far in the western diaspora. Unlike any other diaspora in the developed countries, it was overwhelmingly composed of poor Ostjuden, and far too large to fit into what there was of an existing acculturated German-Jewish framework in the US. It also remained culturally rather marginalized, except perhaps in jurisprudence, until after the Second World War. The modernizing effect on the Jewish population in Poland and Russia of a massive awakening of political consciousness, reinforced by the Russian Revolution, transformed the nature of Jewish emancipation, even in its Zionist version. So, too, did both the enormous expansion of jobs in higher education, notably in the second half of the last century, the rise of fascism, the foundation of Israel and the dramatic decline of western anti-Semitic discrimination since 1945. The sheer scale of the Jewish cultural presence would have been inconceivable before the First or even the Second World War. So, obviously, would the size of the identity-conscious, book-buying Jewish public, which clearly affected the shape of the literary mass market, first in the Weimar Republic, later elsewhere. A distinction between the two periods must therefore be made.

From the start, the contribution of emancipated Jews to their host societies had been disproportionately large; but, by the nature of emancipation, it was culturally unspecific: they wanted to be simply un-hyphenated French, Italian, German and English. Conversely, and even allowing for widespread anti-Semitic feeling, in their liberal phase these societies also welcomed a prosperous and educated minority which reinforced their political, cultural and national values. Consider pre-Second World War show business, in which Jews really were dominant: operetta and musicals in both Europe and the US, theatre and later the movies, or for that matter popular song on both sides of the Atlantic. In the nineteenth century Offenbach was French, Strauss was Austrian. Even in the twentieth century Irving Berlin was American, and in Jewish-controlled Hollywood of the great period you will search in vain for anything other than what Zukor and Loew and Mayer considered 100 per cent white American values, or even for stars whose names hinted at immigrant origin. In the public life of united Italy the 0.1 per cent of Jews played a far larger role than in any other state: seventeen of them sat in the Senate; they provided prime ministers and ministers, even generals. Yet they were so hard to distinguish from other Italians that it wasn't until after the war that we find historians drawing attention to their extraordinary over-representation.

It was the same in the high arts. Jewish composers produced

German and French music, while the takeover of concert halls and orchestra pits by Jewish musicians and virtuoso performers was the first sign of emancipation in the benighted east. But the great twentieth-century Jewish violinists and pianists reinforced the repertoire of western classical music, unlike the modest Gypsy fiddlers, the black jazz and Latin American musicians who extended its reach. A handful of London Irish writers (Wilde, Shaw, Yeats) left a larger recognizably 'Irish' mark on English literature than Jewish writers left on any nineteenth-century European literature. In the Modernist period, on the other hand, the Jewish contribution became much more identifiable as well as influential both in literature and the visual arts, perhaps because Modernist innovation in these fields made them more attractive to a group uncertain of its situation in the world, and perhaps, too, because the crisis of nineteenth-century society moved gentile perceptions closer to the unfixed situation of Jewry. It was the twentieth century that imbued western culture with ideas derived from the very consciously Jewish father of psychoanalysis. A Jew becomes central in *Ulysses*; Thomas Mann becomes preoccupied with these themes; and Kafka makes his enormous posthumous impact on the century. Conversely, moved by the general American – perhaps global – meanings of Arthur Miller's *Death of a Salesman*, we barely notice, as David Mamet has reminded us, how recognizably Jewish is the experience on which it is based.

In the visual arts, one or two distinguished figures who happened to be Jews (Max Liebermann, Camille Pissarro) gave way to a cosmopolitan twentieth-century diaspora in which Jews were more numerous – something like 20 per cent of the artists in the catalogue of the great *Berlin/Moscow 1900–50* exhibition appear to be Jewish – as well as more prominent (Modigliani, Pascin, Marcoussis, Chagall, Soutine, Epstein, Lipchitz, Lissitzky, Zadkine) and sometimes, as in Chagall's case, more recognizably Jewish. More recently, Yiddish locutions have been introduced into journalists' English thanks to the Americanized culture of the mass media. Today, most anglophone gentiles understand the word *chutzpah*: forty years ago hardly anyone who wasn't Jewish used or even understood it.

As for the natural sciences, the contribution of Jews increased dramatically after 1914, as the record of the relevant Nobel Prizes demonstrates. However, they offer very little scope for national and cultural coloration, and only the ideologies of the radical right could link the two as 'Jewish science'. For obvious reasons the social and human sciences have been a very different matter, and issues to do with the nature, structure and possible transformations of society in an era of radical historical change both in practice and in theory have attracted emancipated Jews disproportionately almost from the beginning, starting with the Saint-Simonians and Marx. This fits in with that understandable Jewish proclivity to support movements for global revolutionary transformation, which is so striking in the epoch of the Marx-inspired socialist and communist movements. Indeed, one might say that western Jews of the earlier nineteenth century were emancipated thanks to an ideology not associated with them, while the eastern Ashkenazim largely emancipated themselves through a universalist revolutionary ideology with which they were closely associated. This is even true of the original Zionism, deeply penetrated by Marxist thinking, that actually built the state of Israel.

Correspondingly, in the twentieth century new fields opened up or evolved, such as, in certain regions of Europe, sociology, and especially psychoanalysis, which again could seem as disproportionately populated by Jews as, say, the international club of violin virtuosos. But what characterized these sciences, like all the others to which Jews contributed so signally, was not genetic association, but lack of fixity, leading to innovation. Daniel Snowman has pointed out in *The Hitler Emigrés* (2002) that in Britain 'the greatest impact of the exiles' from central Europe 'was probably in the newer, more cross-disciplinary fields (art history, psychology, sociology, criminology, nuclear physics, biochemistry), and the most rapidly changing professions (film, photography, architecture, broadcasting) rather than in those long established'. Einstein has become the best-known face of twentieth-century science not because he was a Jew, but because he became the icon of a science in revolution in a century of constant intellectual upheaval.

Why, one might ask, has the Jewish contribution to the wider world of western culture and knowledge been so much more marked in some regions than in others? Take the Nobel Prizes in the serious sciences. Of the seventy-four British prizes, eleven were won by Jews, but, with one possible exception, none of them was born in Britain. Of the eleven Russian prizes won since 1917, six or seven went to Jews, presumably all natives of the region. Until 2004, no Nobel Prizes in science had been won by Israeli researchers in any country, although Israel has one of the highest outputs per capita of scientific papers: 2004, however, produced two, one native-born and one born in Hungary. On the other hand, two or perhaps three have been won since Israel became independent by members of the modest Lithuanian-Jewish population of South Africa (*c.*150,000), though all outside that continent. How are we to explain such striking differences?

Here we can only speculate. In the sciences clearly the enormous increase in the research professions is crucial. The total number of university teachers in Prussia in 1913 was less than two thousand; the number of public secondary teachers in Germany was little more than 4200. It's very unlikely that the exiguous number of academic posts in the field has no bearing on the surprising absence of Jews from the list of eminent conventional academic economic theorists before the Second World War (with the notable exception of Ricardo). Conversely, the fact that it was in chemistry that Jews chiefly won Nobel Prizes before 1918 is surely connected with the fact that this was the field in which academically trained specialists were first employed in substantial numbers – the three big German chemical companies alone employed about a thousand. The only one of my seven paternal uncles who had a professional career before 1914 was a chemist.

These may be superficial criteria, but they are not negligible. Patently, without both the opening of US academia to the Jews after 1948 and its vast expansion, the enormous wave of home-grown US Nobels after 1970 would have been impossible. A more important factor, I believe, is segregation, whether of the pre-emancipation kind or by territorial/genetic nationalism. This may explain the relatively disappointing contribution of Israel, considering the relative size of its Jewish population. It would seem that living among gentiles and addressing a gentile audience is as much a stimulus for physicists as it is for film-makers. In this respect it is still much better to come from Brooklyn than from Tel Aviv.

On the other hand, given equal rights, at least in theory, a certain degree of unease in relations between Jews and gentiles has proved historically useful. This was clearly the case in Germany and the Habsburg Empire, as well as in the US until well after the Second World War, in the first half of the twentieth century in Russia/the USSR, and in both South Africa and Argentina. The substantial support given by Jews to other groups suffering official discrimination, as in South Africa and the US, is surely a symptom of this unease, though it isn't found in all Jewish communities. Even in the countries of the fullest toleration – France in the Third Republic, western Austria under Franz Joseph, the Hungary of mass Magyar assimilation – the times of maximum stimulus for Jewish talent may have been those when the Jews became conscious of the limits of assimilation: the *fin-de-siècle* moment of Proust, who came to maturity in the Dreyfus decade, the era of Schoenberg, Mahler, Freud, Schnitzler and Karl Kraus. Is it possible for diaspora Jews to be so integrated as to lose that stimulus? It has been argued that this was the situation of the established Anglo-Jews of the nineteenth century; and certainly British Jews were less than prominent in the leadership of the socialist and social-revolutionary movements, or even among the groups' intellectuals – one has only to compare them with their counterparts east of the Rhine and north of the Alps. I am unqualified to come to a conclusion one way or the other. Whatever may have been the case up to the time of Hitler and the Holocaust, it is no longer so.

The paradox of the era since 1945 is that the greatest tragedy in Jewish history has had two utterly different consequences. On the one hand, it has concentrated a substantial minority of the global Jewish population in one nation-state: Israel, which was itself once upon a time a product of Jewish emancipation and of the passion to enter the same world as the rest of humanity. It has shrunk the diaspora, dramatically so in the Islamic regions. On the other hand, in most parts of the world it has been followed by an era of almost unlimited public acceptance of Jews, by the virtual disappearance of the anti-Semitism and discrimination of my youth, and by unparalleled and unprecedented Jewish achievement in the fields of culture, intellect and public affairs. There is no historic precedent for the triumph of the *Aufklärung* in the post-Holocaust diaspora. Nevertheless, there are those who wish to withdraw from it into the old segregation of religious ultra-Orthodoxy and the new segregation of a separate ethnic-genetic state-community. If they were to succeed I do not think it will be good either for the Jews or for the world.

# 20

## The Jews and Germany

Reviews of *Jews and the German State: The Political
History of a Minority, 1848–1933* by Peter Pulzer and
*The Jews of Germany: A Historical Portrait* by Ruth Gay.

Most of world history until the late eighteenth century could
be written without more than marginal reference to the Jews,
except as a small people which pioneered the monotheistic
world religions, a debt acknowledged by Islam, but creating
endless problems for Christianity, or rather for the Jews unlucky
enough to live under Christian rulers. Practically the entire
intellectual history of the western world, and all that of the great
cultures of the east, could be written without more than a few
footnotes about the direct Jewish contribution to them, though
not without paying considerable attention to the role of Jews as
intermediaries and cultural brokers, notably between the classic
Mediterranean heritage, Islam and the medieval west. This is
rather surprising when we consider the extraordinary prominence in twentieth-century cultural, intellectual and public life
of members of this small people which, even at its demographic

peak before the Holocaust, formed less than 1 per cent of the world population.

Since most public life was closed to them, their absence from it before the French Revolution was perhaps to be expected. Yet it is also clear that Jewish intellectual activity for most of the last two millennia, perhaps with the exception of the Hellenistic era, was overwhelmingly inward-looking. Only the occasional sage between Philo the Jew and Spinoza appeared to be seriously concerned with non-Jewish thinking, and these, like Maimonides, were, not fortuitously, apt to be born in the open civilization of Muslim Spain. The great rabbis, whose commentaries on the sacred texts, in all their Babylonian subtlety, still form the main subject in the Talmudic academies, were not interested in the views of unbelievers. With the possible exception of medicine, where the acknowledged Jewish expertise crossed communal frontiers, Jewish learning and intellectual effort focused on holy matters. The Yiddish word for the place of worship, the 'synagogue', is the old German word for 'school'.

It is evident that an enormous oilfield of talent was waiting to be tapped by that most admirable of all human movements, the eighteenth-century Enlightenment, which, among its many other benefits, brought about the emancipation of the Jews. When we consider that for almost a century after Joseph II's Toleranzedikte of 1781–2, emancipation was still virtually confined to the small Jewish communities of western and west-central Europe, and that Jews had hardly begun to make their mark in some of the major fields of their subsequent intellectual achievement, the size of the contribution which Jews immediately began to make to nineteenth-century history is quite extraordinary. Who could write world history without paying attention to Ricardo and Marx, both products of the first half-century of emancipation?

For understandable reasons most writers on Jewish history, predominantly Jews themselves, tend to concentrate on the impact of the outside world on their people rather than the other way round. Even Peter Pulzer's excellent 'political history of a minority' does not quite escape from such introversion. The two Jews whose impact on German politics was the greatest, the founders of the German labour movement, Marx and Lassalle, barely appear (there are precisely three references to Lassalle, one of which concerns his father), and the author is clearly ill at ease with the 'disparity between the large number of Jews prominent in the Wilhelmine Social Democratic Party's leadership and debates and the slower growth of its electoral following among Jews', preferring to concentrate on the latter.

Nevertheless, his perceptive, though sometimes over-detailed, analysis avoids most of the temptations of Jewish historical separatism. *Jews and the German State* can be seen as belonging with the work of the group of historians associated with the Leo Baeck Institute in London, perhaps the last survivors of the German-Jewish liberal tradition. It has the quiet, low-key strength and balance characteristic of the studies of Jewry that issued from this admirable institution under the auspices of such scholars as Arnold Paucker and Werner Mosse. Like his colleagues, Pulzer understands what has, since Hitler, become almost incomprehensible: namely, why German Jews felt themselves to be profoundly German, and indeed why 'the "fourth Reich" that established itself in Hampstead and Washington Heights, in Hollywood and Nahariya, with battered tomes of Lessing, Kant and Goethe and scratched records of Furtwängler and *The Threepenny Opera*, bore witness to the tenacity of roots in the German *Kulturnation*'. In short, why emancipated nineteenth-century Jews wanted passionately 'to proclaim that they had left the ghetto, that they had entered civilisation'.

For 'the German-Jewish community enjoyed a leading, even dominant, intellectual position among other Jewries'. But then emancipated Jewry contained more German-speakers than any others, even if we count only those in what was to become the German Reich in 1871. Moreover, as Ruth Gay's illuminating and copiously illustrated *The Jews of Germany* makes clear, even as it, too, overlooks Marx and Lassalle, German Jewry was overwhelmingly indigenous, even after the mass migration from the east began, and, with school education, abandoned Yiddish for German speech.

The German *Kulturnation* was far larger than this, however. The very fact, recorded (but not stressed) by Pulzer, that so many of the leading intellectual figures in German Social Democracy – including all but one of its prominent Marxists – had transferred their field of activity to Germany from the Habsburg Empire (Kautsky, Hilferding) or Tsarist Russia (Luxemburg, Parvus, even Marchlewski and Radek) demonstrates that German was the language of culture from the Greater Russian marches to the French borders. The major difference between the Jews of Germany and emancipated Jews from the rest of the German culture zone was that the former were *only* German, whereas a substantial number of the others were pluricultural if not plurilingual. They, and probably they alone, constituted that idealised Mitteleuropa of which dissident Czechs and Hungarians dreamed in the 1880s, linking otherwise non-communicating cultures and peoples in the multinational empires.

Moreover, it was they who carried, perhaps even established, the German language in the remoter outposts of the Habsburg Empire since, as the largest component of the educated middle class in those parts, they were the people who actually used the standard literary German instead of the dialects spoken by the emigrant German diasporas of the east – Swabian, Saxon and (as German philologists confirmed, sometimes not without regret) Yiddish. German was the name of freedom and progress. Yeshiva students from Poland, like Jakob Fromer, recorded by Ruth Gay, secretly studied German among the Talmudic commentaries by means of two dictionaries – Russian-Hebrew and German-Russian. Schiller brought emancipation from what another Polish seeker after liberation called 'the fetters of superstition and prejudice'. It is easier to sentimentalize the *shtetl* now that it no longer exists than it was when young men and women had to live in it.

The German Jews wished passionately to be German, though, as Pulzer observes acutely, they wanted to assimilate 'not to the German nation but to the German middle class'. Yet the commonest of the criticisms of assimilation, the great dream of nineteenth-century social mobility, plainly did not apply to them. Assimilation did not entail a denial of their Jewish identity, not even in the very unusual case of conversion. As Pulzer shows, in spite of massive secularization and their overwhelming commitment to being German, the German Jews survived as a group conscious of their Judaism until extirpated by Hitler. Nor was this due only to anti-Semitism which, as he reminds us, was in any case mild by the standards of other countries. As the refugee physicist Sir Rudolf Peierls put it, 'in pre-Hitler Germany being Jewish was a bearable handicap'. It was not German or the much more palpable Viennese anti-Semitism that converted Herzl to Zionism, but the Dreyfus case in France.

One wishes, however, that Pulzer had not chosen the term 'ethnicity' to describe what bound Jews together, since the bond was not felt to be biological, but historical. They did not see themselves as a community of blood or even ancestral religion, but, in Otto Bauer's words, a 'community of fate'. Still, whatever we call it, emancipated Jews as a group did not behave quite like non-Jews. (Eastern ones, of course, behaved very differently indeed.) Most of Pulzer's book is devoted to demonstrating the specificity of their political behaviour. Not surprisingly, as a community they stood on the moderate liberal left of the German political spectrum, and not by any means on the far left. Even the collapse of liberalism in the years of Hitler's rise didn't push them towards the Communists, but towards the Social Democrats. Unlike the Jews of the Habsburg and tsarist regions of Europe, their politics were not messianic. Relatively few, it is argued, joined or voted for the Communist Party, and before 1933 German Zionists, also a smallish minority, saw

Zionism as a personal rebirth but not as a programme of emigration. Unlike eastern Jews, they did not consider themselves strangers in (to quote one of them) 'the land of Walther and Wolfram, Goethe, Kant and Fichte'.

In short, German Jews were at ease in Germany. Hence theirs was a double tragedy. Not only were they to be destroyed, but they had not expected their fate. Pulzer does his best to make sense of the failure, indeed the refusal of liberal German Jewry to recognise what Hitler meant, even after 1933. It is, of course, true that nobody, not even the eastern Jews who lived among those who had massacred their relatives by the thousands in 1918–20, could expect, or even imagine, what eventually took place at Majdanek and Treblinka. Few could even bring themselves to believe it when the first credible reports of the genocide filtered through to the west in 1942. There was no precedent in human history for it. Nevertheless, I, who experienced 30 January 1933 as a schoolboy in Berlin, can testify that already then there were those who took a fairly apocalyptic view of Hitler's regime. And indeed, despite their reluctance to give up Germany, many Jews prepared for the worst, even though they underestimated it. After all, almost two-thirds of the 1933 Jewish population of Germany emigrated in the next six years and therefore, unlike their unhappy Polish brethren, survived. And yet, they did not leave willingly. Some, like a descendant of the founder of the Deutsche Bank, sent his wife and children to safety, but committed suicide after the Kristallnacht of 1938 rather than give up Germany.

Even the survivors' tragedy was real. Only those who have experienced the force, the grandeur and beauty of that culture, which made the Bulgarian Jew Elias Canetti write in the middle of the Second World War that 'the language of my intellect will remain German', can fully realise what its loss meant. Only those whose surnames still record the Hessian, Swabian and Franconian villages and market towns of their ancestors, know the pain of torn roots. Their loss was irreparable. The Jewish communities of central Europe can never be reconstituted, and even if they could be, the German culture to which they belonged is no longer a world culture.

And what did Germany lose? Paradoxically, probably less than the countries of the old Habsburg Empire: Germany's Jews had fitted themselves into an existing middle-class culture, whereas the emancipated Jews of the Habsburg Empire created new cultures, often, as in Vienna's case, very different from that of the Reich. Culturally, the expulsion or destruction of the Jews left Germany much as before, though more provincial and peripheral than it had been before 1933. And yet this is to underestimate Germany's loss. German is no longer the language of modernity for aspiring Europeans from the backwoods. It is no longer the language of scholarly publications which every academic from Tokyo to Cambridge must be able to read. No doubt that isn't a consequence exclusively of the exodus or death of the Jews. However, their disappearance clearly had at least one dramatic effect. From 1900 to 1933 almost 40 per cent of all Nobel Prizes in physics and chemistry went to Germany; since 1933 only about one in ten. History records, with tragic irony or black humour, that one of the refugee Nobel laureates insisted on revisiting Germany after 1945, because of his 'inextinguishable homesickness for the German language and landscape'.

# 21

# *Ethnicity and Nationalism*

I speak to you not simply as a historian who has been interested in the development of nationalism and has written something about it, but as part of my subject. For historians are to nationalism what poppy-growers are to heroin addicts: we supply the essential raw material for the market. Nations without a past are contradictions in terms. What makes a nation *is* the past, what justifies one nation against others is the past, and historians are the people who produce it. So my profession, which has always been mixed up in politics, becomes an essential component of nationalism. More so even than the ethnographers, philologists and other suppliers of ethnic and national services who have usually also been mobilized. In what terms do Armenians and Azeris argue about who has the right to Mountain Karabakh, which, I remind you, is in Azerbaijan, but inhabited mainly by Armenians? In terms of arguments about the Caucasian Albanians, a people which no longer exists but which in the Middle Ages inhabited the disputed region. Were they more like, or unlike the Armenians who are there now? This is essentially a problem for historical research, in this case endlessly speculative historical debates. Unfortunately the history that nationalists want is not the history that professional academic historians, even ideologically committed ones, ought to supply. It is a retrospective mythology. Let me repeat yet again the words of Ernest Renan in his famous lecture 'What is a Nation' in 1882: 'Forgetting history, or even getting history wrong (*l'erreur historique*), are an essential factor in the formation of a nation, which is why the progress of historical studies is often dangerous to a nationality.' So a historian who writes about ethnicity or nationalism cannot but make a politically or ideologically explosive intervention.

Let me begin with a semantic query. If there is any standard criterion today of what constitutes a nation with a claim to self-determination, i.e. to setting up an independent territorial nation-state, it is ethnic-linguistic, since language is taken, wherever possible, to express and symbolize ethnicity. But of course it is sometimes not possible, because historical research demonstrates conclusively that the kind of standardized written language which can be used to represent ethnicity or nationality is a rather late historic construction – mostly of the nineteenth century or even later – and in any case quite often it does not exist at all, as between Serbs and Croats. Even then, however, the ethnic distinction, whatever it may signify, is made. I spend my holidays in a cottage in Wales which is administratively and legally less distinct from England than Connecticut is from New York State. Yet even though in my part Welsh has not been spoken for a long time, and indeed the natives have even forgotten the Welsh pronunciation of our Celtic place-names, it would not cross my neighbours' minds that just living there makes me Welsh. Of course I must add that the concept of ethnicity is available to them, as it would not be available to my neighbours if I bought a cottage in Suffolk, unless they were anti-Semitic. There I would be just as much a stranger, but they would have to define themselves against me as natives against incomers, or in terms of social classification. This would probably be a less effective form of making collective distinctions than 'ethnicity', but I am by no means clear why.

Every separatist movement in Europe that I can think of bases itself on 'ethnicity', linguistic or not, that is to say on the assumption that 'we' – the Basques, Catalans, Scots, Croats or Georgians – are a different people from the Spaniards, the English, the Serbs or the Russians, and therefore we should not live in the same state with them. This is not, by the way, the case as yet in most of Asia, Africa and the Americas south of the Canadian border. I shall return to this point later. Why then do we need two words, which help us to distinguish *nationalism* from ethnicity, though both are so closely identified today? Because we are dealing with different, and indeed non-comparable, concepts.

*Nationalism* is a political programme, and in historic terms a fairly recent one. It holds that groups defined as 'nations' have the right to, and therefore ought to, form territorial states of the kind that have become standard since the French Revolution. Without this programme, realized or not, 'nationalism' is a meaningless term. In practice the programme usually means exercising sovereign control over a, so far as possible, continuous stretch of territory with clearly defined borders, inhabited by a homogeneous population that forms its essential body of citizens. Or rather, according to Giuseppe Mazzini, it includes the totality of such a population: 'Every nation a state and only one state for the entire nation.' Within such states a single language, that of the 'nation' in question, is dominant, or rather enjoys privileged official status or monopoly. I observe in passing that probably not more than a dozen or so out of the 170-odd political entities in the world conform to even the first half of the Mazzinian programme, if nations are defined in ethnic-linguistic terms. Nationalism, or rather, to use the more lucid nineteenth-century phrase 'the principle of nationality', assumes 'the nation' as given, just as democracy assumes 'the people' as given. In itself it tells us nothing about what constitutes such a nation, although since the late nineteenth century – but not, commonly, much before then – it has increasingly been defined in ethnic-linguistic terms.

Ethnicity and Nationalism

However, I must remind you that earlier versions of the principle of nationality, which I describe in my *Nations and Nationalism since 1780* as the 'revolutionary-democratic' and 'liberal', are not so based, although there are overlaps. Neither language nor ethnicity are essential to the original revolutionary nationalism, of which the USA is the major surviving version. Classical nineteenth-century liberal nationalism was the opposite of the current search for a definition of group identity by separatism. It aimed to *extend* the scale of human social, political and cultural units: to unify and expand rather than to restrict and separate. This is one reason why Third World national liberation movements found the nineteenth-century traditions, both liberal and revolutionary-democratic, so congenial. Anti-colonial nationalists dismissed, or at least subordinated, 'tribalism', 'communalism' or other sectional and regional identities as anti-national, and serving the well-known imperialist interests of 'divide and rule'. Gandhi and Nehru, Mandela and Mugabe, or for that matter the late Zulfikhar Bhutto, who complained about the absence of a sense of Pakistani nationhood, are or were not nationalists in the sense of Vytautas Landsbergis (the first president of Lithuania after the end of communism) or Franjo Tudman (first president of Croatia after the collapse of Yugoslavia). They were on exactly the same wavelength as Massimo d'Azeglio who said, after Italy had been politically unified: 'We have made Italy, now we have to make Italians', i.e. out of the inhabitants of the peninsula who had all sorts of identities, but not one based on a language they did not speak, and a state that had come into existence over their heads. There was nothing primordial about Italianness, just as there is not about the South Africanness of the ANC.

*Ethnicity* on the other hand, whatever it may be, is not programmatic and even less is it a political concept. It may acquire political functions in certain circumstances, and may therefore find itself associated with programmes, including nationalist and separatist ones. There are plenty of good reasons why

319

nationalism thirsts for identification with ethnicity, if only because it provides the historical pedigree 'the nation' in the great majority of cases so obviously lacks. At least it does so in regions of ancient written culture like Europe, where the same names for ethnic groups persist over long periods, even though they may describe quite different and changing social realities. Ethnicity, whatever its basis, is a readily definable way of expressing a real sense of group identity which links the members of 'we' because it emphasizes their differences from 'them'. What they actually have in common beyond not being 'them' is not so clear, especially today, and I shall return to this point. Anyway ethnicity is one way of filling the empty containers of nationalism. Thus Sabino Arana invents the name Euskadi for the country of the people who had long given themselves, and been given, a collective name (Basques, Gascons or whatever) but without feeling the need for the sort of country, state or nation Arana had in mind. In other words, nationalism belongs with political theory, ethnicity with sociology or social anthropology. It can take the state or any other form of political organization or it can leave it alone. If it becomes political, it has no special affinity for ethnically labelled politics. All it requires is that the political label, whatever it is, should make a disproportionately strong appeal to the members of the ethnic group. An extreme case, now long forgotten, is the appeal of the passionately non-ethnic Bolshevik Party in the revolutionary period to the inhabitants of what has become Latvia. The prominence of some Lettish names in the last days of Soviet communism is a reminder of the days when the Lettish riflemen were to Lenin what the Swiss Guards are to the pope. There is Colonel Alksnis on the hard-line side and Otto Latsis of Kommunist and Izvestia on the reforming side. If this is so, why then the general European mutation of ethnic politics into nationalist politics?

This mutation takes two forms, which have little or nothing in common except the need or desire to control state policy: national separatism and national xenophobia, i.e. being against foreigners by setting up 'our' own state, and being against them by excluding them from 'our' already existing state. The second variant I find more difficult to account for than the first, for which there are both specific and general explanations today. But before I try to answer these questions, let me remind you once again that there are vast areas of the globe, where ethnic politics, however embittered, are not nationalist, sometimes because the idea of an ethnically homogeneous population has been abandoned at some time in the past, or never existed – as in the USA – or because the programme of setting up separate territorial, ethnic-linguistic states is both irrelevant and impractical. The USA is once again a case in point, but the situation also arises in the majority of the decolonized Third World states. Whatever the bitterness of interethnic and ghetto conflicts in the USA, separatism is not a serious option, and serves no purpose for any ethnic or other groups.

To return to the main question. The specific reason for the wave of nationalist separatism in Europe today is historical. The chickens of the First World War are coming home to roost. The explosive issues of 1989–91 are those created in Europe and, I am tempted to add, in the Middle East, by the collapse of the multi-ethnic Habsburg, Ottoman and Russian empires in 1917–18, and the nature of the post-war peace settlements in respect of their successor states. The essence of these, you may recall, was the Wilsonian plan to divide Europe into ethnic-linguistic territorial states, a project as dangerous as it was impracticable, except at the cost of forcible mass expulsion, coercion and genocide which was subsequently paid. Let me add that the Leninist theory of nations on which the USSR was subsequently constructed (and Yugoslavia) was essentially the same, though in practice – at least in the USSR – supplemented by the Austro-Marxist system of nationality as an individual choice, which every citizen has the right to make at the age of sixteen, wherever he or she comes from. I don't want to document my thesis at length, but I will just remind you that Slovak

321

conflict with Czechs, Croat conflict with Serbs, could not exist before 1918, when these peoples were put into the same states. Baltic nationalism, which had been the least of the tsar's political worries and barely existed in 1917, was nurtured by setting up independent little states as part of the quarantine belt against the Bolshevist infection. Conversely, national issues which *were* serious or even explosive before 1914 have receded: I am thinking of the famous 'Macedonian Question', Ukraine, or even the demand for the restoration of historic Poland. Ukraine (except in the formerly Habsburg part) and Macedonia showed no signs of wanting to break away until the USSR and Yugoslavia had been destroyed by other hands, and they found they had to take some action in self-defence.

It is therefore more important than ever to reject the 'primordialist' theory of ethnicity, let alone of national self-determination. Since this is an audience of anthropologists I hope that I may assume that this is an uncontroversial statement. It is the historians who need to be reminded how easily ethnic identities can be changed, as witness the nationalist animus against 'assimilation', so familiar in Jewish debates about Judaism. Early twentieth-century Europe was full of men and women who, as their very names indicates, had *chosen* to be Germans or Magyars or French or Finns, and even today the name of President Landsbergis and a number of prominent Slovenes suggests German parents opting for another collective identity. Conversely, a German anthropologist, Georg Elwert, reminds us that the concept of the *Volksdeutsche*, the ethnic German who, by the constitution of the Federal Republic, has a 'right of return' to his homeland as Jews have in Israel, is an ideological construct. Some of those who have, like the east European Mennonites, were not Germans by origin at all (unless all speakers of Germanic languages are counted), but Flemings or Frisians. And the only east European settlers from Germany who actually saw themselves, among other things, as cultural

322

and linguistic Germans – to the point of organizing German schools teaching the standard German language – do not enjoy the 'right of return' except to Israel. They were the upper- and middle-class eastern Jews, whose very choice of surnames – Deutscher, Ginsburg, Shapiro – echoes unforgotten origins. Elwert even notes that there are Transylvanian villages where High German (as distinct from the Teutonic dialects actually spoken) was known before the Hitler period as 'Judendaitsch'.

Such are the paradoxes of primordial ethnicity. And yet there is no denying that 'ethnic' identities which had no political or even existential significance until yesterday (for instance being a 'Lombard', which is now the title of the xenophobic leagues in north Italy) can acquire a genuine hold as badges of group identity overnight. In my *Nations and Nationalism since 1780* I suggest that these short-term changes and shifts of ethnic identities constitute 'the area of national studies in which thinking and research are most urgently needed today', and I maintain this view. There are good reasons why ethnicity (whatever it is) should be politicized in modern multi-ethnic societies, which characteristically take the form of a diaspora of mainly urban ghettoes, combined with a sharp increase in the occasions for friction between ethnic groups. Electoral democracy produces a ready-made machine for minority groups to fight effectively for a share of central resources, once they learn to act as a group and are sufficiently concentrated for electoral purposes. This gives ghettoized groups a lot of potential leverage. At the same time, for reasons both of politics and ideology, and also of changing economic organization, the mechanism for defusing interethnic tensions by assigning separate niches to different groups, atrophies. They now compete, not for comparable resources ('separate but equal', as the phrase went) but for the same resources in the same labour or housing or educational or other markets. And in this competition, at least for the disadvantaged, group pressure for special favours ('affirmative action') is the most powerful weapon available. Where, for whatever reason, participation in elections is low, as in the USA today, or traditional mass support weakens, as in the US Democratic and the British Labour parties, politicians pay even more attention to minorities, of which ethnic groups are one variant. We can even see pseudo-ethnic groups being invented for political purposes, as in the attempt by some on the British left to classify all Third World immigrants as 'Black' in order to give them more leverage within the Labour Party for which most of them vote. So the new 'Black sections' of the party which have been set up will include Bangladeshis, Pakistanis, West Indians, Indians and presumably Chinese.

Yet the core of ethnic politicization is not instrumental. What we see very generally today is a retreat from social into group identity. It is not necessarily political. One thinks of the familiar nostalgia for 'roots' which makes the children of assimilated, secularized and anglicized Jews rediscover comfort in the ancestral rituals and sentimentalize the memories of the *shtetl* which, thank God, they have never known. Sometimes when it calls itself political it is so only by semantic innovation, as in the phrase 'the personal is political'. Yet, inevitably it has a political dimension. But under what circumstances does it become politically separatist? Miroslav Hroch has tried to answer this question for contemporary central and eastern Europe by comparison with nineteenth-century small-nation linguistic nationalism. One element he stresses in both cases is that it is a lot easier to understand language demands than the theory and institutions of democracy and constitutional society, especially for people who lack both political education and political experience. But more crucially he stresses social disorientation:

> In a social situation where the old regime was collapsing, where old relations were in flux and general insecurity was growing, the members of the 'non-dominant ethnic group' [in English in the original German text] would see the community of language and culture as the ultimate certainty, the

unambiguously demonstrable value. Today, as the system or planned economy and social security breaks down, once again – the situation is analogous – language acts as a substitute for factors of integration in a disintegrating society. When society fails, the nation appears as the ultimate guarantee.

The situation in the ex-socialist societies and especially in the ex-USSR is clear. Now that both the material framework and the routines of everyday life have broken down, now that all the established values are suddenly denied, what is the citizen of the USSR, what can he or she believe in? Assuming the past is irrecoverable, the obvious fall-back positions are ethnicity and religion, singly or in combination. And ethnicity turns into separatist nationalism for much the same reasons as colonial liberation movements established their states within the frontiers of the preceding colonial empires. They are the frontiers that exist. Only more so, for the Soviet constitution itself had divided the country into theoretically ethnic territorial sub-units, ranging from autonomous areas to full federal republics. Supposing the union fell to pieces, these were the fracture lines along which it would naturally break. It is a curious joke of history that it was Stalin who gave Lithuania its capital city, Vilnius (between the wars it was in Poland), and Tito who, in order to weaken great-Serbian chauvinism, created a much larger Croatia with a much larger Serbian minority.

However, let us not – or not yet – infer mass nationalism from separatist movements in all cases. So far the Yugoslav civil war has been waged mainly by activist minorities plus the professionals. Has it yet become, will it become, a real peoples' war? We don't know, but there are at least 2.8 million Yugoslav families – those who produced the 1.4 million mixed marriages, mostly Croat-Serb, for whom the choice of an exclusive ethnic identity must be a complex matter. If the roots of ethnic politics in social disorientation are plain in the ex-socialist countries, the same social disorientation is found for other reasons elsewhere. Is it an accident that Quebec separatism became a major force at the end of a decade during which the Quebec birth rate had virtually halved and (for the first time) fallen well below that of Canada?[1]

The decades since 1950, the forty most revolutionary years in the history of human society, should lead us to expect a massive disintegration of old values, a collapse of old certainties. The 'nation' is not as obvious a fall-back position everywhere as it is in those parts of the globe whose frontiers were drawn on Wilsonian-Leninist lines after 1918, and neither is that old-time religion. But it is one such position, and the demonstration effect of central and eastern Europe naturally encourages it, where local conditions are favourable. However, separatism is exceptional in Europe outside the ex-Soviet zone. National xenophobia shading into racism is almost universal. And it poses a problem which I cannot solve. What exactly is being defended against 'the other', identified with the immigrant strangers?

Who constitutes 'us' poses less of a problem, for the definition is usually in terms of existing states. 'We' are French, or Swedes, or Germans or even members of politically defined subunits like Lombards, but distinguished from the invading 'them' by being the 'real' Frenchmen or Germans or Brits, as defined (usually) by putative descent or long residence. Who 'they' are is also not difficult. 'They' are recognizable as 'not we', most usually by colour or other physical stigmata, or by language. Where these signs are not obvious, subtler discriminations can be made: Quebecois who refuse to understand anglophones who talk in a Canadian accent will respond to anglophones who talk with a British or US intonation, as Flemings who claim not to understand French spoken with a Belgian accent understand 'French' French. I am not sure how far, without these visible or audible marks of strangeness, 'they' would be recognized by cultural differences, though in racist reactions much is made of such things: how good Frenchmen are insulted by the smells of north African cooking, or good Brits by that of curry emanating from their neighbours.

In fact, as the global expansion of Indian and Chinese restaurants suggests, xenophobia is directed against foreign people, not foreign cultural imports. It would be tempting to say, what is being defended against strangers is jobs, and there is a certain truth in the proposition. The major social base of European racist movements such as the French National Front appears to be in the native working class, the major activists or such movements appear to be working-class young men – skinheads and the like – and a long era of full or virtually guaranteed employment ended, in western Europe during the 1970s, in central and eastern Europe at the end of the 1980s. Since then Europe is once again living in societies of mass unemployment and job uncertainty. Moreover, as I already observed, the social mechanisms which assigned each group different and non-competitive niches are eroding or are politically unacceptable. The relatively sudden rise of xenophobic parties, or of the xenophobic issue in politics, is largely due to this. Nevertheless, this is clearly only part of the answer. What is being defended is not simply the position of *individuals* in group A against challenge by outsiders. If this were so we would not find the genuine uneasiness about an influx of strangers (or outside influences) which cannot in any realistic sense threaten the members of the group as individuals, for instance the insistence by sections of US citizens that English – of all languages – has to be given protection against immigrant languages by the grant of an official monopoly of public use.

In some sense it is the idea of 'us' as a body of people united by an uncountable number of things 'we' have in *common* – a 'way of life' in the widest sense, a *common* territory of existence in which we live, whose landscape is familiar and recognizable. It is the existence of *this* which the influx from outside threatens. Virtually every single item on the list of what 'we' as English, French, Germans or Czechs are said to have in common can be acquired by immigrants who wish to do so, except physical appearance, where this differs very markedly from the norm of the receiving population. (This is one of the things that makes racism so hard to eradicate.) Moreover, some of the countries where xenophobia has been politically mobilized very powerfully, like France, are also countries which in the past received, even encouraged, and successfully assimilated mass immigration to an extent almost comparable at times to the USA: Italians, Spaniards, Poles, even north Africans. Some countries which are very much exercised about the alien danger actually have very little immigration. Indeed they do their best not to have any. This is the case of the Scandinavian countries – I am thinking of Finland and Iceland in particular – though the prevailing liberal ideology in those parts makes it embarrassing to admit to this form of intolerance. Finland virtually makes permanent immigration impossible, but until the collapse of the USSR it could hardly be described as a clear and present danger. On the contrary, Finland is, as it has long been, a country mass-producing emigrants.

I am not, of course, denying that societies may exist within a specific set of habits and ways of life, which may be destroyed or transformed by, among other things, excessive immigration. Emotionally, most of us can understand the sentiments of the Pyrenean village which decided to block its public water fountain, so that not even the thirsty cyclists touring the region should have any incentive to pass through it. It would be disingenuous, even for those of us who take another view, to pretend that we do not know what made an intelligent British traditionalist like Enoch Powell call for a halt to mass immigration some twenty years ago, and what made British governments of both parties follow his lead. What is more, all of us apply the same criteria when it comes to saving our own favourite environments, human or non-human, from 'being ruined' by too many people or the wrong kind of people. The point is not whether some places, or even some regions and countries should be, or could still be, protected from the disruption by change of their ancient collective character, but whether this is what modern political xenophobia is actually trying to do.

In fact, fear of the alien today is rarely a traditional nationalist defence of old ways of life against the foreign virus. This form of cultural xenophobia was indeed common in the 1950s, mainly in anti-American versions – some of us remember the campaign against 'coca-colonization' – but that battle has long been forgotten. Culturally, the most militant gangs who beat up immigrants in the name of the nation belong to the international youth culture and reflect its modes and fashions, jeans, punk rock, junk food and all. Indeed, for most of the inhabitants of the countries in which xenophobia is now epidemic, the old ways of life have changed so drastically since the 1950s that there is very little of them left to defend. It actually takes someone who has lived through the past forty years as an adult to appreciate quite how extraordinarily the England of even the 1970s differed from the England of the 1940s, and the France, Italy or Spain of the 1980s from those countries in the early 1950s. And this seems to me to be the clue. This is the point of contact with separatism, or the rush into fundamentalism (as we see it, for instance, in Latin America). All are comprehensible as symptoms of social disorientation, of the fraying, and sometimes the snapping, of the threads of what used to be the network that bound people together in society.

The strength of this xenophobia is the fear of the unknown, of the darkness into which we may fall when the landmarks which seem to provide an objective, a permanent, a positive delimitation of our belonging together, disappear. And belonging together, preferably in groupings with visible badges of membership and recognition signs, is more important than ever in societies in which everything combines to destroy what binds human beings together into communities.

A recent documentary film, *Paris Is Burning* (1990), presents a population of the most marginalized, excluded, anomic individuals imaginable: black drag queens in New York. Nothing is more touching and sad than to see how these people – cast out and despised by everyone including their kin, living in and for their regular 'balls' where they compete to dress up to act out, for a moment, the roles they would like to play in real life, and know they can't reconstruct their own human groups. In these so-called 'families', each with an invented family name, each with a senior 'mother' who takes responsibility for the rest of the group, individuals can feel that they are not entirely weak and alone. But for those who can no longer rely on belonging anywhere else, there is at least one other imagined community to which one can belong: which is permanent, indestructible, and whose membership is certain. Once again 'the nation', or the ethnic group, 'appears as the ultimate guarantee' when society fails. You don't have to do anything to belong to it. You can't be thrown out. You are born in it and stay in it.

As Eugeen Roosens says in *Creating Ethnicity: The Process of Ethnogenesis* (1989), the book which, with Fredrik Barth's *Ethnic Groups and Boundaries. The social organization of culture difference* (1998), I have found particularly helpful: 'After all, nobody can change "the past" from which one descends, and nobody can undo who one is.' (Well, of course you can change, or at least invent a past – but they don't know it.) And how do men and women know that they belong to this community? Because they can define the others who do not belong, who should not belong, who never can belong. In other words, by xenophobia. And because we live in an era when all other human relations and values are in crisis, or at least somewhere on a journey towards unknown and uncertain destinations, xenophobia looks like becoming the mass ideology of the twentieth century *fin de siècle*. What holds humanity together today is the denial of what the human race has in common.

And where does that leave you anthropologists whose very name commits you to some conceptual universalism'? And us historians, who are not only being told that only Blacks or Whites or Basques or Croats can properly understand the history of these respective groups, but to invent the sort of history that they want to 'understand'? At least it leaves us, it should leave us, the freedom to be sceptical. No good will come of it, but it won't last for ever.

# Notes

1  See Gérald Bernier, Robert Boily et al., *Le Québec en chiffres de 1850 à nos jours* (Montreal, 1986), p. 28.

# 22

## *The Perils of the New Nationalism*

At a time when the Marshall Islands have just been admitted to the United Nations (September 1991), nearly twenty of whose members have a population of less than 250,000, the argument that a territory is too small to constitute a state can no longer be convincingly maintained. Of course such states – even much larger ones – are not independent in any meaningful sense. Politically and militarily they are helpless without outside protection, as Kuwait and Croatia show. Economically they are even more dependent. Few separatist movements hope to go it alone. They want to exchange dependence on a single-state economy for dependence on the European Community or some other larger unit that limits its members' economic sovereignty just as much. Still, if a territory wishes to run up its flag outside the UN building in New York and acquire all the other fringe benefits of statehood – a national anthem, a national airline and a few embassies in attractive or politically important capitals – the chances today seem better than ever. But why should anyone wish to set up such a state, mostly by breaking up existing political units in Eurasia and Africa? (There is so far no significant tendency to do so in the Americas, except in

Canada.) The usual reason given by would-be state-builders is that the people of the territory concerned have constituted a 'nation' from the beginning of time, a special ethnic group, usually with its own language, which cannot live under the rule of strangers. The right of self-determination, they argue, implies states that coincide.

Almost everything about this argument is historically wrong, but as Ernest Renan noted more than a century ago, 'Forgetting history, and even historical error, are an essential factor in the formation of a nation.' However, we are concerned not with history or with rationality but with politics. Here one thing has to be stated very clearly. The nationalist belief, first expressed in the nineteenth century by Giuseppe Mazzini, that every nation should form a state, and that there should be only one state for each nation, is and always was quite unworkable in ethnic-linguistic terms. There are, with the exception of some island mini-states, probably not more than a dozen ethnically and linguistically homogeneous states among the 170 or so of the world's political entities, and probably none that include anything like the totality of the 'nation' they claim to embody. The territorial distribution of the human race is older than the idea of ethnic-linguistic nation-states and therefore does not correspond to it. Development in the modern world economy, because it generates vast population movements, constantly undermines ethnic-linguistic homogeneity. Multi-ethnicity and plurilinguality are quite unavoidable, except temporarily by mass exclusion, forcible assimilation, mass expulsion or geno-cide – in short, by coercion. There is only a dark future for a world of nation-states such as the new government of Georgia, which wants to deny citizenship rights to any inhabitant who cannot prove that his or her ancestors were Georgian speakers and lived in the territory before 1801. There are today four rather different reasons such sentiments, and their political expression in separatism, are widely supported. The first is that the collapse of the communist system, which imposed political

333

stability over a large part of Europe, has reopened the wounds of the First World War, or, more precisely, of the misconceived and unrealistic peace settlements after it. The explosive nationalist issues in central and eastern Europe today are not ancient ethnic conflicts but those created during the formation of the successor states to the collapsing multi-ethnic Habsburg, Ottoman and Tsarist Russian empires. Baltic and Caucasian separatism, and conflicts between Serbs and Croats, and Czechs and Slovaks, were not serious problems in 1917, or could not have existed before the establishment of Yugoslavia and Czechoslovakia. What has made those problems acute is not the strength of national feeling, which was no greater than in countries like Britain and Spain, but the disintegration of central power, for this forced even Soviet or Yugoslav republics that did not dream of separation, like Kazakhstan and Macedonia, to assert independence as a means of self-preservation.

The breakdown of communist systems has given separatist agitations elsewhere enormous encouragement, but it has no direct bearing on them. Such as they are, the prospects of independence for, say, Scotland, Quebec, Euskadi (the Basque country) or Corsica remain the same as before. They do not depend on what happens in the east. The second reason is more general, though probably more important in the west than in the east. The massive population movements of the past forty years – within and between countries and continents – have made xenophobia into a major political phenomenon, as the earlier mass migrations of 1880–1920 did to a smaller extent. Xenophobia encourages ethnic nationalism, since the essence of both is hostility to other groups (the 'not-we'). United States nationalism is by origin entirely non-linguistic. It is only because of mass Hispanic immigration that today demands are made, for the first time, that English should be the official language of the United States. However, mutual ethnic hatred does not necessarily produce separatism, as the United States also proves. The third reason is that the politics of group identity are easier to understand than any others, especially for peoples who, after several decades of dictatorship, lack both political education and experience.

In central Europe, argues Miroslav Hroch, a leading Czech historian, language is once again replacing complicated concepts like constitutions and civil rights. Nationalism is among the simple, intuitively comprehensible beliefs that substitute for less understandable political programmes. It is not the only one. The fourth reason is perhaps the most fundamental. To quote Hroch: 'Where an old regime disintegrates, where old social relations have become unstable, amid the rise of general insecurity, belonging to a common language and culture may become the only certainty in society, the only value beyond ambiguity and doubt.' In the former communist countries this insecurity and disorientation may derive from the collapse of the predictable planned economy and the social security that went with it. In the west there are other forms of disorientation and insecurity that have built up during the past decades, when the world and human life changed more rapidly and profoundly than ever before in human history. Is it an accident that Quebec separatism as a serious political factor emerged at the end of a decade when a traditional, Catholic, pious and clerical community that had preserved the values of seventeenth-century French peasants suddenly gave way to a society in which people no longer went to church and the birth rate fell almost vertically?

After two generations, when continents of peasants have become continents of city dwellers, when the relations between the generations, and increasingly between the sexes, have been transformed and past wisdom seems irrelevant to present problems, the world is full of people who long for something that still looks like an old, and unchallengeable, certainty. It is not surprising that at such times they turn to group identity, of which national identity is one form, or that the demand for a political unit exclusively for the members of the group, in the form of ethnic-linguistic nation-states, once again comes to the fore.

However, if we can understand the forces that lead to a revival of the politics of national consciousness, and even sympathize with the feelings that inspire it, let us have no illusions. Adding another few dozen to the member-states of the UN will not give any of them any more control over their affairs than they had before they became independent. It will not solve or diminish the problems of cultural or any other autonomy in the world, any more than it did in 1919. Establishing nation-states on the post-First World War model is not necessarily a recipe for disaster. Among the potential new nation-states there may well be one or two future Netherlands and Switzerlands, bastions of toler-ance, democracy and civilization. But who, looking at Serbia and Croatia, at Slovakia and Lithuania, at Georgia, Quebec and the rest, would today expect many of the newly separated nation-states to go that way? And who would expect a Europe of such new states to be a zone of peace?

# 23

# *Reframing Nationalism*

Review of *Nationalism Reframed: Nationhood and the*
*National Question in the New Europe* by Rogers Brubaker.

The present collection of occasionally overlapping studies con-
firms Brubaker's standing as the most impressive of the younger
generation of scholars in the, now vast, field of nationalism. At
all events, he is the one whose merits are most readily appre-
ciated by historians, since his analyses always rest on, or are
documented by, comparative historical case studies. It consists of
six essays. A chapter on 'Rethinking Nationhood: Nation as an
Institutionalized Form, Practical Category, Contingent Event' is
followed by studies of the nationalist heritage inherited from the
USSR by its successors, by three essays developing the theme of
the interaction between 'national minorities, the newly nation-
alizing states in which they live, and the external "homelands"
to which they belong'. They are also overshadowed by the
problem of the former USSR, so, in practice, is the last chapter
on 'Aftermaths of Empire and the Unmixing of Peoples', that is,
ethnic homogenization by migration and terror.

Although the author's range of reference is worldwide in theory, in practice the studies are confined to central and eastern Europe, and, in effect, to the ethno-political consequences of the collapse of the great multi-ethnic European empires after the two world wars and after 1989: the Ottomans, the Habsburgs, the Russian Empire (whose fall was postponed for three-quarters of a century by the October Revolution) and the theoretically mono-ethnic German Empire, whose conquests made it briefly, and disastrously, poly-ethnic. More specifically, the book focuses on Russia. It is much more cursory, though excellent, on the explosive zone of the Balkans.

The focus is thus both geographically and historically specific. Even in Europe, topics that cannot be fitted into the pattern of the three great twentieth-century breakdowns do not quite fit into the book's pattern – for instance, the neo-separatist ethnic nationalism that became a factor in the politics of old-established Western 'nation-states' such as Britain or even Switzerland, well before it began to devastate the communist region.

The restricted focus of these essays limits its practical rather than its theoretical interest. 'The analytical task at hand,' Brubaker argues, 'is to think about nationalism without nations', that is, without supposing that the 'nation' exists as any kind of real entity or substantial collectivity. Following Bourdieu, he sees it as 'produced – or better ... induced – by political fields of particular kinds', and these rather than the properties of collectivities govern its dynamics. To make sense of what has happened in post-communist Europe, all the analyst needs to know is that 'Nation is widely, if unevenly, available and resonant as a category of social vision and division' in the modern world. This is certainly the case in Europe, and it may be argued that, like other Western innovations, it is still conquering the rest of the globe. How it got to be such a 'category of practice' is not immediately relevant to his purpose, although he is plainly aware of the complex debates about the way it did so in the USSR.

Yet the availability – both practical and emotional – of the category 'nation' in its classical Western form can no longer be taken for granted, even though the category 'sovereign territorial state' remains and, via censuses with ethnic classifications and the conflicts between the governments and national sports teams, keeps it alive. Could the Indian BJP [Bharatiya Janata Party], Hamas, or the Taliban be adequately described as a religiously tinted nationalism, like the Catholicism of the nationalist Irish or Poles? Ethnic diasporas are worldwide; 'homeland nationalism' is not. As Brubaker himself notes, the United States is by its construction unsuited to 'national minorities' of the European kind. His global scepticism about the 'nation' in theory cannot conceal a Eurocentric perspective in practice.

Nevertheless, his theoretical stance enables him to focus on certain important and neglected general aspects of the problem. The most urgent of these is 'nationness as an event, as something that suddenly crystallizes', as tragically exemplified during the collapse of Yugoslavia and the USSR. He is equally perceptive about the peculiarities of the nationalism of 'state peoples' in multinational societies, such as the Russians, or for that matter the English, for whom being Russian (or English) was only incidentally something that distinguished them from Finns or Scots, but primarily an overarching super-ethnic identity that was actually reinforced by the variety of intermarrying peoples who lived under a tsar or queen. He sees the asymmetry of nationalist discourse between the Russians and the other nationalities who defined themselves against Russians as a different people. (As Brubaker notes, the Russian language distinguishes, as the English language does not, between the territorial-political and the ethno-linguistic description of its people.) It is only today that Russians, English and Spaniards are forced to think of themselves as 'nations' in the same way as Poles, Scots and Catalans. It is far from clear how they are to do so. He also, incidentally, reminds us that, not least in the Balkans, 'in the protracted course of post-imperial migratory unmixings, the phases of greatest intensity have for the most part been closely linked to actual or threatened violence, especially during or immediately after wars'. In other words, if you wish to see ethnic injustice transformed into mass expulsion and genocide, the best way to do so is to start a war. Alas, it is too late to heed this lesson in 1999.

# Dates and Sources of Original Publication

341

7 The Production of 'National' Traditions
Extracts from 'Mass-producing traditions: Europe, 1870–1914', in Eric Hobsbawm and Terence Ranger (eds), *The Invention of Tradition* (Cambridge: Cambridge University Press, 1983), chapter 7.

8 Ethnicity, Migration and the Nation-State
'Ethnicity, Migration, and the Validity of the Nation-State', in Michael Walzer (ed.), *Toward a Global Civil Society* (Oxford, Berghahn Books, 1995), chapter 20.

9 Working-Class Internationalism
First published in Frits L. van Holthoon and Marcel van der Linden (eds), *Internationalism in the Labour Movement, 1830–1940* (Leiden: E. J. Brill, 1988).

10 Defining Nationalism: The Problems
'Some Reflections on Nationalism', in T. J. Nossiter, A. H. Hanson and S. Rokkan (eds), *Imagination and Precision in the Social Sciences. Essays in memory of Peter Nettl* (London: Faber & Faber, 1972).

11 The State, Ethnicity and Religion
'Nation, State, Ethnicity, Religion: Transformation of Identity', in J. G. Beramendi, R. Máiz and X. M. Núñez (eds), *Nationalism in Europe Past and Present* (Santiago de Compostela: Universidade de Santiago de Compostela Press, 1994).

12 The Celtic Fringe
'The Attitude of Popular Classes Towards National Movements for Independence: Great Britain: The Celtic Fringe', in Ernest Labrousse (ed.), *Mouvement Nationaux d'Indépendance et Classes Populaires aux XIXe et XXe Siècles en Occident et en Orient*, 2 vols (Paris: Armand Colin, 1971).

13 The Limits of Nationalism
*New Society*, 2 October 1969.

14 Tower of Babel
*New Society*, 19 February 1970.

# Dates and Sources of Original Publication

15  The Unconvincing 'Sociobiology' of Nationalism
    Published as 'Lynn and Nationalism', *New Society*, 8 July 1976.

16  State of the Nations
    *New Society*, 2 February 1978.

17  Are All Tongues Equal?
    Published as 'Are all tongues equal? Language, Culture, and
    National Identity', *Social Research*, 63:4 (winter 1996).

18  Falklands Fallout
    *Marxism Today*, January 1983.

19  Benefits of Diaspora Jews
    *London Review of Books* 27:20 (October 2005). Reprinted in
    *Fractured Times* (London: Little, Brown, 2013).

20  The Jews and Germany
    Published as 'Homesickness', *London Review of Books*, 7 (8 April
    1993).

21  Ethnicity and Nationalism
    Plenary lecture to the American Anthropological Association,
    published as 'Ethnicity and Nationalism in Europe Today',
    *Anthropology Today*, 8:1 (February 1992).

22  The Perils of the New Nationalism
    *The Nation*, 4 November 1991.

23  Reframing Nationalism
    *American Journal of Sociology*, 105:3 (November 1999).

# Index

# Index

x, 114, 118, 128, 138, 291;
nationalism, 21; nationhood,
60; 'nations' within, xxii;
patriotism, 118, 145; racism,
177–8; Raj rebellions, 24;
Social Democrats, 174;
suffrage, 129
Brubaker, Rogers, 337–9
Budapest, 78
Buddhism, 214
Bulgaria, xx, 4, 36, 46, 60
bureaucracy, xxiii, 67, 75, 282
Bush, George H. W., 154
Byron, Lord, xix, 26

Campbell-Bannerman, Henry, 231
Canada, xxiv, 158, 326, 333, *see
also* Quebec
Canetti, Elias, 314
Castilian language, 63
Castilians, 208
Castro, Fidel, xiii
Catalan language, viii, 63, 95, 271,
272–3
Catalans, 42, 198, 208, 211, 339
Catalonia, viii, xxii, 95, 228,
272–3, 274
Catholic Emancipation struggle,
23–4
Caucasian separatism, 334
Caucasian tribes, 25
Cavour, Camillo Benso, Count of,
41, 298
Charlemagne, ix
Chávez, Hugo, xiii
Chevallier, Gabriel, 282
China, 198
Christianity, 309, *see also* religion
Churchill, Winston, xiv, 284, 290
Cisleithania, 4, 174
citizenship: American, 44, 67,
141; democratic politics,
207; Georgian restrictions,

333; invented traditions,
119; of new state, 4; political
nationalism, 184; state's
power to admit people to, 262;
working class, 171–2
classes: bourgeoisie, 164–5;
business classes, 18–19, 27;
educated classes, 19–21,
27, 44; lesser gentry, 17–18;
magnates, 17; middle classes,
145; petty bourgeoisie, 74,
197; sports, 148–9; support for
nationalism, 74–5, 81; urban
middle-classes, 74–5; working
classes, *see* working class
Clovis, King, ix
Cluseret, Gustave, 49
Cobden, Richard, 163–4, 167
Colombia, xi
colonial peoples, 69, 182
colonialism, xi, 29, 31, 210, 325
Common Market, 246
Communist International, xxi, 170,
173, 289
*Communist Manifesto*, 49, 162, 165
community: ethnic and national
identity, 219; 'homeland',
64–5; homogeneous, xxiii;
linguistic, 266; migrants,
72; 'the nation', xvii, 65,
197, 206–7, 258–9, 262,
330; political, 207; religious,
214; role of sport, 143; term,
216; traditional bonds, 218;
traditions, 117–18
Congress of Berlin (1878), xix–xx,
79
Connolly, James, 5, 92, 104, 120–1
conscription, military, xiv, 23, 50,
112, 188
continuity, historic, 108–9, 114–15,
135–6, 188, 208, 242
conventions and routines, 109–10

# Index

Engels, Friedrich, xx, 120, 161, 164–5, 167–8, 177

England: Christmas carols, 114–15; John Bull, 114; nationalism, 43; nationhood, 37; working class, 98

English: language, 63, 67, 250, 265, 269, 270, 272, 273, 327, 339; people, 208, 339

Esperanto, 249

Estonia, 23, 39

Estonian language, 272

Estonians, 61, 193, 218

ethnicity: categories and units, 210–11; concept, 317–18; creating mono-ethnic territories, 216; distinguished from nationalism, 318–21; 'ethnic cleansing', xxiii, 216, 262; ethnic frontiers, 166; ethnic identities, 322–3, 325; ethnic movements, 154–5, 211–12; ethnic nationalism, 216, 218, 334, 338; ethnic politicization, 323–4; exclusive, 159; homogeneous national territories, 155–6; identity, 212, 219–20, 322–3; Jews, 313; mass migration, 157–9; minority groups, 156–7; multi-ethnic non-national empires, 215, 338; politicization, 323–4; politics of identity, 11; nation defined in terms of, 59; role of language, 317–19, 333; 'state identity', 206–8; term, 209, 216, 319–20; USSR territorial sub-units, 325

Europe: 'advanced' and 'backward', 5–6; central and eastern, 4–8, 78, 136, 155, 324, 326–7, 334, 338; education, 21, 52, 67; ethnic groups, 320; mass migration, 155, 158; Mazzini's ideal, 39–40, 59, 183; monarchs, xxiv–xxv, 143; nationalism, xi, xiii–xiv; new national states, 60, 79; nationalist movements among small European nationalities, 193–5; racist movements, 327; restructuring of states, 217–18; separatist movements, 318, 321; students, 20, 145; western, 6, 74, 101, 105, 197, 327; Wilsonian plan, 39, 59, 155–6, 321

European Community, 217, 262, 332

European Economic Community, 167, 175

European Union, 272, 275

Euskadi (Basque country), 320, 334

Falklands War, x, 276–7; British tradition, 287–9; *Clochemerle* rides again, 282–3; decline of the empire, 280–1; extraordinary 1945, 289–90; irresistible decline, 279–80; a new alliance, 281–2; patriotism and the left, 286–7; a question of neglect, 277–8; Rule Britannia, 290–1; saviour on a white horse, 291–3; short-term effects, 284–5; split in public opinion, 283–4; upsurge of popular feeling, 278–9

Fenians: Catholicism, 47, 83, 102; Green flag, 104; history, 12, 16, 47–9; mass nationalism, 48, 83, 102; radical insurrection, 35; 'Republican tradition', 47–8; supported from USA, 48, 49

# Index

# Index

Hungarian language, 20

Hungarians, 35

Hungary: Compromise of 1867, 35, 60; education, 77; end of Austro-Hungarian Empire, xxii, 4; frontier, 30; Jews, 78, 299, 307; languages, 73, 77, 272; lesser gentry, 17–18, 45; literature, 300; magnates, 17; Magyarization, 53, 67, 77, 299, 307; nationalism, xv; nationhood, 37

Hunt, Leigh, xix

Hyndman, Henry Mayers, 174

Iceland, 264, 328

identity: choosing, 176, 205–6; collective, 36, 81, 217, 218, 322; concept, xxiii; documents, 4; ethnic, xix, 46, 155, 210–12, 322–3, 325; German, xi–xii, 136; group, 211–12, 213, 214, 319–20, 324, 334–5; 'identity politics', xiv, 11, 219–20, 266; Jewish, 313; linguistic, 275; multiple identities, 88–9, 263–4; national, ix, xii, xv, xviii, 88, 140, 213, 335; state, 206–7; term, 216

Illyria, 30, 39

immigrants: assimilation, 212; bans on non-white, 71; 'Black sections' of Labour Party, 324; citizenship and 'foreigners', 262; communities, 54, 72; ghetto movements, 217; Icelandization, 264; languages, 68, 265, 268, 301, 327; multiple identities, 89, 212; 'natives' and 'foreigners', 92–4, 326–7; repatriation issue, 178; rituals in USA, 141; xenophobia, 329

India: Aodhya mosque, 9–10; BJP, 339; bourgeoisie, 30; ethnicity, 211; identification, 88; invented traditions, 117; language of administration, 264; languages, xxiv, 246; mathematics, 295; Muslim League, 192; National Congress, 192; 'national language', 192–3, 267, 270–1; nationalism, 24, 192–3; rebellions against British Raj, 25; unification movement, 198

Industrial Revolution, xi, 109, 116

International Institute of Social History, 160–1, 178

internationalism: bourgeois-liberal, 163–4; 'cultural', 45; international cadres, 172–3; labour movements, 175–8; left, xx–xxi, xxv, 49, 72; Marx and Engels, 165; 'the nation' and, 162–3; nationalism and, 174; working-class, 160–2, 166–72, 176–8

Iran, 214

Ireland: agrarian economy, 228; emigration, 35–6, 92; famine, 35; Fenian insurrection, 35–6; Fianna Fáil, 176; Gaelic football, 144, 222; history, 12–13; Home Rule question, 226, 230, 237; Irish Republican Brotherhood, 16; labour movement, 100–1, 102–4, 106; Labour Party, 176; language, xxiv, 62, 77, 78, 250; national movement, 41–2, 45; nationalism, 21, 38–9, 77, 83, 168, 213, 221, 226, 244, 339; nationalists, xv, xxiv; peasants, 24; political identifications,

# Index

Palestine, 155, 242; political behaviour in Germany, 313–14; relationship with Israel, 244, 245; 'right of return', 210, 322; in science, 305–7; Sephardi, 295, 297; women's emancipation, 299; Zionism, *see* Zionism

Joan of Arc, 188, 289

Joseph II, Emperor, 310

Kant, Immanuel, xi

Katanga, xxii

Katz, Jacob, 296

Kautsky, Karl, xx, 58, 72, 172, 312

Kazakhstan, 216, 334

Kedourie, Elie, xi

Khomeini, Ayatollah, 8, 214

Koloktrones rebellion, 28

Kolowrat, Franz Anton von, 30

Kosovo, xxii

Kosovo, battle (1389), 10, 25

Kossuth, Louis, xv, 23

Kuliscioff, Anna, 173

Kurdistan, xxii

Kurds, 155, 207

Kuwait, 332

Ladino, 53

'Lallans' language, 274

Landsbergis, Vytautas, 319, 322

language: Austrian censuses, 61; bilingual education, 266; bilingualism, 247–8; constructed languages, 273–4; dialects, xviii, xxiii, 40–1, 43, 63, 75–6, 266, 301; ethnicity and, 317; importance, xiii, xxiii–xxiv, 37, 62–3, 189–90, 246–50, 335; of instruction, 5, 67–8, 75–8, 266–7, 272, 301, 322–3; lingua franca, 62, 188, 247, 270, 273; linguistic engineering, 77–8; multilingualism, 76, 189, 247–50, 264, 267, 300; national constructs, 121–2; 'official', 53; publications, 20–1; on radio, 270; single national language, 265–71; survival of, 75; on television, 270; translation, 272, 275

Larkin, James, 92, 104

Lassalle, Ferdinand, 311, 312

Latin America, xi, 29, 158, 190, 329

Latin language, 20, 265, 272, 273

Latsis, Otto, 320

Latvia, 38, 174, 267, 320

Latvians, 218

Le Bon, Gustave, 130

Lebanon, 91

Lenin: attitude to nationalism, xx, 182, 244; debate on 'the national question', 58, 174; First World War, 287; Lettish guard, 320; location of Communist International, 170; theory of nations, 321; on 'trade-union' consciousness, 171; on working-class consciousness, 100

Leopold I, King, xvii

liberation movements: colonial, 182, 325; internationalism, 174; Irish national, 12, 48; national and social, 58, 83, 96, 182, 191, 258, 289; role of Marxists, 104; Third World national, 319; world liberation, 16, 170

Liebknecht, Wilhelm, 50

List, Friedrich, 163

literacy, 21, 268, 270

Lithuania, 319, 325, 336

Lithuanians, 193

# Index

# Index

Russia – *continued*
(1917), 85, 98, 170, 215,
338; royal ceremonials, 142;
Russification, 67; Tsarist, xii,
xvii, 60, 66, 155, 215, 312,
334
Russian Empire, 215, 321, 334,
338
Russian language, 63, 269, 339
Russians, 339
Ruthenes, 73, 274

Saint-Simonians, 31
San Martín, José de, 29
Savoy, kingdom, 35, 43, 128, 298
Saxons, 208, 263–4
Scandinavia, literacy, 21
Schiller, Friedrich, 300–1
Schnitzler, Arthur, 301
Schönerer, Georg von, 145
Schopenhauer, Arthur, xvii–xviii
Scotland: bourgeoisie, 228;
devolution, 225–6; 'historic
nation', 222; Home
Rule question, 233–4,
334; immigration, 223;
industrialism, 228; Irish
immigrants, 233, 236–7;
labour movement, 226–7,
232–4; law, 224–5; Liberal
Party, 226, 229–32, 234,
236; migration to England,
224; 'nation' in UK, xxii;
national institutions, 221,
222, 224, 225; nationalism,
xxi, 221, 227, 234, 235;
politicians, 224, 231;
religion, 222, 236; 'Scottish
Covenant', 234; Scottish
Labour Party, 233; Socialist
Labour Party, 234; sport,
222; unemployment, 228,
229; working class, 235

Scots, 224–6, 228, 254, 258, 318,
339
Second International, xxi, 83, 98,
170, 171–2, 174
Second World War, xiii
Sedlnitzky, Josef von, 30
Selbourne, David, 263
Serbia, xx, xxii, 36, 60, 156, 336
Serbo-Croat language, 62, 275
Serbs: in Bosnia, 215; in Croatia,
325; conflict with Croats,
322, 334; Kosovo, 10, 25;
mixed marriages, 211, 325;
nationalism, 39, 84; rising
(1804–7), 26; in Yugoslavia,
156, 215
Seton-Watson, Hugh, 256–60
Shamyl movement, 25
Shelley, Percy Bysshe, xix
Sherifian Empire, 32
Siebenpfeiffer, Philipp Jakob, 15
Sieyès, Abbé, 262
Sikhs, xix, 25, 26
Singapore, xxii
Sinhalese (Sinhala) language, 267,
270
Skanderbeg, Albanian
commander, 25
Slavs, 29–30, 39, 40, 46
Slezkine, Yuri, 302
Slovak language, 72
Slovakia, 4, 7, 156, 336
Slovaks: conflict with
Czechs, 321–2, 334; in
Czechoslovakia, 73, 156;
emigration, 72, 73; Hungarian
treatment of, 41; national
movement, 60, 73, 193
Slovene language, 77
Slovenes, 41, 53, 58
Slovenia, 4
Snowman, Daniel, 305
songs: Christmas carols, 114–15;

# Index

Internationale, 131, 146; national anthems, x, 57, 114, 118, 128, 131, 138, 291, 332; new song repertoires, 113; 'Rule, Britannia!', 291; sentimental homesick, 22; traditional folksongs, xiv, 38, 113

South Africa, 71, 159, 178, 307, 319

South Sudan, xxii

Southern Slavs: language, 275; literacy, 21; unification movement, 198

Soviet republics, xxi

Soviet Union (USSR): Bolshevik model, 6–7; collapse, 217–18, 339; construction, 321; international communist movement, 170, 173, 189; Jews, 307; nationalist heritage, 337; Polish territory, xxii

Spain: Basque National Party, 61; flag, xiii; frontiers, 206; identification, 88; languages, xxiv, 274; literacy, 21; monarchy, 215; Muslim rule, 310; nationhood, xx, 37; 'nations', xxii; regional identities, 208; religion, 22; trade union movements, 97

Spanish language, 269, 273, 301

Spencer, Jonathan, 219

Spinoza, Baruch, 310

sport, 143–9; cricket, 144; cycling, 144; football, 120, 144–5, 222; gymnastics, 45, 79, 120, 136, 143, 144, 146; Irish, 222; rifle-shooting, 144; rugby, 144, 222; Scottish, 222; Welsh, 222

Sri Lanka: conflict, 211, 213; education, 219; 'identity politics', 219; national language, 267, 270, 271; religion, 214; Tamils, 211

Stalin, Joseph, xx, 7, 58, 174, 215, 325

state: 'civic religion', 199–200; creation, 332–3; definition, 261–2; demands of, 209; education, 126; embodying the people, xvii; French model, 63; generating nationalism, 187–91; identity, 206–8; imposing national uniformity, 50; inventions of tradition, 125, 131–43, 146–50; nation and, 50, 64, 65, 206, 215, 242, 259, 318, 333; new states, 128–9; patriotism, 208–9, 213, 220; role of language, xxiii–xxiv, 67, 99; role of sport, 143–6; size, 332–3; territorial, 63, 78, 184, 186–9, 199, 206–7, 254, 259, 261–2, 339; working class, 87

students, 8, 19–20, 44–5, 51, 112, 145

Suez Canal, 31

Swabians, 208, 263–4

Swahili language, 270

Sweden: education, xiv, 67; emigration, 158; Norwegian separation, xx; suffrage, 129

Swedish language, xiii, 267, 271

Swiss mercenaries, 23

Switzerland: formation of federal state, 113; languages, xxiv, 189, 267, 272; literacy, 21; 'nation', xx; nationalism, 113; rifle-shooting, 144; suffrage, 129

Széchenyi, Count, 17

Taliban, 339

Tamils, 211

territory: ethnic issues, 216,
217, 325; ethnic-linguistic
territorial states, 321;
identification of nations,
64–5; nation-states, 37,
210, 216, 259, 317; national
territory, 194; nations
and states, 242; size of
state, 332–3; territorial
state, 63, 121, 154–5, 184,
186–8, 206–8, 253–4, 259,
261–2, 318; territorial state
nationalism, 70, 77–8, 83;
written languages, 63
Thatcher, Margaret, 7, 278–81,
283–4, 286, 290–3
Thernstrom, Stephen, 297
Thomas, P. A., 229
Thucydides, ix
Tito, 325
tradition: British working-
class patriotism, 287–9;
convention and, 109–11;
custom and, 108–9;
difference between old and
invented, 118–19; French
invention, 131–4, 139;
genuine, 115; German
invention, 135–40; invented,
107–8, 111–22, 146–9;
Irish history, 12–13; myth-
making, ix; pacifist, 283,
286; production of 'national',
124–5, 131–4; songs, 113;
types of invented, 116–17;
USA invention, 140–2, 188
Tranmæl, Martin, 92, 169
Treitschke, Heinrich von, 136
tribes, 25, 208, 210, 252
Trieste, 30
Tsarist Empire, xxi, xxii, 313,
334
Tudman, Franjo, 11, 319

Turkey: army, 4; Balkans, 36;
Greek diaspora, 30; Trojan
treasure, 8–9; written
language, xxiii; *see also*
Ottoman Empire

Ukraine, 4, 156, 322
Ulster: Catholics and Protestants,
101–3, 105, 168; civil war,
47–8, 95; class unity, 94;
industrialization, 101–3;
new and old unions, 103;
Protestant identification, 90;
'Republican tradition', 47–8;
terror and counter-terror, 211;
working class, 106, 168
uniforms, 81, 110–11, 128, 134, 146
United Kingdom (UK), *see* Britain
United Nations (UN), xxii, 206,
242, 261, 332, 336
uprooting of peoples, xviii, 22–3,
73, 188
Urdu language, 247, 267
USA: African-American
language, 269;
'Americanism', 190; black
drag queens, 329–30; Black
Power, 243; Civil War, 36;
Constitution, 213, 275;
Democratic Party, 73, 96,
157, 324; education, 51,
141; English immigrants,
43; English language, 67,
69, 265–6, 327, 334; ethnic
politics, 321; ethnicity, 154;
European immigrants, 54;
flag ritual, 67, 118, 141, 146,
188; German immigrants,
54, 68; ghettoization,
157; immigration, 54, 93,
140, 158; Immigration
Restriction League, 71;
invented traditions, 140–1;

# Index

Irish Americans, 212; Irish immigrants, 35–6, 48, 54; Jewish community, 302, 307; languages, 265–6; literacy, 21; middle classes, 141; migration to, 23; nation-state, 208, 215; national loyalty, 188–9; nationalism, xi, 21, 334; 'native Americans', 210; race-prejudice, 70–1; racism, 157; religion, 213; rituals, xii, 141–2; Scottish immigrants, 44; suffrage, 129; 'un-American', 105, 141; Uncle Sam, 114; urban ethnicity, 159; Welsh immigrants, 43–4; working class, 89, 141–2

Vandervelde, Emile, 169
Varnhagen, Rahel, 300
Venetians, xviii
Venezuela, xi, xiii, 29
Victor Emmanuel II, King, xxv
Victor Emmanuel III, King, xxv
Victoria, Queen, xvii, xxiv–xxv, 66, 142, 143
Vienna: architecture, 148; culture, 5–6; Czech education, 266; Greek-language newspapers, 27; Hobsbawm's childhood, vii, 302; Jews, 78, 297, 298, 301, 302, 315; Social Democratic Party, 93; workers' movement, 168
Vietnamese language, xxiv

Wales: classes, 223, 224, 228–9, 234; education, 68, 76–7, 221, 225, 227, 271; eisteddfodau, viii, 113; ethnicity, 211; industrialism, 228; Irish immigrants, 236–7; labour

movement, 232–4; Liberal Party, 74, 227, 229–32, 234; local government, 227; migration to England, 224, 225; miners, 89, 91, 168–9, 232, 233; 'nation' in UK, xxii; national movement, 225; nationalism, xxi, 221, 227, 244, 274; nationalists, 176; 'non-historic nation', 223; Plaid Cymru, 91, 286; politicians, 225, 231, 232–3; religion, 223–4, 227, 236; sport, 222; unemployment, 228, 229; 'Welshness', 223–4, 233, 241–2, 317; working class, 91; Young Wales movement, xv, 61, 74, 227

Wallas, Graham, 130
Wallonia, xxii, 101, 195
Walloons, 89, 93, 195, 246, 250
Walther von der Vogelweide, 120
Weber, Max, 70
Weizmann, Chaim, 83
Wells, H. G., 56
Welsh language: attitudes to decline, 40, 68; bilingual teaching, 227, 248; concern of Welsh nationalists, 225, 274; miners, 91, 168–9; oratory, 232; prohibition, 75; road signs, 246, 250; standardized, viii; use, 211, 317; vocabulary, 269; 'Welshness', 223–4
Wheeler, Mortimer, ix
William (Wilhelm) I, Emperor, 125, 137
William (Wilhelm) II, Emperor (Kaiser), xxv, 135, 138, 139
Wilson, Woodrow, 6, 39, 59, 155, 215, 321
Wister, Owen, 71
Wolf, Eric, 195